EXCEL
HACKS™

Other resources from O'Reilly

Related titles	Windows XP Hacks	Word Pocket Guide
	PC Annoyances	Windows XP Pocket
	Excel Pocket Guide	Reference

Hacks Series Home   *hacks.oreilly.com* is a community site for developers and power users of all stripes. Readers learn from each other as they share their favorite tips and tools for Mac OS X, Linux, Google, Windows XP, and more.

Windows Books Resource Center   *windows.oreilly.com* is a complete catalog of O'Reilly's Windows and Office books, including sample chapters and code examples.

oreillynet.com is the essential portal for developers interested in open and emerging technologies, including new platforms, programming languages, and operating systems.

Conferences   O'Reilly & Associates brings diverse innovators together to nurture the ideas that spark revolutionary industries. We specialize in documenting the latest tools and systems, translating the innovator's knowledge into useful skills for those in the trenches. Visit *conferences.oreilly.com* for our upcoming events.

Safari Bookshelf (*safari.oreilly.com*) is the premier online reference library for programmers and IT professionals. Conduct searches across more than 1,000 books. Subscribers can zero in on answers to time-critical questions in a matter of seconds. Read the books on your Bookshelf from cover to cover or simply flip to the page you need. Try it today with a free trial.

EXCEL
HACKS™

David and Raina Hawley

O'REILLY®

Beijing · Cambridge · Farnham · Köln · Paris · Sebastopol · Taipei · Tokyo

Excel Hacks™

by David and Raina Hawley

Published by O'Reilly Media, Inc., 1005 Gravenstein Highway North, Sebastopol, CA 95472.

O'Reilly Media, Inc. books may be purchased for educational, business, or sales promotional use. Online editions are also available for most titles (*safari.oreilly.com*). For more information, contact our corporate/institutional sales department: (800) 998-9938 or *corporate@oreilly.com*.

Editor:	Simon St.Laurent	**Production Editor:**	Mary Brady
Series Editor:	Rael Dornfest	**Cover Designer:**	Hanna Dyer
Executive Editor:	Dale Dougherty	**Interior Designer:**	David Futato

Printing History:

March 2004:	First Edition.

 This book uses RepKover™, a durable and flexible lay-flat binding.

ISBN: 0-596-00625-X
[C]

For our girls, Aleisha and Kate

Contents

Credits

About the Authors

David and Raina Hawley provide business applications, training and tutoring in all aspects of Excel and VBA for Excel through OzGrid Business Applications in Western Australia.

David Hawley has spent the last 12 years creating business applications using Excel and VBA for Excel on a day-to-day basis. He produces a monthly newsletter containing information on the use of Excel and VBA for Excel. He runs and maintains a popular Excel forum on the OzGrid site.

Raina Hawley lectures in industry and in the college education system, and is a registered workplace assessor. Raina runs the OzGrid office and administration side of the business, and works in Excel solutions alongside her husband. They offer hundreds of Excel Add-Ins and business software designed for data analysis in all industry areas through their web site at *http://www.ozgrid.com*. They live in Bunbury, Western Australia with their two children.

Contributors

The following people contributed their hacks, writing, and inspiration to this book:

- Andy Pope started working for Digitab in 1986 as a junior programmer, mostly using Fortran. Digitab is a data-processing bureau situated in London. Andy now deals with all IT issues for Digitab and has installed the companies network infrastructure, purchased IT hardware and software, installed and maintained mainframes, mini-frames, servers, and desktop PC's, and now also provides support to users with both software and hardware support. He currently writes customized solutions for reporting projects, using Office and VBA. He has his own web site at *http://www.andypope.info/*.

- Paul Bausch is an accomplished Web Application Developer and is a cocreator of the popular weblog software Blogger (see *http://www. blogger.com/*). He cowrote *We Blog: Publishing Online* with Weblogs (John Wiley & Sons), and posts thoughts and photos almost daily to his personal weblog, onfocus (*http://www.onfocus.com/*).
- Simon St.Laurent is an Editor with O'Reilly and Associates, Inc. Prior to that, he'd been a web developer, network administrator, computer book author, and XML troublemaker. He lives in Dryden, NY. His books include *XML: A Primer*, and *XML Elements of Style*. He is a contributing editor to xmlhack (*http://www.xmlhack.com*) and an occasional contributor to XML.com (*http://www.xml.com*). For more information about Simon's books and projects, see *http://simonstl.com*.

Acknowledgments

First and foremost, we would like to thank our parents, Walter and Beryl Fenlon and Mike and Marlene Hawley, for without their love and support, we never would have made it through.

Thanks must also go to John Read, who gave us great guidance along the way, and to the team at O'Reilly, especially Simon, for all the hard work that has been put into this book. Andy Pope must be thanked also for the hacks he contributed, and we have to mention all the visitors to our web site and forum, who helped us identify some of the most common issues that people face.

Finally, we must thank Aleisha and Kate, as always, our inspiration. Their understanding and extra efforts to be good while the book was in progress will be remembered!!

Preface

Millions of Microsoft Excel users are busy creating and sharing spreadsheets every day. Indeed, the spreadsheet has grown from a powerful convenience to a transformative foundation for many businesses, driving decision-making around the planet.

Although Excel is a critical tool, many Excel users know only about a subset of its functionality. They utilize the pieces they need, often reusing more complex pieces from existing templates, and don't dive too deeply into everything Excel has to offer. Odds are good that no one user actually needs every feature in Excel, so this approach is pretty reasonable. At the same time, though, it means a lot of people never get far enough along the learning curve to see the techniques they can use to make their work much easier.

Why Excel Hacks?

Although it's possible to accomplish an enormous amount of work using a relatively simple subset of Excel's capabilities, the software offers a lot of powerful techniques that can leapfrog your work beyond the ordinary without requiring that you spend years using and studying Excel. However, most people focus on the content they create—data and formulas, with the occasional chart—so moving to these more advanced levels of Excel usage looks difficult.

There are lots of ways to take advantage of Excel's capabilities to greatly extend your ability to create great spreadsheets, but that don't require years of study. These tools, or *hacks*—quick and dirty solutions to problems, or clever ways of doing things—were created by Excel users looking for simple solutions to complex issues. The hacks in this book are designed to show you what's possible and how to make them work immediately.

You can benefit from these hacks in two important ways. First, you can use the hacks directly as you build and improve your spreadsheets. Second, by studying the hacks and possibly learning a little Visual Basic for Applications (VBA) code, you can customize the hacks to meet your needs precisely.

Getting and Using the Hacks

To save you the time and effort of typing scripts and spreadsheets by hand, all the hacks (except those that are only a few lines long or use only the GUI) are available for download from the authors' web site at *http://www.ozgrid.com/ BookExamples/excel-hack-examples.htm*.

You'll undoubtedly want to cut and paste from the examples and modify their contents to make them fit your spreadsheets more precisely. Excel spreadsheets are tremendously diverse, and you'll want to change things to make them fit your work.

Finally, please note that although all the scripts, tools, procedures, and resources described and contained in this book have been tested, the author and the experts who contributed them make no guarantee or warranty that they will work as intended in your networking environment. Nor do we assume any liability or responsibility for any loss or damage arising from their use. In other words, the information provided in this book is presented on an *as is* basis, and we strongly recommend that you experiment with a hack before using it in a production environment.

How to Use This Book

Although this book is divided into chapters, as described in the following section, you can use it in a variety of different ways. One approach is to think of the book as a toolbox and start by becoming familiar with the tools in each chapter. Then, when a need arises or a problem occurs, you can simply use the right tool for the job. Or, you might decide to browse through the book or read it from cover to cover, studying the procedures and scripts to learn more about Excel. Some of the hacks are helpful in this area because they contain tutorials about complex subjects or well-documented scripts. You also might pick one chapter and see what you find useful to your current situation or what you might find helpful in the future.

How This Book Is Organized

Whichever way you choose to use this book, you probably will want to familiarize yourself with the contents first, so here's a brief synopsis of each chapter and what you'll find:

Chapter 1, *Reducing Workbook and Worksheet Frustration*
Workbooks and worksheets are the primary interface to data in Excel, but sometimes this set of giant open grids doesn't do precisely what you want. These hacks enable you to manage how users interact with worksheets, help you find and highlight information, and teach you how to deal with debris and corruption.

Chapter 2, *Hacking Excel's Built-in Features*
Excel includes many built-in features for analyzing and managing data. However, these features often have limitations. The hacks in this chapter enable you to extend and automate these features, moving beyond the limited tasks they were designed to perform originally.

Chapter 3, *Naming Hacks*
Although cell references such as A2 and IV284:IN1237 are certainly useful, as spreadsheets become larger, it's often easier to reference information by name. These hacks show you not only how to name cells and ranges, but also how to create names that adapt to the data in your spreadsheet.

Chapter 4, *Hacking PivotTables*
For many Excel users, PivotTables already seem like a complicated but magical hack. The hacks in this chapter show you how to get the most out of PivotTables, avoiding the problems that make them frustrating and showing you how to extend them.

Chapter 5, *Charting Hacks*
Excel's built-in charting capabilities are very useful, but they don't always provide the best method for viewing spreadsheet data. These hacks teach you how to tweak and combine Excel's built-in charting capabilities so that you can create customized charts.

Chapter 6, *Hacking Formulas and Functions*
Formulas and functions are at the heart of most spreadsheets, but sometimes the way Excel handles them just isn't quite what you want. These hacks cover subjects ranging from moving formulas around to dealing with datatype issues to improving recalculation time.

Chapter 7, *Macro Hacks*
Macros (and VBA) are Excel's escape hatch, enabling you to build spreadsheets that go well beyond Excel's own capabilities or develop spreadsheets that look more like programs. These hacks help you make the most of macros, from managing them to using them to extend other features.

Chapter 8, *Connecting Excel to the World*

> Although most spreadsheets are self-contained, this chapter shows you how you can take advantage of web sites and services from Google and Amazon, as well as use XML, to get information into and out of your spreadsheets.

Windows and Macintosh Users

The hacks in this book were written for Windows versions of Excel and were tested on a Macintosh using Excel.X. Most of the differences between the two platform versions are cosmetic, and most involve changes to key combinations and the occasional menu. Where the key combinations differ, they are written with the Windows modifier first, as in Alt/Command(⌘)-Q, which means Alt-Q for Windows and ⌘-Q on the Macintosh. There are a few cases, especially in the Visual Basic Editor (VBE), where the interfaces look different and have different menu choices, and these are explained on first encounter. There also are a few Windows-only hacks, using the Windows registry and other features that are supported only on Windows versions of Excel. These are noted in the text.

Macintosh users with one-button mice should also note that holding down the Control key while clicking is the equivalent of right-clicking. (Macintosh users with two or more buttons can just right-click.)

Most of the hacks should work with any version of Excel from Excel 97 onward; the text will indicate when this isn't the case. Screenshots were taken using a variety of different versions of Excel and are not an indicator of which hacks work with which versions.

Conventions Used in This Book

The following typographical conventions are used in this book:

Plain text
> Indicates cell identifiers, named ranges, menu titles, menu options, menu buttons, and keyboard accelerators (such as Alt and Ctrl).

Italic
> Indicates new terms, URLs, email addresses, filenames, file extensions, pathnames, directories, and variables in text.

Constant width
> Used for commands, options, switches, variables, attributes, keys, functions, types, classes, namespaces, methods, modules, properties, parameters, values, objects, events, event handlers, XML tags, HTML tags, macros, the contents of files, or the output from commands.

Constant width bold

> Used to show commands or other text that should be typed literally by the user, as well as to emphasize important lines of code.

Constant width italic

> Used in examples, tables, and commands to show text that should be replaced with user-supplied values.

Color

> The second color is used to indicate a cross-reference within the text.

↵

> A carriage return (↵) at the end of a line of code is used to denote an unnatural line break; that is, you should not enter these as two lines of code, but as one continuous line. Multiple lines are used in these cases due to page width constraints.

You should pay special attention to notes set apart from the text with the following icons:

 This icon signifies a tip, suggestion, or general note.

 This icon indicates a warning or caution.

The thermometer icons, found next to each hack, indicate the relative complexity of the hack:

 beginner   moderate   expert

Using Code Examples

This book is here to help you get your job done. In general, you may use the code in this book in your programs and documentation. You do not need to contact us for permission unless you're reproducing a significant portion of the code. For example, writing a program that uses several chunks of code from this book does not require permission. Selling or distributing a CD-ROM of examples from O'Reilly books *does* require permission. Answering a question by citing this book and quoting example code does not require permission. Incorporating a significant amount of example code from this book into your product's documentation *does* require permission.

We appreciate, but do not require, attribution. An attribution usually includes the title, author, publisher, and ISBN. For example: *"Excel Hacks: 100 Industrial-Strength Tips and Tools*, by David and Raina Hawley. Copyright 2004 O'Reilly & Associates, Inc., 0-596-00625-X."

If you feel your use of code examples falls outside fair use or the permission given above, feel free to contact us at *permissions@oreilly.com*.

How to Contact Us

Please address comments and questions concerning this book to the publisher:

O'Reilly & Associates, Inc.
1005 Gravenstein Highway North
Sebastopol, CA 95472
(800) 998-9938 (in the United States or Canada)
(707) 829-0515 (international or local)
(707) 829-0104 (fax)

We have a web page for this book, where we list errata, examples, and any additional information. You can access this page at:

http://www.oreilly.com/catalog/excelhks

A collection of spreadsheet files for each individual hack is available at:

http://www.ozgrid.com/BookExamples/excel-hack-examples.htm

To comment or ask technical questions about this book, send email to:

bookquestions@oreilly.com

For more information about our books, conferences, Resource Centers, and the O'Reilly Network, see our web site at:

http://www.oreilly.com

CHAPTER ONE

Reducing Workbook and Worksheet Frustration

Hacks 1-15

Excel users know that workbooks are a powerful metaphor. But many users are equally aware that dealing with workbooks can cause a huge number of snags. The hacks in this chapter will help you avoid some of these snags while taking advantage of some of the more effective but often overlooked ways in which you can control your workbooks.

Before we leap into the hacks, though, it's worth taking a quick look at some basics that will make it much easier to create effective hacks. Excel is a very powerful spreadsheet application, and you can do incredible things with it. Unfortunately, many people design their Excel spreadsheets with little foresight, making it difficult for them to reuse or update the spreadsheets they've so carefully built. In this section, we provide several tips you can follow to ensure that you're creating spreadsheets that are as efficient as possible.

The 80/20 Rule

Perhaps the most important rule to follow when designing a spreadsheet is to take a long-term view and never assume you will not need to add more data or formulas to your spreadsheet because chances are good that you will. With that in mind, you should spend about 80% of your time planning your spreadsheet and about 20% implementing it. Although this can seem extremely inefficient in the short run, we can assure you that the long-term gain will far outweigh the short-term pain, and the planning gets easier after you've done it for a while. Remember that spreadsheets are about making it easy for users to get correct information, not just about presenting information that looks good only once.

Structural Tips

Without a doubt, the number one mistake most Excel users make when creating their spreadsheets is that they do not set up and lay out the data in the manner in which Excel and its features expect. Here are, in no particular order, some of the most common mistakes users make when setting up a spreadsheet:

- Unnecessarily spreading data over many different workbooks
- Unnecessarily spreading data over numerous worksheets
- Unnecessarily spreading data over different tables
- Having blank columns and rows in tables of data
- Leaving blank cells for repeated data

The first three items on the preceding list add up to one thing: you should always try to keep related data in one continuous table. Time and time again we see spreadsheets that do not follow this simple rule and thus are limited in their ability to take full advantage of some of Excel's most powerful features, including PivotTables, subtotals, and worksheet formulas. In such scenarios, you can use these features to their full potential only when you've laid out your data in a very basic table.

It is no coincidence that Excel spreadsheets can comprise 65,536 rows but only 256 columns. With this in mind, you should set up tables with column headings going across the first row of your table, and related data laid out in a continuous manner directly underneath their appropriate headings. If you find you are repeating the same data over and over for two or more rows in one of these columns, resist the temptation to omit the repeated data by using blank cells to indicate repetition.

Make sure your data is sorted whenever possible. Excel has a rich set of lookup and reference formulas, some of which require that your data be sorted in a logical order. Sorting also will speed the calculation process of many functions significantly.

Formatting Tips

Moving beyond structure, formatting also can cause problems. Although a spreadsheet should be easy to read and follow, this should rarely be at the expense of efficiency. We are big believers in "keeping it simple." Far too many people spend tremendous amounts of time formatting their spreadsheets. Although they don't necessarily realize it, this time frequently comes at the expense of efficiency. Often the overuse of formatting adds size to your workbook, and although your workbook might look like a work of art to you, it might look terrible to someone else. Some very good universal colors to consider using in your spreadsheets are black, white, and gray.

It is always a good idea to leave at least three blank rows above your table (*at least* three, preferably more). These can then be used for criteria for features such as Advanced Filter and Database functions.

People also tinker with the alignment of cell data. By default, numbers in Excel are right-aligned and text is left-aligned, and there are good reasons to leave it this way. If you start changing this formatting, you will not be able to tell at a glance if the contents of a cell are text or numeric. It is very common for people to reference cells, which look like numbers but in reality are text. If you have altered the default alignment, you will be left scratching your head. Perhaps headings are an exception to this rule.

Format cells as text only when completely necessary. All data entered into cells formatted as text become text, even if you meant for them to be numbers or dates. Worse still, any cell housing a formula that references a text-formatted cell also will be formatted as text. Generally, you do not want formula cells to be formatted as text!

Merged cells can also cause problems. The Microsoft knowledge base is full of frequently encountered problems with merged cells. As a good alternative, use "Center across selection," found on the Alignment tab of the Format Cells dialog under the Horizontal tab.

Formula Tips

Another enormous mistake users often make in Excel formulas is referencing entire columns. This forces Excel to examine potentially thousands, if not millions, of cells it otherwise could have ignored.

Assume, for example, that you have a table of data ranging from cell A1 to cell H1000. You might decide you want to use one or more of Excel's lookup formulas to extract the required information. Because your table might continue to grow (as you add new data), it is common to reference the entire table, incorporating all rows. In other words, your reference might look something like A:H, or possibly A1:H65536. You would use this reference so that when new data is added to the table, it will be referenced in the formulas automatically.

This is a very bad habit to form and you should almost always avoid it. You still can eliminate the need to constantly update your formula references to incorporate new data as it is added to a table by using dynamic named ranges, discussed in "Create Ranges That Expand and Contract" [Hack #42]).

Another common problem with poorly designed spreadsheets is painfully slow recalculation. Many people suggest that shifting calculation mode into Manual via Tools → Options → Calculations will solve this problem.

However, this is generally very poor advice, fraught with potential disasters. A spreadsheet is all about formulas and calculations and the results they produce. If you are running a spreadsheet in manual calculation mode, sooner or later you will read some information from your spreadsheet that will not have been updated. Your formulas might be reflecting old values and not the updated values because when you go into manual calculation mode, you must force Excel to recalculate by pressing the F9 key. However, it is very easy to forget to do this! Think of it this way. If your car brakes were rubbing and slowing down your car, would you disconnect the brake pedal and rely on the hand brake instead of fixing the problem? Most of us wouldn't dream of doing this, but many people don't hesitate to put their spreadsheets into manual calculation mode. If you need to run your spreadsheet in manual calculation mode, you have a design problem. Address it properly and do not apply a "Band-Aid" approach.

Array formulas are another common cause of trouble. They are best suited to referencing single cells. If you use them to reference large ranges, do so as infrequently as possible. When large numbers of arrays reference large ranges, your workbook's performance will suffer, sometimes to the point where it becomes unusable and you are forced to run your spreadsheet in manual calculation mode.

Excel's database functions provide many alternatives to array formulas, as discussed in "Sum or Counting Cells While Avoiding Error Values" [Hack #66]. Also, the Excel Help offers some very good examples on how you can use these formulas on large tables of data to return results based on multiple criteria. Another alternative that is often overlooked is the use of Excel's Pivot-Table feature, discussed in Chapter 4. Although PivotTables might seem very daunting when first encountered, we highly recommend that you familiarize yourself with this powerful Excel feature because once you master PivotTables, you will wonder how you survived without them!

At the end of the day, if you remember nothing else about spreadsheet design, remember that Excel works best when all related data is laid out in one continuous table. That should make the rest of your hacking much easier.

Create a Personal View of Your Workbooks

Excel enables you to have multiple workbooks showing simultaneously, and to have a customized view of your workbooks arranged in different windows. Then you can save your *view* workspaces as *.xlw* files and use them when it suits you.

Sometimes when working in Excel, you might need to have more than one workbook open on your screen. This makes it easier to use or view data from multiple workbooks. The next few paragraphs describe how to do this in a neat and organized way.

Open all the workbooks you will need.

To open more than one workbook at a time, select File → Open..., press the Ctrl key while selecting the workbooks you want to open, and then click Open.

From any of the workbooks (it doesn't matter which one), select Window → Arrange. If "Windows of active workbook" is checked, uncheck it, and then select the window arrangement you prefer and click OK.

If you select Tiled, you will be presented with your workbooks in a tiled fashion, as shown with blank workbooks in Figure 1-1.

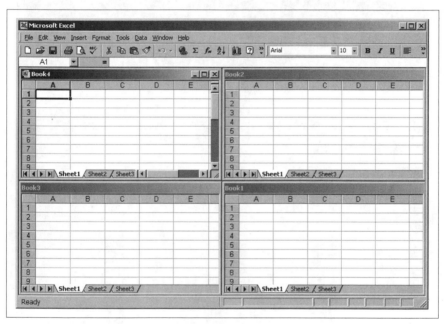

Figure 1-1. Four workbooks in a tiled view

Selecting Horizontal gives you a view of your workbooks in a single stack, one on top of the other, as in Figure 1-2.

Checking the Vertical option will place all your open workbooks side by side, as shown in Figure 1-3.

Finally, as shown in Figure 1-4, selecting the Cascade option will layer all your open workbooks one on top of the other.

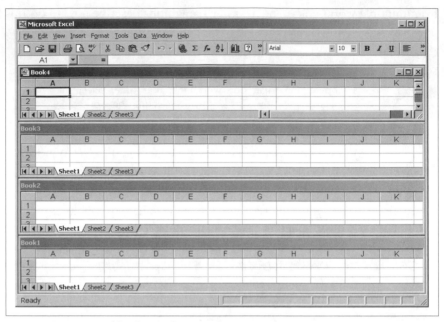

Figure 1-2. Four workbooks in a horizontal view

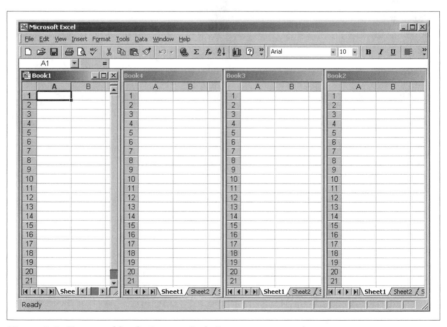

Figure 1-3. Four workbooks in a vertical view

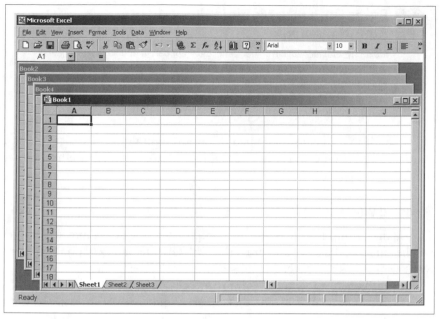

Figure 1-4. Four workbooks in a cascade view

Once your workbooks are displayed in your preferred view, you can easily copy, paste, drag-and-drop, etc., between them.

If you think you might want to return to a view you created, you can save this preferred view as a workspace. To save a workspace, simply select File → Save Workspace, enter the workspace's filename in the File Name box, and click OK. When saving your workspace, the file extension will be *.xlw* rather than the standard *.xls*. To restore your Excel workspace to one full window of a particular workbook, just double-click the blue titlebar appearing on any one of your workbooks. You can also click the Maximize button on any of the windows in your workspace. Close your workbooks as usual when you're finished.

Whenever you need to open those same workbooks, simply open the *.xlw* file, and the view you initially set up will be magically restored for all workbooks. If you need to open just one of these workbooks, open the file as usual. Any changes you make to the workbooks in the *.xlw* file will be saved automatically as you close the workspace as a whole, or you can save workbooks individually.

If you spend a small amount of time setting up some custom views for repetitive tasks that require multiple open workbooks, you'll find that these tasks become easier to manage. You might decide to use different views for different repetitive tasks, depending on what the task is or how you're feeling that day.

HACK #2   Enter Data into Multiple Worksheets Simultaneously

It's fairly ordinary to have the same data appear in multiple worksheets simultaneously. You can use Excel's tool for grouping so that data in one workbook can be entered into multiple worksheets at the same time. We also have a quicker and more flexible approach that uses a couple of lines of Visual Basic for Applications (VBA) code.

Excel's built-in mechanism for making data go to multiple places at once is a feature called *Group*. It works by grouping the worksheets together so that they're all linked within the workbook.

Grouping Worksheets Manually

To use the Group feature manually, simply click the sheet into which you will be entering the data, and press the Ctrl key (the Shift key on the Macintosh) while clicking the Name tabs of the worksheets where you want the data to go. When you enter data into any cells on your worksheet, they will be entered automatically in the other grouped worksheets. Mission accomplished.

To ungroup your worksheets, either select one worksheet that is not part of the group or right-click any Name tab and select Ungroup Sheets.

When your worksheets are grouped together, you can look up to the titlebar and you will see the word Group in square brackets. This lets you know your worksheets are still grouped. Unless you have eagle eyes and a mind like a steel trap, however, it is highly likely that you won't notice this or you'll forget you have your worksheets grouped. For this reason, we gently suggest you ungroup your sheets as soon as you finish doing what you need to do.

Although this method is easy, it means you need to remember to group and ungroup your sheets as needed or else you will inadvertently overtype data from another worksheet. It also means simultaneous data entries will occur regardless of the cell you are in at the time. For example, you might want the simultaneous entries to occur only when you are in a particular range of cells.

Grouping Worksheets Automatically

You can overcome these shortcomings by using some very simple VBA code. For this code to work, it must reside within the private module for the Sheet object. To quickly go to the private module, right-click the Sheet Name tab and select View Code. You can then use one of Excel's sheet events, which are events that take place within your worksheet, such as changing a cell, selecting a range, activating, deactivating, and so on, to move the code into the private module for the Sheet object.

The first thing to do to make grouping work is to name the range of cells you want to have grouped so that the data shows automatically on other worksheets.

Enter this code into the private module:

```
Private Sub Worksheet_SelectionChange(ByVal Target As Range)
    If Not Intersect(Range("MyRange"), Target) Is Nothing Then
    'Sheet5 has purposely been placed first as this will
    'be the active sheet we will work from
        Sheets(Array("Sheet5", "Sheet3", "Sheet1")).Select
    Else
        Me.Select
    End If
End Sub
```

In this code, we used the named range MyRange. (If you aren't familiar with named ranges, see "Address Data by Name" [Hack #39]) Change MyRange to the range name you are using on your worksheet. Also change the three sheet names in the code, as shown in Figure 1-5, to the sheet names you want to be grouped. When you're done, either close the module window or press Alt/⌘-Q to get back to Excel.

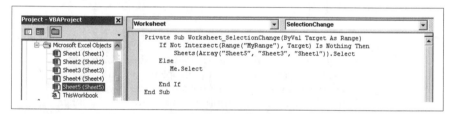

Figure 1-5. Code for automatically grouping worksheets

It is important to note that the first sheet name used in the array must be the sheet housing the code, and thus the worksheet on which you will enter the data.

Once the code is in place, each time you select any cell on the worksheet, the code checks to see whether the cell you selected (the target) is within the range named MyRange. If it is, the code will automatically group the worksheets you want grouped. If it isn't, it will ungroup the sheets simply by activating the sheet you are already on. The beauty of this hack is that there is no need to manually group the sheets and therefore run the risk of forgetting to ungroup them. This approach can save lots of time and frustration.

If you want the same data to appear on other sheets but *not* in the same cell addresses, code like this:

```
Private Sub worksheet_Change(ByVal Target As Range)
    If Not Intersect(Range("MyRange"), Target) Is Nothing Then
        With Range("MyRange")
        .Copy Destination:=Sheets("Sheet3").Range("A1")
        .Copy Destination:=Sheets("Sheet1").Range("D10")
        End With
    End If
End Sub
```

This code also needs to live within the private module of the Sheet object. Follow the steps described earlier in this hack to get it there.

HACK #3 Prevent Users from Performing Certain Actions

Although Excel provides overall protection for workbooks and worksheets, this blunt instrument doesn't provide limited privileges to users—unless you do some hacking.

You can manage user interactions with your spreadsheets by monitoring and responding to events. *Events*, as the term suggests, are actions that occur as you work with your workbooks and worksheets. Some of the more common events include opening a workbook, saving it, and closing it when you're through. You can tell Excel to run some Visual Basic code automatically when any one of these events is triggered.

> Users can bypass all these protections by disabling macros entirely. If their security is set to Medium, they'll be notified of macros in the workbook upon opening it and will be offered the opportunity to turn them off. A security setting of High will simply turn them off automatically. On the other hand, if using the spreadsheet requires the use of macros, users might be more likely to have macros turned on. These hacks are a convenience and do not provide heavy-duty data security.

Preventing Save As… in a Workbook

You can specify that any workbook be saved as read-only by checking the "Read-only recommended" checkbox in the File → Save options. Doing so can prevent a user from saving any changes he might make to the file, unless he saves it with a different name and/or in a different location.

Sometimes, however, you might want to prevent users from being able to save a copy of your workbook to another directory or folder with or without a different name. In other words, you want to be able to save on top of the existing file and not save another copy elsewhere. This is particularly handy when more than one person is saving changes to a workbook because you do not end up with a number of different copies of the same workbook, saved with the same name in different folders.

The Before Save event you'll be using has existed since Excel 97. As its name suggests, this event occurs just before a workbook is saved, enabling you to catch the user before the fact, issue a warning, and stop Excel from saving.

 Before trying this at home, be sure to save your workbook first. Putting this code into place without having saved will prevent your workbook from ever saving.

To insert the code, open your workbook, right-click the Excel icon immediately to the left of the File item on the worksheet menu bar, and select View Code, as shown in Figure 1-6.

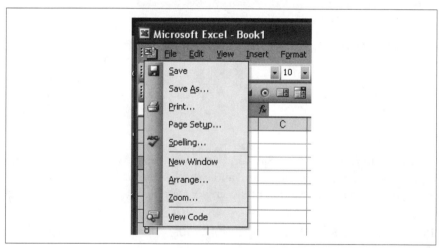

Figure 1-6. Quick access menu to the private module for the workbook object

 This shortcut isn't available on the Mac. You'll have to open the Visual Basic Editor (VBE) by pressing Option-F11, or by selecting Tools → Macro → Visual Basic Editor. Once you're there, Ctrl-click or right-click This Workbook in the Projects window.

Type the following code into the VBE, as shown in Figure 1-7, and then press Alt/⌘-Q to get back to Excel proper.

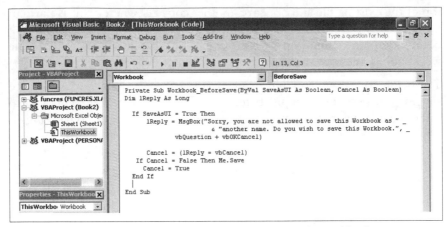

Figure 1-7. Code once it's entered into the private module (ThisWorkbook)

```
Private Sub workbook_BeforeSave(ByVal SaveAsUI As Boolean, ⌐
    Cancel As Boolean)
Dim lReply As Long
  If SaveAsUI = True Then
lReply = MsgBox("Sorry, you are not allowed to save this" & _
    "workbook as another name. Do you wish to save this " & _
    "workbook?", vbQuestion + vbOKCancel)
    Cancel = (lReply = vbCancel)
    If Cancel = False Then Me.Save
      Cancel = True
  End If
End Sub
```

Give it a whirl. Select File → Save and your workbook will save as expected.
Select File → Save As..., however, and you'll be informed that you're not
allowed to save this workbook under any other filename.

Preventing Users from Printing a Workbook

Perhaps you want to prevent users from printing your workbook—and
probably having it end up in a recycling bin or left on a desk somewhere in
plain sight. Using Excel's Before Print event, you can stop them in their
tracks. Enter the following code, as before, into the VBE:

```
Private Sub workbook_BeforePrint(Cancel As Boolean)
    Cancel = True
    MsgBox "Sorry, you cannot Print from this workbook", vbInformation
End Sub
```

Press Alt/⌘-Q when you're done entering the code to save it and get back to
Excel. Now each time users try to print from this workbook, nothing will
happen. The MsgBox line of code is optional, but it's always a good idea to

include it to at least inform users so that they do not start hassling the IT department, saying there is a problem with their program!

If you want to prevent users from printing only particular sheets in your workbook, use this similar code instead:

```
Private Sub workbook_BeforePrint(Cancel As Boolean)
    Select Case ActiveSheet.Name
        Case "Sheet1", "Sheet2"
            Cancel = True
            MsgBox "Sorry, you cannot print this sheet from this workbook",_
vbInformation
        End Select
End Sub
```

Notice you've specified Sheet1 and Sheet2 as the only cases in which printing should be stopped. Of course, these can be the names of any sheets in your workbook; to add more sheets to the list, simply type a comma followed by the sheet name in quotation marks. If you need to prevent the printing of only one sheet, supply just that one name in quotes and drop the comma.

Preventing Users from Inserting More Worksheets

Excel lets you protect a workbook's structure so that users cannot delete worksheets, rearrange the order in which they appear, rename them, and so forth. Sometimes, though, you want to prevent just the addition of more worksheets, while still allowing other structural alterations.

The following code will get the job done:

```
Private Sub Workbook_NewSheet(ByVal Sh As Object)
  Application.DisplayAlerts = False
    MsgBox "Sorry, you cannot add any more sheets to this workbook",_
vbInformation
    Sh.Delete
  Application.DisplayAlerts = True
End Sub
```

The code first displays the message box with the message and then immediately deletes the newly added sheet when the user clicks OK from the message box. The use of Application.DisplayAlerts = False stops the standard Excel warning that asks users if they really want to delete the sheet. With this in place, users will be unable to add more worksheets to the workbook.

Another way to prevent users from adding worksheets is to select Tools → Protection → Protect Workbook..., ensure that the Structure checkbox is checked, and click OK. However, as mentioned at the beginning of this hack, Excel's worksheet protection is a rather blunt instrument and will prevent many other Excel features from working as well.

Prevent Seemingly Unnecessary Prompts

HACK
#4

Excel's chattiness can get a little old; always prompting you to confirm actions you just asked it to perform. Quit the conversation and let Excel get back to the action.

The types of prompts we are talking about are those that ask you whether you want to enable macros (when you do not have any), or whether you are sure you want to delete a worksheet. Here is how to get rid of the most common prompts once and for all.

Enabling Macros When You Don't Have Any

Excel's memory is like a steel trap when it comes to remembering that you recorded a macro in your workbook. Unfortunately, its memory of macros persists even though you might have since deleted one or more macros via Tools → Macro → Macros (Alt/Option-F8). Reopen the workbook and you'll still be prompted to enable macros, even though there are none to enable.

> You'll be prompted to enable macros only if your security level is set to Medium. If it's set to Low, macros are enabled without a peep; if it's set to High, macros are disabled automatically for your protection.

When you record a macro, Excel inserts a Visual Basic module to hold your commands and home-brewed functions. Upon opening a workbook, Excel checks for the presence of modules, whether empty or macro-filled. Deleting a workbook's macros deletes any code within the module, not the module itself—kind of like drinking the last of the milk, yet putting the empty carton back in the fridge. To avoid the unnecessary macro prompt, you need to remove the module. Here's how to do that.

Open the VBE by selecting Tools → Macro → Visual Basic Editor (or by pressing Alt/Option-F11) and select View → Project Explorer. (On the Macintosh, the Projects window is always open, so you don't need to open the Project Explorer.) You'll see a window such as that shown in Figure 1-8.

Find your workbook in the Project Explorer and click the plus sign (+) to its left to expose the workbook's component parts, particularly the modules. Click the plus sign to the left of the Modules folder to list any modules on board.

Right-click each module in turn and choose Remove Module from the context sensitive menu. Decline the offer to export the modules. Before blithely removing modules that might contain useful code, double-click each module in turn to make certain you don't need them. Press Alt/⌘-Q as usual to get back to Excel's spreadsheet view.

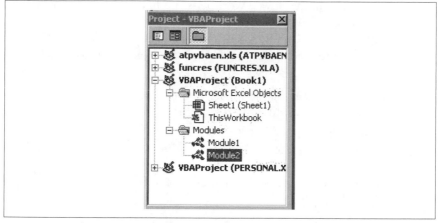

Figure 1-8. Project Explorer modules with Modules folder expanded

Prompting to Save Nonexistent Changes

You might have noticed that sometimes simply opening a workbook and taking a look around is enough to trigger Excel to prompt you to save changes to your personal macro workbook—despite the fact that you've made no changes whatsoever. Whether you know it or not, you most likely have a volatile function within your personal macro workbook.

A *personal macro workbook* is a hidden workbook created the first time you record a macro and opened each time you use Excel. A *volatile function* (or formula) is one that automatically recalculates each time you do almost anything in Excel, including opening and closing either the workbook or the entire application. Two of the most common volatile functions are the Today( ) and Now( ) functions.

So, although you might believe you've made no changes to the workbook at hand, those volatile functions running in the background might have. This counts as a change and triggers Excel's prompt to save said invisible changes.

If you want Excel to stop prompting you to save changes you didn't make, you have a couple of options open to you. The most obvious is not to store volatile functions within your personal macro workbook in the first place, and to delete any volatile functions that are already there. Or, if you need volatile functions, you can use this rather simple snippet of code to circumvent the check by tricking Excel into thinking your personal macro workbook has been saved the moment it opens:

```
Private Sub workbook_Open( )
    Me.Saved = True
End Sub
```

This code must live in the private workbook module of your personal macro workbook. To get there from any workbook, select Window → Unhide, select *Personal.xls* from Unhide Workbook, and click OK. Visit the VBE and enter the aforementioned code. Press Alt/⌘-Q to get back to Excel when you're done.

Of course, if you have a volatile function you want to recalculate and you want to save the changes, you need to explicitly tell Excel to do so:

```
Private Sub workbook_Open( )
    Me.Save
End Sub
```

This macro will save your personal macro workbook automatically each time it is opened.

Stopping Excel's Warning Prompts for Recorded Macros

One of the many drawbacks of recorded macros is that, although they're pretty good at mimicking just about any command, they tend to forget your responses to prompts. Delete a worksheet and you're prompted for confirmation; run a macro for the same and you'll still be prompted. Let's turn off those prompts.

Select Tools → Macro → Macros (Alt/Option-F8) to bring up a list of your macros. Make sure All Open Workbooks is selected in the Macros In: box's pull-down menu. Select the macro you're interested in and click the Edit button. Put the cursor before the very first line of code—the first line without an apostrophe in front of it, that is—and prepend the following:

```
Application.DisplayAlerts = False
```

At the very end of your code, append the following:

```
Application.DisplayAlerts = True
```

Your macro should look something like this:

```
Sub MyMacro( )
'
' MyMacro Macro
' Deletes the Active worksheet
'

'
    Application.DisplayAlerts = False
    ActiveSheet.Delete
    Application.DisplayAlerts = True
End Sub
```

Note that you've turned alerts back on at the end of your macro to reenable standard Excel prompts while working in Excel. Leave this out, and you'll see no alerts at all, not even those that might have been good to include.

> If your macro does not complete for any reason—a runtime error, for instance—Excel might never get to the line of code that turns alerts back on. If this happens, it's probably wise to quit and restart Excel to set things back to the way they were.

Now you know how to use Excel without prompts. Be aware, though, that these prompts are there for a reason. Make sure you fully understand the purpose of a prompt before summarily turning it off.

HACK #5 Hide Worksheets So That They Cannot Be Unhidden

Sometimes you want a place for information that users can't read or modify. Build a backstage into your workbook, a place to keep data, formulas, and other minutiae consumed by, but not seen in, your sheets.

A useful practice when setting up a new Excel workbook is to reserve one worksheet for storing information users do not need to see: formula calculations, data validation, lists, useful variables and special values, sensitive data, and so forth. Although you can hide the sheet by selecting Format → Sheet → Hide..., it's a good idea to ensure that users can't unhide it by selecting Format → Sheet → Unhide....

You can, of course, simply protect the worksheet. However, this still leaves it in full view—sensitive data, scary formulas, and all. Also, you can't protect a cell linked into any of the controls available to you from the Forms toolbar.

Instead, we'll fiddle with the worksheet's Visible property, making it xlVeryHidden. From the VBE (Tools → Macro → Visual Basic Editor or Alt/Option-F11), make sure the Project Explorer window is visible by selecting View → Project Explorer. Find the name of your workbook within the Project Explorer and expand its hierarchy by clicking the + to the left of the workbook's name. Expand the Microsoft Excel Objects folder within to reveal all your workbook's worksheets.

Select the sheet you want to hide from the Project Explorer and reveal its properties by selecting View → Properties Window (or by pressing F4). Make sure the Alphabetic tab is selected, and look for the Visible property at the very bottom. Click the value box on the right associated with the

`Visible` property and select the last option, `2 - xlSheetVeryHidden`, as shown in Figure 1-9. Press Alt/⌘-Q to save your changes and return to Excel. The sheet will no longer be visible via the Excel interface and won't appear as a choice under Format → Sheet → Unhide....

> Once you have selected `2 - xlSheetVeryHidden` from the Properties window, it might appear as though your selection had no effect. This visual bug sometimes occurs and shouldn't concern you; if the sheet no longer appears in the Format → Sheet → Unhide... choices, you know it had the desired effect.

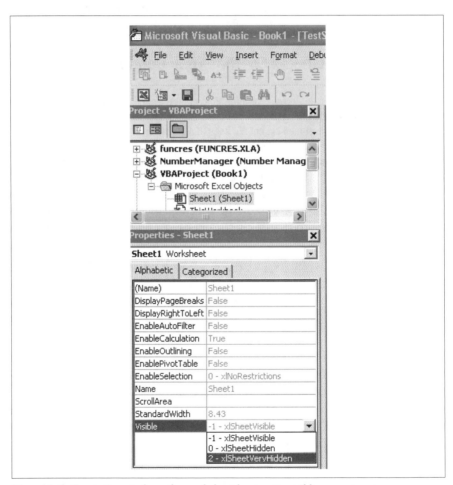

Figure 1-9. Properties window of a worksheet having its visible property set to 2 - xlSheetVeryHidden

To reverse the process, simply follow the preceding steps, this time selecting -1 – xlSheetVisible.

Customize the Templates Dialog and Default Workbook

If you tend to perform the same tasks or use the same spreadsheet layouts again and again, you can build your own Template tab into Excel's standard Insert Template dialog to provide a quick starting point.

Imagine you have a spreadsheet containing days of the year and formulas summarizing various data for the days. You have formatted this spreadsheet beautifully with your company colors, logo, and required formulas, and you need to use it on a daily basis. Instead of reinventing the wheel (or copying and deleting what you don't need) each day, you can save yourself a lot of time and trouble by creating a template.

Excel's worksheet and workbook templates provide you with a running start on your next project, enabling you to skip the initial setup, formatting, formula-building, and so on. Saving a template worksheet simply means opening a new workbook, deleting all but one worksheet, and then creating the basic template you will be using. Once you're finished, select File → Save As... and choose Template from the dialog's Save As Type drop-down list. If your template is to be a workbook template—i.e., it will contain more than one worksheet—again add a new workbook, make all the necessary changes, select File → Save As..., and save as a template.

Template in hand, you can create a clone at any time by either selecting File → New... and selecting a workbook template, or by right-clicking the Worksheet tab and selecting Insert... from the context sensitive menu to insert a new worksheet from a template. Wouldn't it be nice, though, to have those templates available to you right from Excel's standard Insert Template dialog, or to set your preferred workbook as the default? You can, by creating your own Template tab.

This hack assumes you have a single installation of Excel running on your computer. If you have multiple copies or versions of Excel installed, this may not work.

Creating Your Own Template Tab

If you have a slew of templates—workbooks, worksheets, or both—that you use on a regular basis, you can group them together right there on the Insert dialog.

From within any workbook, select File → Save As... and, from the Files of Type pop-up menu, select Template (*.xlt). Excel will, by default, select the standard Templates or My Templates folder in which all your homegrown templates are kept. If you don't already have a My Templates folder, create one as a subfolder of the Templates folder using the New Folder button.

Select File → New... on the worksheet menu bar (for Excel 2000 and above, choose General Templates from the New Workbook dialog that will appear). You should now see the tab you created (My Templates as depicted in the screen shot in Figure 1-10) on the dialog floating over your screen. You also should now see your Template workbooks and worksheets, as long as you saved them to this folder.

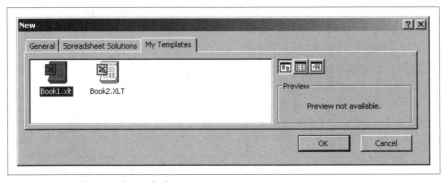

Figure 1-10. The Templates dialog

Using a Custom Default Workbook

Starting Excel opens a blank default workbook called *Book1* containing three blank worksheets. This is fine and dandy if you want a clean slate each time you start Excel. If you're like us, however, you tend to favor one workbook over the others. So, for us, opening Excel involves dismissing the default workbook and searching for our regular workbook. It sure would be handy to have that favored workbook open at the outset, ready for action.

To do so, save your default workbook (template) in the *XLSTART* folder (generally found in *C:\Documents* and *Settings\Owner\Application Data\ Microsoft\Excel\XLSTART* on Windows, and in *Applications/Microsoft Office X/Office/Startup/Excel* under Mac OS X). Once you have done this, Excel will automatically use whichever workbook(s) you have in here as the default.

The *XLSTART* folder is where your personal macro workbook is created and saved automatically when you record a macro. The personal macro workbook is a hidden workbook. You also can have your own hidden workbooks open in the background if you want by opening the required workbook, selecting Window → Hide, closing Excel, and clicking Yes to save changes to the workbook you just hid. Now place this workbook in your *XLSTART* folder. All the workbooks you hide and place within the *XLSTART* folder will open as hidden workbooks each time you start Excel.

Don't be tempted to place too many workbooks into this folder, especially large ones, as all of them will open when you start Excel. Too many open workbooks can greatly slow down Excel's performance.

Naturally, if you change your mind and decide to go back to a blank default workbook, simply remove the appropriate workbook or workbook template from the *Startup* folder.

HACK #7 Create an Index of Sheets in Your Workbook

If you've spent much time in a workbook with many worksheets, you know how painful it can be to find a particular worksheet. An index sheet available to every worksheet is a navigational must-have.

Using an index sheet will enable you to quickly and easily navigate throughout your workbook so that with one click of the mouse, you will be taken exactly where you want to go, without fuss. You can create an index in a couple of ways.

You might be tempted to simply create the index by hand. Create a new worksheet, call it **Index** or the like, enter a list of all your worksheet's names, and hyperlink each to the appropriate sheet by selecting Insert → Hyperlink... or by pressing Ctrl/⌘-K. Although this method is probably sufficient for limited instances in which you don't have too many sheets and they won't change often, you'll be stuck maintaining your index by hand.

The following code will automatically create a clickable, hyperlinked index of all the sheets you have in the workbook. The index is re-created each time the sheet that houses the code is activated.

This code should live in the private module for the Sheet object. Insert a new worksheet into your workbook and name it something appropriate—**Index**, for instance. Right-click the index sheet's tab and select View Code from the context menu. Enter the following Visual Basic code (Tools → Macro → Visual Basic Editor or Alt/Option-F11):

```
Private Sub Worksheet_Activate( )
Dim wSheet As Worksheet
Dim l As Long
l = 1
    With Me
        .Columns(1).ClearContents
        .Cells(1, 1) = "INDEX"
        .Cells(1, 1).Name = "Index"
    End With

    For Each wSheet In Worksheets
     If wSheet.Name <> Me.Name Then
      l = l + 1
      With wSheet
         .Range("A1").Name = "Start" & wSheet.Index
         .Hyperlinks.Add Anchor:=.Range("A1"), Address:="", SubAddress:= _
           "Index", TextToDisplay:="Back to Index"
      End With
         Me.Hyperlinks.Add Anchor:=Me.Cells(l, 1), Address:="",_
            SubAddress:="Start" & wSheet.Index, TextToDisplay:=wSheet.Name
     End If
    Next wSheet
End Sub
```

Press Alt/⌘-Q to get back to your workbook and then save your changes. Notice that the code *names* (such as when you *name* a cell or range of cells in Excel) cell A1 on each sheet Start, plus a unique whole number representing the index number of the sheet . This ensures that A1 on each sheet has a different name. If A1 on your worksheet already has a name, you should consider changing any mention of A1 in the code to something more suitable—an unused cell anywhere on the sheet, for instance.

You should be aware that if you select File → Properties → Summary and enter a URL as a hyperlink base, the index created from the preceding code possibly will not work. A hyperlink base is a path or URL that you want to use for all hyperlinks with the same base address that are inserted in the current document.

Another, more user-friendly, way of constructing an index is to add a link to the list of sheets as a context-menu item, keeping it just a right-click away. We'll have that link open the standard workbook tabs command bar. You generally get to this command bar by right-clicking any of the sheet tab scroll arrows on the bottom left of any worksheet, as shown in Figure 1-11.

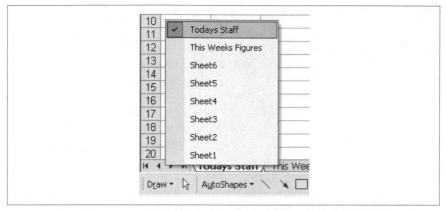

Figure 1-11. Tabs command bar displayed by right-clicking the sheet scroll tabs

To link that tab's command bar to a right-click in any cell, enter the following code in the VBE:

```
Private Sub Workbook_SheetBeforeRightClick(ByVal Sh As Object, ByVal Target
As Range, Cancel As Boolean)
Dim cCont As CommandBarButton
    On Error Resume Next
    Application.CommandBars("Cell").Controls("Sheet Index").Delete
    On Error GoTo 0
        Set cCont = Application.CommandBars("Cell").Controls.Add _
                        (Type:=msoControlButton, Temporary:=True)
        With cCont
        .Caption = "Sheet Index"
            .OnAction = "IndexCode"
      End With
End Sub
```

Next, you'll need to insert a standard module to house the IndexCode macro, called by the preceding code whenever the user right-clicks in a cell. It is vital that you use a standard module next, as placing the code in the same module as Workbook_SheetBeforeRightClick will mean Excel will not know where to find the macro called IndexCode.

Select Insert → Module and enter the following code:

```
Sub IndexCode( )
 Application.CommandBars("workbook Tabs").ShowPopup
 End Sub
```

Press Alt/⌘-Q to get back to the Excel interface.

Now, right-click within any cell on any worksheet and you should see a new menu item called Sheet Index that will take you right to a list of sheets in the workbook.

Limit the Scrolling Range of Your Worksheet

HACK #8

If you move around your spreadsheet a lot, or if you have data you don't want readers to explore, you might find it convenient to limit the visible area of your spreadsheet to only that which has actual data.

All Excel worksheets created in Excel 97 and above are 256 columns wide (A to IV) and 65,536 rows long. More often than not, your worksheet uses only a small percentage of the cells available to you. A nice bit of spring cleaning limits the worksheet's scrollable area to just the part containing the data you want a user to see. You then can place data you do not want a user to see outside the scrollable area. Doing this also can make it less daunting to scroll around in a worksheet, as it is not uncommon for users to find themselves at row 50,000 and then start screaming that they are unable to find any data in a worksheet.

The easiest way to establish boundaries is simply to hide all the unused columns and rows. On your sheet, locate the last row containing data and select the entire row below it by clicking the row label. Press the Ctrl and Shift keys while pressing the down arrow to select all rows beneath. Select Format → Row → Hide to hide them all. Do the same thing for unused columns; find the last-used column, select the entire column to the right of it, press the Ctrl and Shift keys while pressing the right arrow, and select Format → Column → Hide. If all went according to plan, your useful cells should be surrounded by a gray moat past which you cannot scroll.

The second way to establish boundaries is to specify a valid range in the worksheet's Properties window. Right-click the sheet's tab at the bottom left of the window and select View Code from the context menu. Select View → Project Explorer (Ctrl-R) on Windows, or press ⌘-R under Mac OS X to visit the Project Explorer. If the Properties window isn't visible, press F4 to make it appear. Select the appropriate worksheet and visit the ScrollArea property in the Properties window.

Now, from within the Project Explorer, select the worksheet you want the scroll area limited to, and then, from the Properties window (shown in Figure 1-12), go down to the ScrollArea property. In the associated value field to the right, enter the preferred boundaries of your worksheet—$A$1: $G$50, for instance.

You will be unable to scroll outside the area you have specified. Unfortunately, Excel will not save this setting after closing it. This means you need a very simple macro to automatically set the scroll area to the desired range by placing some code in the worksheet_Activate event.

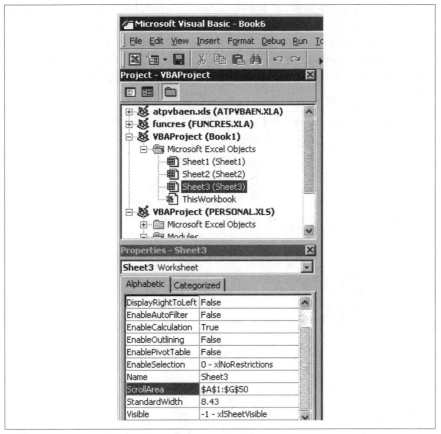

Figure 1-12. Project Explorer Properties window

Right-click the Sheet Name tab on which the scroll area should be limited and select View Code, then enter the following:

```
Private Sub Worksheet_Activate ( )
Me.ScrollArea = "A1:G50"
End Sub
```

As usual, press Alt/⌘-Q to return to Excel proper and save your workbook.

Although you will not see a visible clue, such as the gray moat of the first method, you won't be able to scroll or select anything outside the specified area.

> Any macro that tries to select a range outside this scroll area (including selections of entire rows and columns) will no longer be able to do so. This is true particularly for recorded macros, as they often use selections.

If your macros do select a range outside the scrollable area, you can easily modify any existing macros so that they are not limited to a specific scroll area while operating. Simply select Tools → Macro → Macros... (Alt-F8), locate your macro name, select it, and click Edit. Place the following line of code as the very first line of code:

```
ActiveSheet.ScrollArea = ""
```

As the very last line of code in your macro, place the following:

```
ActiveSheet.ScrollArea = "$A$1:$G$50"
```

So, your code should look something like this:

```
Sub MyMacro( )
'
' MyMacro Macro
' Macro recorded 19/9/2003 by OzGrid.com
'


'
ActiveSheet.ScrollArea = ""
    Range("Z100").Select
    Selection.Font.Bold = True
ActiveSheet.ScrollArea = "$A$1:$G$50"
Sheets("Daily Budget").Select
ActiveSheet.ScrollArea = ""
    Range ("T500").Select
    Selection.Font.Bold = False
ActiveSheet.ScrollArea = "$A$1:$H$25"

End Sub
```

Our recorded macro selects cell Z100 and formats it to boldface. It then selects the worksheet named Daily Budget, selects cell T500 on that sheet, and "unbolds" it. We added `ActiveSheet.ScrollArea = ""` so that any cell on the worksheet can be selected and then the scroll area can be set back to our desired range. When we select another worksheet (`Daily Budget`), we again allow the code to select any cell on this worksheet and set the scroll area for this worksheet back to the desired range.

A third method, the most flexible, automatically limits the scroll area to the used range on the worksheet within which you place the code. To use this method, right-click the Sheet Name tab on which you want the scroll area limited, select View Code, and enter the following code:

```
Private Sub Worksheet_Activate( )
    Me.ScrollArea = Range(Me.UsedRange, Me.UsedRange(2,2)).Address
End Sub
```

Now press Alt/⌘-Q or click the X in the top righthand corner to get back to Excel and save your workbook.

The preceding macro will run automatically each time you activate the worksheet in which you placed it. However, you might encounter a problem with this macro when you need to actually enter data outside the existing used range. To avoid this problem, simply use a standard macro that will reset your scroll area back to the full sheet. Select Tools → Macro → Visual Basic Editor, then select Insert → Module, and enter the following code:

```
Sub ResetScrollArea()
    ActiveSheet.ScrollArea = ""
End Sub
```

Now press Alt/⌘-Q or click the X in the top righthand corner to get back to Excel and save your workbook.

If you want to, you can make your macro easier to run by assigning it to a shortcut key. Select Tools → Macro → Macros... (Alt/Option-F8). Select ResetScrollArea (the name of your macro), click Options, and assign a shortcut key.

Each time you need to add data outside the established bounds of your worksheet, run the ResetScrollArea macro to readjust the borders. After you run the macro, make any changes you were unable to make while the scroll area was limited. When you're finished, activate any other worksheet and then activate the worksheet you just modified. Activation of the worksheet will cause the code to run and limit the scroll area to the desired range.

HACK #9

Lock and Protect Cells Containing Formulas

You may want to let users change cells containg data without providing them access to change formulas. You can keep cells containing formulas under lock and key without having to protect your entire sheet or workbook.

When we create a spreadsheet, most of us need to use formulas of some sort. Sometimes, however, you might not want other users to tamper/delete/overtype any formulas you included on your spreadsheet. The easiest and most common way of barring people from playing with your formulas is to protect your worksheet. However, protecting your worksheet doesn't just prevent users from tampering with your formulas, it also stops users from entering anything at all. Sometimes you do not want to go this far.

By default, all cells on a worksheet are locked; however, this has no effect unless worksheet protection has been applied. Here is a very easy way to apply worksheet protection so that only formula cells are locked and protected.

Select all cells on your worksheet, either by pressing Ctrl/⌘-A or by clicking the gray square at the intersecting point of column A and row 1. Then select

Format → Cells → Protection and uncheck the Locked checkbox to remove the tick. Click OK.

Now select any single cell, select Edit → Go To... (Ctrl-G or F5), and click Special. You'll see a dialog box such as that in Figure 1-13.

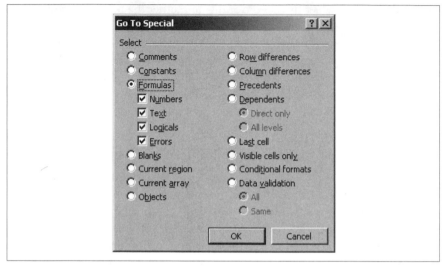

Figure 1-13. The Go To Special dialog

Select Formulas from the Go To Special dialog and, if needed, limit the formulas to the subtypes underneath. Click OK. With only the formula cells selected, select Format → Cells → Protection and check the Locked checkbox to insert a tick. Select OK. Now select Tools → Protection → Protect Worksheet to protect your worksheet and apply a password if required.

The preceding method certainly saves a lot of time and eliminates possible errors locating formulas so that you can protect them. Unfortunately, it can also prevent users from using certain features, such as sorting, formatting changes, aligning text, and many others you might not be concerned with, even when in an unlocked cell. You can overcome this problem in two ways.

The first approach doesn't use worksheet protection at all, and uses data validation instead.

> Data validation is far from bulletproof when it comes to preventing users from entering nonvalidated data into cells. Users can still paste into a validated cell any data they want and, in doing so, remove the validation from that cell unless the copied cell also contains data validation, in which case this validation would override the original validation.

To see what we mean, select any single cell, select Edit → Go To... (Ctrl-G or F5), and click Special. Now select Formulas from the Go To Special dialog and, if needed, limit the formulas to the subtypes underneath. Click OK.

With only the Formula cells selected, select the Data → Validation → Settings page tab, select Custom from the Allow: box, and in the Formula box, enter =" ", as shown in Figure 1-14. Click OK.

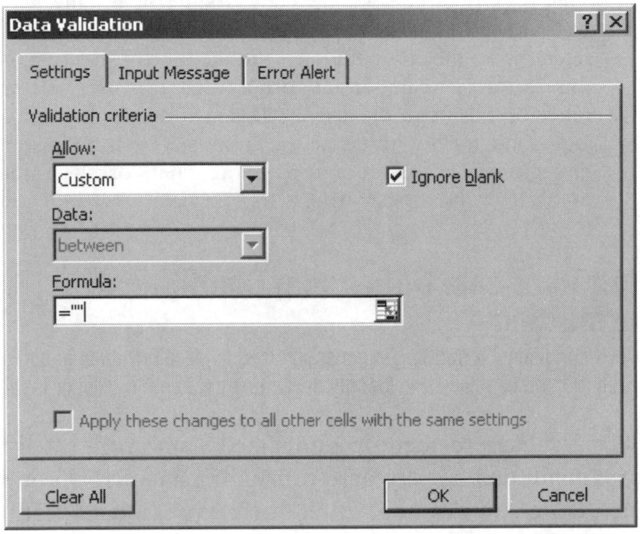

Figure 1-14. Validation formulas

This method will prevent a user from accidentally overtyping into any formula cells—although, as stressed in the earlier warning, it is not a fully secure method and should be used only for accidental overtyping, etc. However, the big advantage to using this method is that all of Excel's features are still usable on the worksheet.

The last method also will enable you to use all of Excel's features, but only when you are in a cell that is not locked. To start, ensure that only the cells you want protected are locked and that all other cells are unlocked. Right-click the Sheet Name tab, select View Code from the pop-up menu, and enter the following code:

```
Private Sub Worksheet_SelectionChange(ByVal Target As Range)
    If Target.Locked = True Then
        Me.Protect Password:="Secret"
    Else
        Me.Unprotect Password:="Secret"
    End If
End Sub
```

If no password is used, omit `Password:="Secret"`. If a password is used, change the word `Secret` to your password. Press Alt/⌘-Q or click the X in the top righthand corner to get back to Excel and save your workbook. Now, each time you select a cell that is locked, your worksheet will automatically protect itself. The moment you select any cell that is not locked, your worksheet will unprotect itself.

> This hack doesn't work perfectly, though it usually works well enough. The keyword used in the code, `Target`, will refer only to the cell that is active at the time of selection. For this reason, it is important to note that if a user selects a range of cells (with the active cell being an unlocked cell), it is possible for him to delete the entire selection because the target cell is unlocked and, therefore, the worksheet automatically will unprotect itself.

HACK #10   Find Duplicate Data using Conditional Formatting

Excel's conditional formatting is generally used to identify values in particular ranges, but we can hack it to identify duplicated data within a list or table.

People frequently have to identify duplicated data within a list or table. Doing this manually can be very time-consuming and error-prone. To make this job much easier, you can hack one of Excel's standard features, conditional formatting.

Take, for example, a table of data with a range of $A$1:$H$100. Select the top-left cell, A1, and drag it over and down to H100. It is important that A1 be the active cell in your selection, so dragging from H100 to A1 isn't quite the same. Select Format → Conditional Formatting... and, in the Conditional Formatting dialog box, select Formula Is from the top-left pop-up menu. In the field to its right, enter the following code:

```
=COUNTIF($A$1:$H$100,A1)>1
```

Click the Format tab (that's the Format button under Mac OS X), followed by the Patterns tab, and select a color you want applied to visually identify duplicate data. Click OK to return to the Conditional Formatting dialog box and click OK again to apply the formatting.

All those cells containing duplicate data should be lit up like a Christmas tree in the color you chose, making it much easier to eyeball duplicate data and delete, move, or alter it as appropriate.

It is vital to note that as A1 was the active cell in your selection, the cell address is a relative reference and is not absolute, as is your table of data,

$A$1:$H$100. By using conditional formatting in this way, Excel automatically knows to use the correct cell as the COUNTIF criterion. By this we mean that the conditional formatting formula in cell A1 will read as follows:

```
=COUNTIF($A$1:$H$100,A1)>1
```

while in cell A2, it will read:

```
=COUNTIF($A$1:$H$100,A2)>1
```

in cell A3, it will read:

```
=COUNTIF($A$1:$H$100,A3)>1
```

and so forth.

If you need to identify data that appears two or more times, you can use conditional formatting with three different conditions and color-code each condition for visual identification. To do this, select cell A1 (the cell in the top lefthand corner of table) and drag it down to H100. Again, it is important that A1 is the active cell in your selection.

Now select Format → Conditional Formatting… and, from the box containing the text "Cell Value Is", select Formula Is. In the box to the right of Formula Is, enter the following code:

```
=COUNTIF($A$1:$H$100,A1)>3
```

Click the Format tab and then the Patterns page tab, and select a color you want to apply to identify data that appears more than three times. Click OK, then click Add, and from the Condition 2 box, select Formula Is and enter the following formula:

```
=COUNTIF($A$1:$H$100,A1)=3
```

 Instead of retyping the formula, highlight it from the Condition 1 box, press Ctrl/⌘-C to copy, click the Formula box for Condition 2, press Ctrl/⌘-V to paste, and then change >3 to =3.

Click the Format tab and then the Patterns page tab and select a color you want to apply to identify data that appears three times. Click OK, and then click Add. From the Condition 3 box, select Formula Is and enter the following formula:

```
=COUNTIF($A$1:$H$100,A1)=2
```

Finally, click the Format tab and then the Patterns page tab. Select a color you want to apply to data that appears twice. Click OK. You will have different cell colors depending on the number of times your data appears within your table of data.

Again, it is vital to note that as A1 was the active cell in your selection, the cell address is a relative reference and is not absolute, as is your table of data, $A$1:$H$100. By using conditional formatting in this way, Excel automatically knows to use the correct cell as the COUNTIF criterion.

HACK #11 Tie Custom Toolbars to a Particular Workbook

Although most toolbars you build apply to just about any work you do, sometimes the functionality of a custom toolbar applies to only one workbook in particular. With this hack, you can tie custom toolbars to their respective workbooks.

If you've ever created a custom toolbar, you have no doubt noticed that the toolbar is loaded and visible regardless of which workbook you have open. What if your custom toolbar contains recorded macros meant only for a specific workbook? It's probably best to tie special-purpose custom toolbars to the appropriate workbooks to reduce both clutter and possible confusion. You can do this by inserting some very simple code into the private module of the workbook.

To get to this private module, right-click the Excel icon, which you'll find at the top left of your screen, next to File, and select View Code.

> This shortcut isn't available on the Mac. You'll have to open the Visual Basic Editor (VBE) by pressing Option-F11 or by selecting Tools → Macro → Visual Basic Editor. Once you're there, Ctrl-click or right-click This Workbook in the Projects window.

Then, enter this code:

```
Private Sub Workbook_Activate( )
    On Error Resume Next
        With Application.CommandBars("MyCustomToolbar")
            .Enabled = True
                .Visible = True
        End With
    On Error GoTo 0
End Sub

Private Sub Workbook_Deactivate( )
    On Error Resume Next
        Application.CommandBars("MyCustomToolbar").Enabled = False
    On Error GoTo 0
End Sub
```

Change the text *"MyCustomToolbar"* to the name of your own custom toolbar. To get back to the Excel interface, close the module window or press Alt/⌘-Q. Whenever you open or activate another workbook, your custom toolbar disappears and isn't accessible. Reactivate the appropriate workbook, and poof! The toolbar's back.

You even can take this down a level, making the custom toolbar available only to a specific worksheet within the workbook. Right-click the Sheet Name tab of the sheet on which you want the toolbar to be accessible and select View Code. Enter this code:

```
Private Sub Worksheet_Deactivate( )
    On Error Resume Next
        Application.CommandBars("MyCustomToolbar").Enabled = False
    On Error GoTo 0
End Sub

Private Sub Worksheet_Activate( )
    On Error Resume Next
        With Application.CommandBars("MyCustomToolbar")
            .Enabled = True
                .Visible = True
        End With
        On Error GoTo 0
End Sub
```

Now press Alt/⌘-Q or close the window to get back to Excel.

The first procedure (Worksheet_Deactivate( )) will fire automatically each time you leave that particular worksheet to activate another one. The firing of the code changes the Enable property of your custom toolbar to False so that it cannot be seen or displayed. The second procedure is fired each time you activate the worksheet and sets the Enable property of your custom toolbar to True so that it can be made visible. The line of code that reads Application.CommandBars("MyCustomToolbar").Visible = True simply displays your custom toolbar again, so the user can see it. Switch worksheets and the toolbar's gone; switch back and it reappears like magic.

HACK #12 Outsmart Excel's Relative Reference Handler

In Excel, a formula reference can be either relative or absolute, but sometimes you want to move cells that use relative references without making the references absolute. Here's how.

When a formula needs to be made absolute, you use the dollar sign ($) in front of the column letter and/or row number of the cell reference, as in $A$1. Once you do this, no matter where you copy your formula, the formula will reference the same cells. Sometimes, however, you already set up a lot of formulas that contain not absolute references, but relative references. You would usually do this so that when you copy the original cell formula down or across, the row and column references change accordingly.

If you already set up your formulas using only relative references, or perhaps a mix of relative and absolute references, you can reproduce the same formulas in either another range on the same worksheet, another sheet in the same workbook, or perhaps even another sheet in another workbook.

To do this without changing any range references inside the formulas, select the range of cells you want to copy and then select Edit → Replace.... In the Find What: box, type an equals sign (=) and in the Replace With: box, type an at sign (@). (Of course, these could be any symbols you are sure are not being used in any of the formulas.) Click Replace All. The equals sign in all the formulas on your worksheet will be replaced with the at sign.

You now can simply copy this range, paste it to its desired destination, select the range you just pasted, and select Edit → Replace.... This time replace the at sign with an equals sign. Your formulas now should be referencing the same cell references as your originals.

Remove Phantom Workbook Links

HACK
#13

Ah, phantom links. You open your workbook and are prompted to "Update Links," but there are no links! How can you update links when they don't exist?

External links are links that reference another workbook. Unexpected external linking can occur for various reasons, many of them stemming from moving or copying charts, chart sheets, or worksheets into another workbook. Knowing why they're there doesn't always help you find them, though. Here are a few ways to deal with the spooky phantom link problem.

First, you need to see whether you have any real external links (nonphantom) that you forgot about. If you are not sure whether you have real external links, start looking in the most obvious place: your formulas. You can do this by ensuring no other workbooks are open and then searching for [*] within the formulas on each worksheet. Close all other workbooks to ensure that any formula links will include [*], where the asterisk represents a wildcard string.

> Excel 97 doesn't provide the option of searching the entire workbook, but you can search all worksheets in a workbook by grouping them. You do this by right-clicking any Sheet Name tab and choosing Select All Sheets. In later versions of Excel, Find... and Replace... provide the option of searching within the sheet or workbook.

Once you find the formula links, simply change the formula accordingly or delete it altogether. Whether you change the formula or delete it depends on the situation, and only you can decide which route to take.

You also might want to consider going to the Microsoft Office Download Center, located at *http://office.microsoft.com/Downloads/default.aspx,* and from the Add-Ins category selecting the Delete Links Wizard. The Delete Links Wizard is designed to find and delete links such as defined name links, hidden name links, chart links, Microsoft query links, and object links. However, in our experience, it does not find phantom links.

Once you're confident there are no formula links, you need to ensure that you don't have any nonphantom links lurking somewhere else. To do this, we like to start from within the Excel workbook containing the phantom links. Select Insert → Name → Define. Scroll through the list of names, clicking to highlight each one and looking in the Refers To: box at the bottom. Check to make sure none of these names is referencing a different workbook.

> Instead of clicking each name in the Define Name dialog, you can insert a new worksheet and select Insert → Name → Paste. Then, from the Paste Name dialog, click Paste Link. This will create a list of all the names in your workbook, with their referenced ranges in the corresponding column.

If any of the names are pointing outside your workbook, you've found the source of at least one link that would prompt the updating question. Now it's up to you to decide whether you want to change this range name to refer only to the workbook itself or leave it as it is.

Another potential source of links is in your charts. It's possible that your charts have the same problem we just explained. You should check that the data ranges and the X-axis labels for the chart aren't referencing an external workbook. Once again, you get to decide whether the link you've found is correct.

Links also can lurk in objects, such as text boxes, autoshapes, etc. Objects can try to reference an external workbook. The easiest way to locate objects is to select any single cell on each worksheet and then select Edit → Go To... (F5). From the Go To... dialog, click Special and then check the Objects option and click OK. This will select all objects on the worksheet. You should do this on a copy of your workbook. Then, with all objects selected, you can delete, save, close, and reopen your copy to see whether this has eliminated the problem.

Finally, the last not-so-obvious place to check for real links is in the hidden sheets that you might have cleverly created and forgotten about. Unhide these sheets by selecting Format → Sheet → Unhide. If the Unhide option on the Sheet submenu is grayed out, that means you have no hidden sheets. (If you think there are sheets that don't turn up in the menu, see "Hide Worksheets So That They Cannot Be Unhidden" [Hack #5] for more information.)

Now that you have eliminated the possibility of real links, it's time to eliminate the phantom links. Go to the haunted workbook with the phantom links and select Edit → Links.... Sometimes you can simply select the unwanted link, click Change Source, and then refer the link back to itself. Often, though, you will be told that one of your formulas contains an error, and you will not be able to do this.

If you can't take the easy way out, note to which workbook Excel thinks it is linking (we'll call it the well-behaved workbook). Create a real link between the two by opening both workbooks. Go to the problem workbook and, in any cell on any worksheet, type =. Now click a cell in the well-behaved workbook and press Enter so that you have a true external link to the other workbook.

Save both workbooks, but don't close them yet. While in the phantom links workbook, select Edit → Links... and use the Change Source button to refer all links to the new workbook to which you just purposely created a link. Save your workbook again and delete the cell in which you created the true external link. Finally, save your file.

This often eliminates the offending phantom link, as Excel now realizes you have deleted the external link to the workbook. If this does not solve the problem, however, try these next steps, but make sure you *save a copy first*.

The following process involves deleting data permanently. Therefore, before you begin, create a backup copy of your workbook. Neglecting to do so could create new problems for you.

With the problem workbook open, delete one sheet, Save, and then close and re-open the workbook. If you are not prompted to update your missing links, the sheet you deleted contained the phantom link. This should solve the problem, but if it doesn't, repeat the first step for each sheet in the workbook. You will need to add a new sheet before you delete the last sheet, as any workbook must have at least one sheet.

We're going to assume this technique worked for you. So, here's what you should do next. Open the copy of your workbook (the one that still has data in it) and make another copy. You've got to work with the problem worksheet (or worksheets) and use the process of elimination to discover where the problem is in the worksheet.

With the problem worksheet active, select a chunk of cells (about 10×10) and then select Edit → Clear → All. (Are you absolutely sure you saved a copy?) Save, close, and reopen the worksheet. If you are not prompted to update those links, you found the problem and your reward is to redo that block of cells. If you are prompted to update the links, continue deleting cells until you aren't are no longer prompted. Then redo the badly behaved cells.

We hope these techniques will save you some of the frustration that arises when those dreaded phantom links appear in your workbooks. They're not easy or fun to perform, but they can get you out of trouble.

Reduce Workbook Bloat

HACK #14

Ever notice that your workbook is increasing in size at an alarming rate for no apparent reason? There are several causes of workbook bloat, and some slimming solutions.

Have you ever eaten so much that you can't function properly? Workbook bloat in Excel is much the same thing. *Workbook bloat* is a term for a workbook that has had so much done to it that it has swollen to such a size it can no longer function correctly.

We checked out the size of a typical workbook containing a fairly large amount of data. With data only, the workbook file size was 1.37 MB. Then we added a pivot table referencing four entire columns for its data source and noted that the file size increased dramatically to 2.4 MB. Add some formatting and your typical workbook size has blown out to almost double by performing a few actions.

One of the more common causes of file bloat, particularly in earlier versions of Excel, is the application of formats to entire columns or rows rather than to just the data range in use. Another mistake is referencing entire columns as the data source for charts and pivot tables rather than just the cells with actual data in them. To fix these problems, you will need to eliminate all the superfluous formatting and restrict your data source to only the useful range of cells.

Before doing such refactoring, *always* make a copy of your workbook for safekeeping.

Eliminating Superfluous Formatting

The first step in eliminating superfluous formatting is to figure out where your worksheet's data ends—the bottom righthand corner of your data, if you will. Don't rely on Edit → Go To... → Special → Last Cell, as this might take you to the last cell containing formatting, not actual data. Having manually located the cell you know to be your last cell containing legitimate data, highlight the row immediately following it. While pressing the Ctrl and Shift keys, press the down arrow on your keyboard to highlight all rows beneath that row and select Edit → Clear → All to clear them.

Now apply the same logic to unwanted formatting lurking in your columns. Locate the cell in the last column containing data and click the column header of the column immediately to the right. Press Ctrl-Shift and the right arrow on your keyboard to highlight all other columns to the right and then select Edit → Clear → All.

> Don't be tempted to actually delete these rows or columns rather than clearing them, as doing so often causes the dreaded #REF! error in any cells of any formulas that might reference them.

Save your workbook and take gleeful note of the change in its file size by selecting File → Properties... → General.

If you have macros, now you need to address the modules that the macro code resides in. This is a fairly quick, painless, and straightforward process that entails exporting all modules and UserForms to your hard drive and then deleting the existing modules and UserForms, pressing Save, and importing the modules you exported.

To do this, go into the Visual Basic Editor and, from within the Project Explorer, right-click each module and select Remove Module1 (or whatever the name of the module happens to be). When you are asked whether you want to export your module before removing it, say Yes, taking note of the path.

Do this for each module in turn, as well as for any UserForms you might have. Don't forget the private modules of your workbook and worksheets if they house code as well. Once you have done all this, save the workbook. Then, select File → Import File and import each module and UserForm back into your workbook. Following this process will create a text file of each module and that, in turn, removes all extra baggage that the modules might be holding.

The Web contains some free utilities that will automate this task to some degree, but we have heard cases of these utilities making a mess of code or even increasing file sizes. If you do use one of these, always save a backup copy first, as the developers will take no responsibility for any loss of data.

Honing Data Sources

If, after performing the previous steps, you still believe your file size is unrealistically large, another possible suspect is referencing unused cells in Pivot-Tables and PivotCharts. This is true particularly of PivotTables, as people frequently reference all 65,536 rows in order to avoid manually updating ranges as new data is added. If this is your modus operandi, use dynamic named ranges [Hack #42] for your data sources instead.

Cleaning Corrupted Workbooks

If you still believe your workbook is too large, it is possible that your workbook or component sheets are corrupt. Unfortunately, determining a point of corruption requires a manual process of elimination.

> Again, we strongly advise you to save a copy of your workbook before proceeding.

To be sure you're not missing anything, unhide any hidden sheets by selecting Format → Sheet → Unhide. If this menu option is grayed out, you have no hidden worksheets to worry about. With all your sheets visible, start from the sheet on the far left and move one-by-one to the right. For each in turn, delete it, save your workbook, and note its file size by selecting File → Properties → General. If the file size drops dramatically considering the amount of data on that sheet, you've probably found your corruption.

To replace a corrupt sheet in your workbook, create a new worksheet, manually select the data in the corrupt sheet, and cut (do not copy) and paste it into the new sheet. Delete the corrupt sheet from your workbook, save, and repeat.

> By cutting rather than copying, Excel automatically will follow the data to the new sheet, keeping references intact.

HACK #15 Extract Data from a Corrupt Workbook

Workbook corruption can mean the loss of vital data, costing you more than just money. This hack explores some methods that might recover your data.

Workbooks sometimes become corrupt for no apparent reason. This can cause all sorts of problems, especially if the workbook is vital and for whatever reason you have no backup. Lesson 1: always back up your data somewhere. Realistically, though, this does not always happen, and corruption can, of course, occur right before your regularly scheduled backup.

To add to your frustration, even though you know your workbook is corrupt, you sometimes might still be able to open it and even perform certain actions in it.

If You Can Open Your Workbook

If you can open the offending workbook, before doing anything else, be sure to save a copy of it; otherwise, you might regret it. If you have a copy, you can always seek professional help!

Now, try opening the workbook in a later version of Excel and simply saving. Obviously this is not possible if you already are using the latest version of Excel.

If this doesn't work, try opening your workbook and saving the file in HTML or HTM format, then close the file and reopen it, this time saving again in the format you require—e.g., *.xls*.

When saving in HTML or HTM format, the following features will be lost:

- Custom views
- Unused number formats
- Unused styles
- Data consolidation settings
- Scenarios
- Natural language formulas (they are converted to standard range references)
- Custom function categories
- Strikethrough, subscript, and superscript elements
- Change History
- Customized page setup settings for charts that are embedded on a worksheet
- List settings for ListBoxes and ComboBoxes from the Forms toolbar
- Conditional formatting that is stored on an XLM macro sheet

Also, shared workbooks will no longer be shared. The "Value (Y) axis crosses at category number" setting on the Scale tab of the Format Axis dialog box is not saved if the "Value (Y) axis crosses a maximum category" checkbox is checked. The "Vary colors by point" setting in the Format Data Series dialog box is not saved if the chart contains more than one data series.

Finally, try opening your file and saving it in SYLK (*.slk*, for symbolic link) format. Note that when you save a workbook in this format, only the active worksheet is saved. So, you will have to do the same for each worksheet. Reopen the file and save it in a desired format such as *.xls*.

If You Cannot Open Your File

If your workbook is corrupt to the point that you cannot even open it, open your spreadsheet in Microsoft Word or via the Spreadsheet viewer, which can be downloaded from the Microsoft web site, then copy your data from the open file. Much of your formatting, formulas, etc., will, however, be lost.

Next, open a new workbook and create an external link to the corrupt workbook—e.g., ='C:\Documents and Settings\Raina\My Documents\[ChookSheet. xls]Sheet1'!A1. Copy this link down as many rows and across as many columns as needed. Do the same for each worksheet in the workbook. If you cannot remember any of the names of the worksheets, create any old sheet name using the correct filename path, and Excel will display the sheet names for you when you press Enter.

One final thing you can do is visit the OpenOffice.org web site and download the free version of OpenOffice.org. Except for different names for different tools and commands, OpenOffice.org is very similar to Excel. OpenOffice.org is based on the same basic spreadsheet structure as Excel, making it simple for Excel users to use. In fact, about 96% of the formulas used in Excel can be created and applied by using the spreadsheet in Open-Office.org.

To download the free version of OpenOffice.org, go to *http://download. openoffice.org/index.html* and download it from the FTP site of your choice. Then install the program. OpenOffice.org is also available for Macs.

In many cases, your Excel data can be recovered. However, no VBA code can be recovered due to incompatibility between OpenOffice.org and Excel.

Sadly, if none of these methods works, you probably will have to pay to try to have your workbook recovered with special software. One source where such reputable software (for Windows) can be purchased belongs to the authors of this book and is located at *http://www.ozgrid.com/Services/ corrupt-file-recovery-index.htm*.

After purchase and installation, run the ExcelFix program. Click Select File, select a corrupt file, and then click Diagnose to recover the file. You should now see the recovered file in the workbook viewer. Click Save Workbook to save the workbook into a new readable file that you can open from Excel.

Also available is a demo version that does not enable you to save the file, but all versions of the program enable you to start again and recover as many files as you want.

Hacking Excel's Built-in Features
Hacks 16-38

Although Excel comes with a wide variety of standard features for managing and analyzing data, the boundaries of these features are often frustrating. The hacks in this chapter provide numerous ways in which you can escape these boundaries and make Excel a much more powerful tool.

 HACK #16 ## Validate Data Based on a List on Another Worksheet

Data validation makes it easy to specify rules your data must follow. Unfortunately, Excel insists that lists used in data validation must appear on the same worksheet as the data being validated. Fortunately, there are ways to evade this requirement.

In this hack, we provide two methods you can use to validate data based on a list on another worksheet. The first method takes advantage of Excel's named ranges (which are covered in more detail in Chapter 3), and the second uses a function call.

Method 1: Named Ranges

Perhaps the easiest and quickest way to overcome Excel's data-validation barrier is by naming the range where the list resides. To create a named range, select the cells containing the list and enter a name in the Name box that appears at the left end of the Formula bar. For the purposes of this example, we will assume your range is called MyRange.

Select the cell in which you want the drop-down list to appear and then select Data → Validation. Select List from the Allow: field, and in the Source: box enter **=MyRange**. Click OK.

Because you used the named range, your list (even though it resides on another worksheet) now can be used for the validation list.

Method 2: the INDIRECT Function

The INDIRECT function enables you to reference a cell containing text that represents a cell address. You then can use that cell as a local cell reference, even though it gets its data from another worksheet. You can use this feature to reference the worksheet where your list resides.

Assume your list resides on Sheet1 in the range $A$1:$A$8. Click any cell on a different worksheet where you want to have this validation list (pick list) appear. Then select Data → Validation and choose List from the Allow: field. In the Source: box, enter the following code:

```
=INDIRECT("Sheet1!$A$1:$A$8")
```

Ensure that the In-Cell drop-down box is checked and click OK. The list that resides on Sheet1 should appear in your drop-down validation list.

If the name of the worksheet on which your list resides contains spaces, you need to use the INDIRECT function in the following way:

```
=INDIRECT("'Sheet 1'!$A$1:$A$8")
```

The difference here is that you used a single apostrophe immediately after the first quotation mark and another single apostrophe immediately before the exclamation point.

> It is a good idea to always use the single apostrophe, regardless of whether your sheet name contains spaces. You still will be able to reference a sheet with no spaces in its name, and it makes it easier to make changes later.

The Pros and Cons of Both Methods

Named ranges and the INDIRECT function each have an advantage and a disadvantage.

The advantage to using a named range is that changes you make to the sheet name will have no effect on the validation list. This highlights the INDIRECT function's disadvantage—namely, that any change you make to the sheet name will not be reflected automatically within the INDIRECT function, so you will have to manually change the function to correspond to the new sheet name.

The advantage to using the INDIRECT function is that if the first cell/row or last cell/row is deleted from the named range, the named range will return a #REF! error. This highlights the disadvantage to using named ranges: if you delete any cells or rows from within a named range, those changes will not affect the validation list.

Control Conditional Formatting with Checkboxes

Although conditional formatting is one of Excel's most powerful features, it's a nuisance to turn it on and off through the menus and dialog boxes of the GUI. Adding checkboxes to your worksheet that turn formatting on and off makes it much easier to read data in any way you want, whenever you want.

Conditional formatting, a feature available since Excel 97, applies formats to selected cells that meet criteria based on values or formulas you specify. Although conditional formatting is usually applied based on cell values, applying it based on formulas provides the flexibility to extend the conditional formatting interface all the way to the spreadsheet grid.

Setting Up Checkboxes for Conditional Formatting

The checkboxes from the Forms toolbar return either a TRUE or FALSE value (checked/not checked) to their linked cell. By combining a checkbox from the Forms toolbar with conditional formatting using the Formula Is option (shown in Figure 2-1), you can turn conditional formatting on and off via a checkbox.

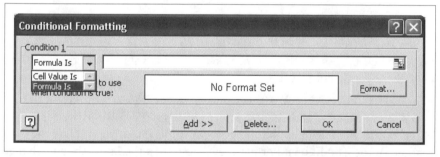

Figure 2-1. The Conditional Formatting dialog with the Formula Is option

 When used in conjunction with a formula (such as the Formula Is option), conditional formatting automatically formats a cell whenever the formula result returns TRUE. For this reason, any formula you use in this hack must return either TRUE or FALSE.

To see what we mean, try this simple example, which hides data via the use of conditional formatting and a checkbox. For this example, we will use the range $A$1:$A$10, filled consecutively with the numbers 1–10. To obtain a

checkbox from the Forms toolbar, select View → Toolbars → Forms and click the checkbox, then click near cell C1 on your sheet to position the checkbox. Right-click the checkbox and select Format → Control → Control. Type **C1** in the Cell Link box, as shown in Figure 2-2, and click OK.

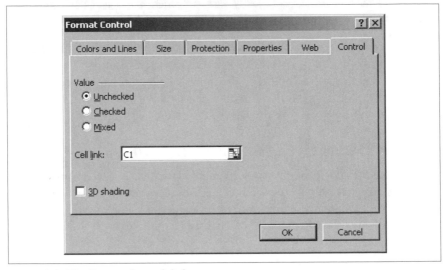

Figure 2-2. The Format Control dialog

When you select the checkbox floating over cell C1, it will return TRUE or FALSE to cell C1. As you do not need to see these values, select cell C1 and change the font color to White.

Now select cells $A$1:$A$10, starting with A1. Select Format → Conditional Formatting..., and then select Formula Is (it will initially read Cell Value Is). In the Formula box to the right, type **=$C$1**. Next, click the Format tab of the Conditional Formatting dialog, then the Font tab, and change the font color to White. Click OK, then OK again.

Select your checkbox so that it is checked, and the font color of the data in range $A$1:$A$10 automatically will change to white. Unchecking the checkbox will set it back to normal.

Toggling Number Highlighting On and Off

The ability to automatically highlight numbers that meet certain criteria can make it a lot easier to find the data you need in a spreadsheet. To do this, start by selecting cell E1 (or any other cell you prefer) and name this cell **CheckBoxLink** using the name box at the far left of the Formula toolbar (see Figure 2-3).

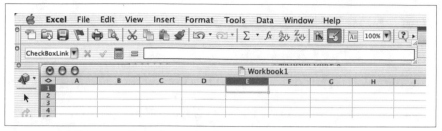

Figure 2-3. Cell E1 named CheckBoxLink

Add a checkbox from the Forms toolbar to a clean worksheet, call this sheet **Checkboxes**, and position it in cell A1. Set the cell link of this checkbox to the cell CheckBoxLink by right-clicking the checkbox and selecting Format Control... → Control. Then type **CheckBoxLink** in the Cell Link box and click OK.

Right-click the checkbox again, select Edit Text, and enter the words **Show Me**. In column A on another worksheet, enter the numbers **25** to **2500** in increments of 25. Name this range **Numbers** and hide this sheet by selecting Format → Sheet → Hide.

> To enter these numbers quickly, enter the number **25** in cell A1. Then, left-click the fill handle (which appears as a small black square at the bottom right of the selection) and, while holding down the left mouse button, drag down to about row 100. Now release the left mouse button, select Series from the pop-up shortcut menu, enter **25** as the step value, and enter **2500** as the stop value. Then click OK.

Select cell B1 of the Checkboxes worksheet and name this cell **FirstNum**. Select cell D1 and name this cell **SecondNum**. In cell C1, type the word **AND**. Now, select cell B1 (FirstNum), and press the Ctrl key while selecting cell D1 (SecondNum). Select Data → Validation → Settings, and from the Allow: box, select List, and in the Source: box, type **=Numbers**. Ensure that the In-Cell drop-down item is checked and then click OK. This will give you a drop-down list of numbers 25 through 2500 in both cells.

In cell A1, type the heading **Amount**. Immediately below this, fill the range A2:A20 with any numbers that fall between the range 25 and 2500. Select cells A2:A20 (ensuring that you start from cell A2 and that it is your active cell in the selection), and select Format → Conditional Formatting....

In the dialog box that appears, shown in Figure 2-4, select Formula Is (it now should read Cell Value Is). Then, in the Formula box, type the following formula:

```
=AND($A2>=FirstNum,$A2<=SecondNum,CheckBoxLink)
```

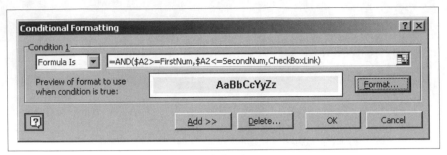

Figure 2-4. The Conditional Formatting dialog box

Click the Format tab and set any desired formatting or combination of formatting. Click OK, and then click OK again to dismiss the dialog boxes. Change the font color for cell CheckBoxLink (E1) to White so that True or False will not show. From cell FirstNum (B1), select any number and then select another number higher than the first from cell SecondNum (D1).

Check the checkbox, and the conditional formatting you just set will be applied automatically to the numbers that fall between the range you specified earlier. Deselect the checkbox and the formatting will revert it to its default.

As you can see, by using a checkbox in combination with conditional formatting, you can do things most people would think is possible only through the use of VBA code.

HACK #18 Identify Formulas with Conditional Formatting

Excel does not have a built-in function that identifies formulas. Once a formula is entered into a cell, you can tell whether the cell is a static value or a value derived from a formula only by clicking in each cell and looking in the Formula bar. This hack fills that gap with a custom function.

The VBA code in this custom function (also called a *user-defined function*) enables you to identify cells that contain formulas without having to click through 10,000 cells and examine each one.

To become a clever formula hunter, start by selecting Tools → Macro → Visual Basic Editor (Alt/Option-F11) and then select Insert → Module. Enter the following function:

```
Function IsFormula(Check_Cell As Range)
    IsFormula = Check_Cell.HasFormula
End Function
```

Close the window (press Alt/⌘-Q, or use the Close button in the window's titlebar). Now this function is available in any cell on any worksheet in this workbook when you enter the formula **=IsFormula($A$1)**. You also can access the function by selecting Insert → Function, then selecting UserDefined from the Category option and choosing IsFormula from the functions displayed.

The formula returns TRUE if the reference cell houses a formula and FALSE if it does not. You can use this Boolean result in conjunction with conditional formatting so that all formulas are highlighted automatically in a format of your choice.

One of the best things about using this method is that your spreadsheet's formula identification capabilities will be dynamic. This means that if you add or remove a formula, your formatting will change accordingly. Here we explain how to do this.

Select a range of cells on your spreadsheet—say, A1:J500—and incorporate some extra cells in case more formulas are added at a later stage.

> Avoid the temptation of selecting an entire worksheet, as this can add unnecessary overhead to your spreadsheet.

With these cells selected, and with A1 the active cell of the selection, select Format → Conditional Formatting.... Under Cell Value Is, select Formula Is and enter **=IsFormula(A1)** in the Formula box. Click the Format button and choose any formatting you want to use to identify formula cells. Click OK, then OK again.

> Sometimes, when entering formulas into conditional formatting, Excel will try to put quotation marks around the formulas after you click OK. This means Excel has recognized what you entered as text, not as a formula. If this happens to you, go back into the Conditional Formatting dialog, remove the quotation marks, and click OK.

At this point, the specified formula should be applied to all cells on your worksheet that contain formulas. If you delete or overtype a cell containing a formula, the conditional formatting will disappear. Similarly, if you enter a new formula into any cell within the range, it too will be highlighted.

This simple conditional formatting hack can make your spreadsheets a lot easier to deal with when it comes time to maintain or modify them.

HACK #19   Count or Sum Cells That Meet Conditional Formatting Criteria

Once you can see the results of conditional formatting, you might want to create formulas that reference only the data that was conditionally formatted. Excel doesn't quite understand this in its calculations, but it can learn.

Excel users regularly ask, "How can I do calculations on only the cells that have a specific background color?" This question arises so often because Excel has no standard function for accomplishing this task; however, it can be accomplished with a custom function, as shown in "Count or Sum Cells That Have a Specified Fill Color" **[Hack #88]**.

The only trouble with using a custom function is that it does not pick up any formatting that is applied using conditional formatting. With a bit of lateral thinking, however, you can achieve the same result without bothering with a custom function.

Say you have a long list of numbers in the range $A$2:$A$100. You applied conditional formatting to these cells so that any numbers that fall between the range 10 and 20 are flagged. Now you have to add the value of the cells that meet the criterion you just set and then specify the sum of the values using conditional formatting. You don't need to worry about what conditional formatting you applied to these cells, but you do need to know the criteria that were used to flag the cells (in this case, cells with values between 10 and 20).

You can use the SUMIF function to add a range of cells that meet a certain criterion—but only one criterion. If you need to deal with more than one factor, you can use an array formula.

You use an array formula like this:

```
=SUM(IF($A$2:$A$100>10,IF($A$2:$A$100<20,$A$2:$A$100)))
```

When entering array formulas, *don't press Enter. Press Ctrl-Shift-Enter.* This way, Excel will place curly brackets around the outside of the formula so that it looks like this:

```
{=SUM(IF($A$2:$A$100>10,IF($A$2:$A$100<20,$A$2:
$A$100)))}
```

If you enter these brackets yourself, it won't work. You must allow Excel to do it for you.

Also, note that using an array formula can slow down Excel's recalculations if there are too many references to large ranges.

To read more about array formulas, visit *http://www.ozgrid.com/Excel/arrays.htm.*

An Alternate Path

Alternatively, you can use a spare column (for instance, column B) to reference the cells in column A. Your reference will return results into column B only if the value meets the conditions you set—e.g., >10, <20. To do this, follow these steps:

Select cell B1 and enter the following formula:

```
=IF(AND(A2>10,A2<20),A2,"")
```

Fill this formula into each cell, down to cell B100. Once the values are filled in, you should have values in column B that are between 10 and 20.

 To quickly copy a formula down to the last used row in the column adjacent, enter the formula in the first cell (B2), reselect that cell, and double-click the fill handle. You also can do this by selecting Edit → Fill → Down.

Now you can select any cell where you want your SUM result to appear and use a standard SUM function to add it up. (You can hide column B if you want so that you do not see an extra column full of the returned values of your formula.)

The preceding methods certainly get the job done, but Excel provides yet another function that enables you to specify two or more criteria. This function is part of Excel's database functions, and is called DSUM. To test it, use the same set of numbers in A2:A100. Select cells C1:D2 and name this range **SumCriteria** by selecting the cells and entering the name in the name box to the left of the Formula bar. Now select cell C1 and enter **=$A$1**, a reference to the first cell on the worksheet. Copy this across to cell D1, and you should have a double copy of your column A heading. These copies will be used as headings for your DSUM criteria (C1:D2), which you called **SumCriteria**.

In cell C2, enter **>10**. In cell D2, enter **<20**. In the cell where you want your result, enter the following code:

```
=DSUM($A$1:$A$100,$A$1,SumCriteria)
```

DSUM is the preferred and most efficient method of working with cells that meet certain criteria. Unlike arrays, the built-in database functions are designed specifically for this purpose, and even when they reference a very large range and are used in large numbers, the negative effects they have on recalculation speed and efficiency are quite small compared to those of array formulas.

Highlight Every Other Row or Column

HACK #20   You've surely seen Excel spreadsheets that have alternating row colors. For instance, odd-numbered rows might be white, while even-numbered rows might be gray. Conditional formatting makes this easy.

Alternating colors or shading looks professional and can make data easier to read. You can apply this formatting manually, but as you can imagine, or might have experienced, it's a rather time-consuming task that requires constant updating as you add and remove data from the table. It also requires infinite patience. Fortunately, *conditional formatting* can reduce the amount of patience required and enhance your professional image.

We'll assume your data occupies the range A1:H100. Select this range of cells, starting with A1, thus ensuring that A1 is the active cell in the selection. Now, select Format → Conditional Formatting.... From the drop-down that currently says Cell Value Is, select Formula Is. In the Formula box, type the following formula, as shown in Figure 2-5:

    =MOD(ROW( ),2)

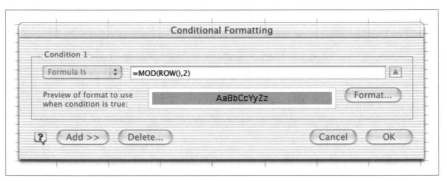

Figure 2-5. Conditional Formatting dialog containing the MOD formula to specify a format to every second row in a range

Click the Format button and choose the format you want to apply to every second row. Click OK, and then click OK again. The format you specified should be applied to every second row in the range A1:H100. You also should have some patience left for the rest of the day.

If you need to apply this to columns rather than rows, use this formula instead:

    =MOD(COLUMN( ),2)

Although this method applies the formatting specified to every second row or column quickly and easily, it is not dynamic. Rows containing no data will still have the formatting applied. This looks slightly untidy and makes reading the spreadsheet a bit more difficult. Making the highlighting of every second row or column dynamic takes a little more formula tweaking.

Again, select the range A1:H100, ensuring that A1 is the active cell. Select Format → Conditional Formatting..., and from the Cell Value Is pull-down menu, select Formula Is. In the Formula box, enter the following formula:

```
=AND(MOD(ROW( ),2),COUNTA($A1:$H1))
```

Note that you do not reference rows absolutely (with dollar signs), but you do reference columns this way.

Click the dialog's Format button and select the desired formatting, then click OK, and OK again. Any row within the range A1:H100 that does not contain data will not have conditional formatting applied. If you remove data from a specific row in your table, it too will no longer have conditional formatting applied. If you add new data anywhere within the range A1:H100, the conditional formatting will kick in.

This works because when you supply a formula for conditional formatting, the formula itself must return an answer of either TRUE or FALSE. In the language of Excel formulas, 0 has a Boolean value of FALSE, while any number greater than zero has a boolean value of TRUE. When you use the formula =MOD(ROW( ),2), it will return either a value of 0 (FALSE) or a number greater than 0.

The ROW( ) function is a volatile function that always returns the row number of the cell it resides in. You use the MOD function to return the remainder after dividing one number by another. In the case of the formula you used, you are dividing the row number by the number 2, so all even row numbers will return 0, while all odd row numbers will always return a number greater than 0.

When you nest the ROW( ) function and the COUNTA function in the AND function, it means you must return TRUE (or any number greater than 0) to both the MOD function and the COUNTA function for the AND function to return TRUE. COUNTA counts all nonblank cells.

HACK #21 Create 3D Effects in Tables or Cells

Whenever you see a nifty 3D effect in a program or application such as Excel, you are actually seeing an illusion created by specific formatting. It is easy to create this illusion yourself by applying formatting to a cell or range of cells.

To start off with a simple example, we'll give a cell a 3D effect so that it appears raised, like a button. On a clean worksheet, select cell D5. (You're selecting D5 because it's not on an edge.) Select Format → Cells → Border. From the Line box, choose the second thickest line style. Ensure that the color selected is Black (or Automatic, if you haven't changed the default for this option). Now click the righthand border and then click the bottom border. Return to the color option and select White. The second thickest border still should be selected, so this time click the two remaining borders of the cell, the top border and the left border. Click the Patterns tab on the Format Cells dialog and make the cell shading Gray. Click OK and deselect cell D5. Cell D5 will have a raised effect that gives the appearance of a button. You did it all with borders and shading.

If, for fun or diversity, you want to make a cell look indented or pushed in, select cell E5 (because it's next to D5 and it makes the next exercise work). Select Format → Cells → Border, select the second thickest border from the line styles, and ensure that the color is black.

Apply the formatting to the top and left border of the cell. Select White for the color option and apply a white line to the right and bottom borders. Click the Patterns tab and change the cell's format to Gray. Click OK. Cell E5 should appear indented. This works even better in contrast with cell D5, which has the raised effect.

Using a 3D Effect on a Table of Data

Next, we'll experiment with this tool to see the sorts of effects you can apply to your tables or spreadsheets to give them some 3D excitement.

Select cells D5 and E5, and click the Format Painter tool (the paintbrush icon) on the standard toolbar. While holding down the left mouse button, click in cell F5, and drag across to cell J5 and release.

Now select cells D5:J5 and again click the Format Painter tool on the standard toolbar. While holding down the left mouse button, select cell D6 and drag it across and down to cell J15, then release. This should produce the effect shown in Figure 2-6.

We have used a fairly thick border to ensure that the effect is seen clearly; however, you might want to make this a little subtler by using a thinner line style. You also could use one of the other line styles to produce an even greater effect. The easiest way to find good combinations is to use trial and error on a blank worksheet to create the effect you want. You are limited only by your imagination and, perhaps, your taste.

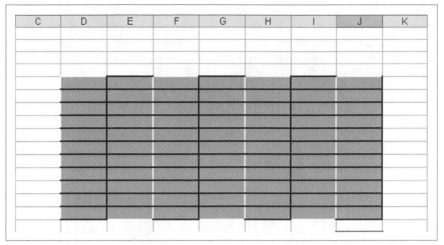

Figure 2-6. A 3D effect applied to a range of cells

Always keep in mind that 3D effects can enhance readability and give spreadsheets a more professional look and feel, but when they're used in excess, they can have the opposite effect. Remember, use everything in moderation.

If you want to take this a step further and apply 3D effects automatically and dynamically, you can combine the 3D with conditional formatting, automating the application of the style choices you prefer.

HACK
#22
Turn Conditional Formatting and Data Validation On and Off with a Checkbox

Data validation can make it far less likely that a user accidentally will enter incorrect data. Sometimes, however, you might need to make it easier to enter data that otherwise would be flagged as incorrect by conditional formatting or blocked completely by the validator.

Usually, you would enable users to enter data that otherwise would be flagged as incorrect by removing conditional formatting and/or data validation from the cells. There is an easier way, however: you can combine a simple checkbox from the Forms toolbar with data validation.

For this example, you'll apply conditional formatting to a range of cells so that any data appearing more than once is highlighted for easy identification. We'll assume your table of data extends from cell $A$1:$H$100. To conditionally format this range of data so that you can identify duplicates requires a few steps.

Select cell K1 and name this cell **CheckBoxLink** by typing the name into the Name box to the left of the Formula bar and pressing Enter. If the Forms toolbar is not already showing, right-click any toolbar and select Forms, then click the Checkbox icon. Now click your worksheet somewhere outside the range A1:H100 to add the checkbox to the worksheet.

Right-click the checkbox and select Format Control → Control. In the Cell Link box, type the name **CheckBoxLink** and click OK. Select cell A1, then drag and select a range down to cell H100. It is important that cell A1 is the active cell in your selection. Select Format → Conditional Formatting..., and from the box with the Value Is cell, select Formula Is. In the box to the right of Formula Is, enter this formula (as shown in Figure 2-7):

    =AND(COUNTIF($A$1:$H$100,A1)>1,CheckboxLink)

Click the Format tab and then the Patterns page tab and select a color you want to be applied to duplicated data. Click OK, then OK again.

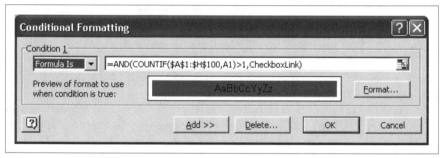

Figure 2-7. Conditional Formatting dialog showing formula to conditionally format a range to highlight duplicates

Although the checkbox you added to the worksheet is checked, the cell link in K1 (CheckBoxLink) will read TRUE and all duplicates within the range $A$1: $A$100 will be highlighted. As soon as you deselect the checkbox, its cell link (CheckBoxLink) will return FALSE, and duplicates will not be highlighted.

The checkbox gives you a switch so that you can turn conditional formatting on and off from the spreadsheet, with no need to return to the Conditional Formatting dialog box. You can apply the same principle to data validation when using the formula option.

This works because you used the AND function. AND means two things must occur: COUNTIF($A$1:$H$100,A1)>1 must return TRUE, and the cell link for the checkbox (CheckboxLink) also must be TRUE. In other words, both conditions must be TRUE for the AND function to return TRUE.

Support Multiple Lists in a ComboBox

HACK #23

When working with multiple lists, you can force a list to change by using a combination of option buttons plus a ComboBox.

Excel offers many ways for users to select items from a list, be they names, products, days of the week—whatever the list is composed of. However, to access more than one list of choices simultaneously generally requires that you use three separate controls, such as three ComboBox controls from the Forms toolbar.

Instead, you can use a ComboBox in combination with option buttons (also called radio buttons and also found on the Forms toolbar) to have a list change automatically according to which option button you choose. To see how this works, enter the numbers **1** through **7** in the range A1:A7 on a new worksheet. In B1:B7, enter the days of the week starting with **Monday** and ending with **Sunday**. In C1:C7, enter the months **January** through **July**.

> Excel's auto-fill features can make this task much easier. Enter **1** in cell A1, select cell A1, press the Ctrl key, and then left-click the fill handle. While holding down the left mouse button and the Ctrl key simultaneously, drag down to row 7. Excel will fill in the numbers for you. Next, enter **Monday** in cell B1 and double-click the fill handle for this cell. Enter **January** in cell C1 and double-click the fill handle for this cell. Excel will fill in the days and months for you!

Select View → Toolbars → Forms and double-click the option button on the toolbar. Then, click the spreadsheet anywhere in three separate spots to place three option buttons on the spreadsheet.

Now, click the ComboBox and again click somewhere on the spreadsheet to insert a ComboBox on it. Using the drag handles, size the ComboBox to a manageable size and position the option buttons so that they're directly below the ComboBox.

Left-click the first option button, select Edit Text, then replace the words Option Button 1 with the word **Numbers**. Use the same process for Option Button 2, replacing with the word **Weekdays**, and for Option Button 3, replacing with the word **Months**. This is shown in Figure 2-8.

While holding down the Ctrl key, click each option button so that all three are highlighted, then right-click and select Format Control → Control. Specify cell $F$1 as the cell link (make sure it is absolute—use those dollar signs).

In cell E6, enter the following formula:

```
=ADDRESS(1,$F$1)&":"&":"ADDRESS(7,$F$1)
```

Select Insert → Name → Define. In Names in Workbook:, type **MyRange**, and in the Refers To: field, type the following:

```
=INDIRECT($E$6)
```

Click Add, and then click OK. Right-click the ComboBox and select Format Control → Control. Make the Input range **MyRange** and the cell link **$G$1**, then click OK. You should be able to select one of the option buttons, and the list within the ComboBox should automatically reflect which option button you chose.

	A	B	C	D	E	F	G	H	I
1		1	Monday	January	This cell will have the		3	5	
2		2	Tuesday	February	number 1, 2 or 3 in it				
3		3	Wednesday	March	depending on the Option			This cell will reflect the item	
4		4	Thursday	April	Button chosen			chosen from the Combobox	
5		5	Friday	May				and can be used as the	
6		6	Saturday	June		$C$1:$C$7		needed argument in a Lookup	
7		7	Sunday	July				formula	
8									
9									
10									
11					May				
12									
13					○ Numbers	This address will change with each			
14					○ Weekdays	selection of the Option Buttons and			
15						will cause the Combobox list to			
16					◉ Months	change.			
17									
18									

Figure 2-8. A multilist ComboBox controlled by option buttons

When setting this up for your own spreadsheet, you should use some off-screen cells for the ComboBox links and lists. You might even want to hide these cells from users so that your links stay where they should. Also, you need to modify the two ADDRESS functions to reflect the cell range you are using. In the ADDRESS functions we used in this example, 1 represents the first row number of the lists, while 7 represents the last row number.

HACK #24   Create Validation Lists That Change Based on a Selection from Another List

Validation needs can vary depending on the context in which the validation is used. However, you can create a spreadsheet in which one validation list changes depending on what you select in another.

To make this hack work, the first thing you need to do is set up a worksheet with some data. On a clean worksheet named Lists and located in cell A1, type the heading **Objects**. In cell B1, type the heading **Corresponding List**. In cells A2:A5, repeat the word **Can**. In cells A6:A9, repeat the word **Sofa**. In cells A10:A13, repeat the word **Shower**. In cells A14:A17, repeat the word **Car**. Then, starting with cell B2 and ending with cell B17, enter the following words (corresponding to the Objects list): **Tin**, **Steel**, **Opener**, **Lid**, **Bed**, **Seat**, **Lounge**, **Cushion**, **Rain**, **Hot**, **Cold**, **Warm**, **Trip**, **Journey**, **Bonnet**, and **Boot**.

In cell C1, enter the heading **Validation List**. Next, to create a list of unique entries, enter the word **Can** in cell C2, the word **Sofa** in cell C3, the word **Shower** in cell C4, and the word **Car** in cell C5.

> You also can use the Advanced Filter to create a list of unique items. Select cells A1:A17, select Data → Filter → Advanced Filter, and then select Unique Records Only, Filter the List in Place. Click OK, and then select cells A2:A14 (which will include the hidden cells). Copy and paste them to cell A18. Select Data → Filter → Show All, select the list of unique objects, and cut and paste them into cell A2. Now you've got your list!

Select Insert → Name → Define, and in the Names in Workbook: field, type the word **Objects**. In the Refers To: box, type the following formula and click Add:

```
=OFFSET($A$2,0,0,COUNTA($A$1:$A$20),1)
```

In the Names in Workbook: box, type the name **ValList**, and in the Refers To: box, enter **$C$2:$C$5**. Click Add. Now insert another worksheet, call it **Sheet1**, and roll up your sleeves as you put this strange data to work.

With Sheet1 still active, select Insert → Name → Define. In the Names in Workbook: field, enter the words **CorrespondingList**, and in the Refers To: field, enter this rather lengthy formula and then click Add:

```
=OFFSET(INDIRECT(ADDRESS(MATCH(Val1Cell,Objects,0)+1,2,,,"Lists")),0,0,COUNT
IF(Objects,Val1Cell),1)
```

Click the Names in Workbook: field and type the word **Val1Cell**. In the Refers To: box, enter **$D$6** and click Add. Click the Names in Workbook: field and type the word **Val2Cell**. In the Refers To: box, enter **$E$6** and again click Add. Click OK to take yourself back to Sheet1 and then select $D$6.

This is a long process, but you are nearly done.

Select Data → Validation → Settings. Select List from the Allow: box, and in the Source: box, type **=ValList**. Ensure that the In-Cell drop-down checkbox is selected and click OK.

Select cell E6 and again select Data → Validation → Settings. Select List from the Allow: box, and in the Source: box, type **=CorrespondingList**. Then, ensure that the In-Cell drop-down box is checked, and click OK. Select one of the objects from the validation list in cell D6, and the validation list in cell E6 will change automatically to reflect the object you selected.

You now have one very user-friendly validation (pick) list, shown in Figure 2-9, whose contents will change automatically based on the item chosen from the other pick list. In any cell or range of cells, you can use one pick list that houses up to five separate lists.

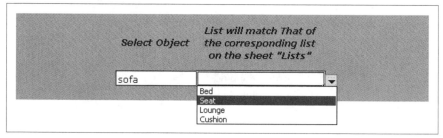

Figure 2-9. Two corresponding validation lists in use

HACK #25 Force Data Validation to Reference a List on Another Worksheet

One of the options available in the data validation feature is the List option, which provides a nice drop-down list of specific items from which the user can choose. One drawback with data validation is that the moment you try to reference a list that resides on another worksheet, you will be told this is not possible. Luckily, you can make it possible by using this hack.

You can force data validation to reference a list on another worksheet using two different approaches: named ranges and the INDIRECT function.

Method 1: Named Ranges

Perhaps the easiest and quickest way to perform this task is by naming the range where the list resides. For this purposes of this exercise, we will assume you called that range MyRange. Select the cell in which you want this drop-down list to appear and select Data → Validation. Select List from the Allow: field, and in the Source: box, enter **=MyRange**. Click OK. Your list (which resides on another worksheet) can now be used for the validation list.

Method 2: the INDIRECT Function

The INDIRECT function enables you to reference a cell containing text that represents a cell address. You can use the cell containing the INDIRECT function as the cell reference, and you can use this feature to reference the worksheet where the list resides.

Assume your list resides on Sheet1 in the range $A$1:$A$10. Click in any cell on another worksheet where you want to have this validation list (pick list) appear. Then select Data → Validation, and select List from the Allow: field. In the Source: box, enter the following function:

```
=INDIRECT("Sheet1!$A$1:$A$10")
```

Ensure that the In-Cell drop-down box is checked and click OK. The list that resides on Sheet1 should be in your drop-down validation list.

If the name of the worksheet on which the list resides contains spaces, use the INDIRECT function as follows:

```
=INDIRECT("'Sheet 1'!$A$1:$A$10")
```

Here you used a single apostrophe immediately after the first quotation mark and another single apostrophe immediately before the exclamation point. The apostrophes identify the boundaries of the sheet name to Excel.

 It is a good idea to always use the single apostrophe, regardless of whether your sheet name contains spaces. You still will be able to reference a sheet with no spaces in its name, and it makes it easier to make changes later.

The Pros and Cons of Each Method

There are advantages and disadvantages to using named ranges and the INDIRECT function to force data validation to reference a list on another worksheet.

The advantage to using a named range in this scenario is that any changes you make to the sheet name will have no effect on the validation list. This highlights the INDIRECT function's disadvantage—namely, that any changes you make to the sheet name will not be reflected automatically within the INDIRECT function, so you will have to manually change the function to correspond to the new sheet name.

The advantage to using the INDIRECT function is that if the first cell or row or last cell or row is deleted from the named range, the named range will return a #REF! error. This highlights the disadvantage to using named ranges: if you delete any cells or rows from within the named range, those changes will not affect the validation list.

HACK #26 Use Replace... to Remove Unwanted Characters

When importing data or copying and pasting data from other sources into Excel, unwanted characters appear throughout your spreadsheet. Using this hack, you can spare yourself the trouble of removing them by hand.

Excel's Replace... feature can help you remove unwanted characters from your spreadsheet, but it takes a few extra steps. For instance, you can replace cells containing unwanted characters with nothing (effectively deleting them) so that they no longer exist. To do this, you need to know the character code of the characters you want removed. All characters have a character code, and Excel will tell you what it is if you apply the CODE function to them. The CODE function returns a numeric code for the first character in a text string. The returned code corresponds to the character set used by your computer.

To make this work, select one of the cells containing an unwanted character. From the Formula bar, highlight the character and copy it to the clipboard. Then select any unused cell (A1, for example) and paste the character into the cell on its own.

In another cell, enter the following formula:

    =CODE($A$1)

This returns the character code of the unwanted character.

Select all your data and select Edit → Replace.... Click the Find What: field, press the Alt or ⌘ key, and enter **0** followed by the code number the CODE function returned. If the code number is 163, press the Alt or ⌘ key and type **0163**. Leave the Replace With: field empty and click Replace All. This will very quickly remove all the unwanted characters matching that character code. Repeat these steps for each unwanted character.

HACK #27 Convert Text Numbers to Real Numbers

The contents of a cell might look like numbers, especially in imported data, but it still might be impossible to use these numbers in calculations. Here are a few ways in which you easily can convert these "text" numbers to true numbers.

Remember that numbers in Excel are right-aligned by default, and text is left-aligned by default. One easy way to identify those problematic text numbers in a column of what you think is composed entirely of true numbers is to select the column, select Format → Cells → Alignment, ensure that the horizontal alignment is set to Excel's default of General, and click OK. Widen the column to a reasonable width, and all true numbers will be aligned to the right while any problematic text numbers will be aligned to the left. Dates will also be aligned to the right, as a date's true underlying value is nothing more than a number.

Now that you know you have numbers that are being seen as text, here is a quick and easy way to convert them all to true numbers, making Excel consider them usable for calculations. Copy any blank cell and then select your list of numbers. Select Edit → Paste Special... and then select Values under the Paste options. Select Add under the Operation options and click OK.

This will change to true numbers any numbers that are being seen as text. This happens because a blank cell has a value of 0, and when you add any number to a number that Excel is treating as text, you will force the text number to become a true number.

You can apply this logic to some of Excel's standard functions—in particular, Excel's TEXT functions. Usually, when you use any of Excel's TEXT functions and the result returned is a number, Excel will still return that number as a text value rather than as a numeric value.

Assume you have a range of cells starting from $A$1. Each cell contains a dollar amount, followed by a space, then a person's name. Using the following formula, which combines the two TEXT functions LEFT and FIND, you can extract this dollar value:

```
=LEFT(A1,FIND(" ",A1)-1)
```

If cell A1 contains the data $22.70 Fred, the formula's result will be $22.70. However, this result will be returned as text rather than as a true numeric value; therefore, by default it will be left-aligned within the cell.

You can modify the formula so that the result is no longer a text value, but rather, a true numeric value, by adding **0** to the value:

```
=LEFT(A1,FIND(" ",A1)-1)+0
```

This will force the dollar value returned to become a true number; therefore, it will be right-aligned by default. All you need to do now is format the cell accordingly.

Another problem that can arise regarding text and numbers occurs when you mix text and numbers in the same cell, with no real way of extracting the numeric portion only. In this case, you can use a custom function to extract the numeric portion from a text string.

To create this custom function, press Alt/Option-F11, select Insert → Module, and enter the following code:

```
Function ExtractNumber(rCell As Range)
Dim lCount As Long, l As Long
Dim sText As String
Dim lNum As String

sText = rCell

  For lCount = Len(sText) To 1 Step -1
      If IsNumeric(Mid(sText, lCount, 1)) Then
          l = l + 1
          lNum = Mid(sText, lCount, 1) & lNum
      End If

      If l = 1 Then lNum = CInt(Mid(lNum, 1, 1))
  Next lCount


ExtractNumber = CLng(lNum)
End Function
```

Press Alt/⌘-Q and save. The function will appear under User Defined in the Paste function (Shift-F3). Use the function as shown in Figure 2-10.

	A	B	C
1	hjl4566klo59	456659	=ExtractNumber(A1)
2	jkh4025lop596	4025596	=ExtractNumber(A2)
3	hgt548kl92	54892	=ExtractNumber(A3)
4			
5			

Figure 2-10. Extracting the numeric portion from a text string

In Figure 2-10, column A contains a mixture of text and numbers, column B contains the result of using the ExtractNumber function, and column C shows how the formula looks in column B.

HACK #28   Customize Cell Comments

Cell comments enable you to place the electronic equivalent of a sticky note to any specified cell in a worksheet. Although many people use cell comments, many don't know that cell comments are customizable.

When you insert a cell comment via Insert → Comment, Excel will, by default, also insert the username for the PC being used. You can change this by selecting Tools → Options → General. The username will appear at the bottom of the dialog box that opens, where you can type whatever you want to be shown by default.

Although cell comments serve the simple purpose of displaying a message to either yourself or another user, you can customize the cell comment so that it better reflects your intentions.

Ensure that the Drawing toolbar is displayed by selecting View → Toolbars → Drawing. Insert a cell comment into a cell by selecting the cell and then selecting Insert → Comment. This automatically places you in Edit mode, ready to enter text into the comment box.

Left-click the outside border of the cell comment so that you are no longer in Edit mode. With the comment selected, select Draw from the Drawing toolbar, then Change AutoShape. You will be presented with a list of options including Basic Shapes, Block Arrow, Flow Chart, Stars and Banners, and Callouts. Choose an option, and the cell comment will change to the shape selected, as shown in Figure 2-11.

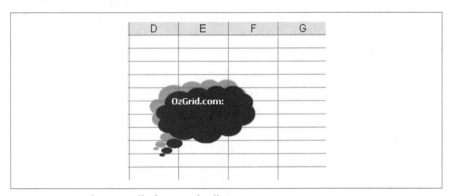

Figure 2-11. A dramatically formatted cell comment

You can take this a step further by applying a shadow style to the comment to give it a more lifelike and three-dimensional look. Ensure that your comment is still selected, but that you are no longer in Edit mode. On the Drawing toolbar, click the Shadow Settings icon shown in Figure 2-12 and choose a shadow setting for the cell comment.

Another interesting thing you can do with cell comments is use them to display pictures without impeding on any associated data. For instance, you could insert a picture of a chart into a cell comment to better illustrate the data in the chart without having to show the chart all the time.

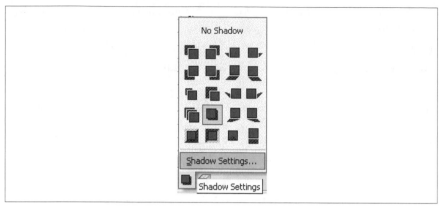

Figure 2-12. Shadow Settings options

To add a picture, ensure that the cell comment is selected, but that you are not in Edit mode. Left-click and select Format → Comment, or double-click the Comment border. Select Colors and Lines from the Format Comment dialog box. From the Color options, select Fill Effects, and from the Fill Effects dialog, select Picture. Now browse to the picture you want to insert into the cell comment.

One last thing you can do to cell comments is extract the text that was placed into a cell comment and have it appear in a cell. To do this, you need to place a simple custom function into a standard module. Select Tools → Macro → Visual Basic Editor (Alt/Option-F11), then select Insert → Module and enter the following code:

```
Function GetCommentText(rCommentCell As Range)
Dim strGotIt As String
    On Error Resume Next
    strGotIt = WorksheetFunction.Clean _
            (rCommentCell.Comment.Text)
    GetCommentText = strGotIt
    On Error GoTo 0
End Function
```

To return to Excel, either click the Close button or press Alt/⌘-Q. Now, in any cell, enter the following formula:

```
=GetCommentText(A1)
```

where A1 has a cell comment in it. The comment text will appear in the cell.

Sort by More Than Three Columns
#29

Excel's Sort feature is limited in that it enables you to nominate no more than three data fields by which to sort. In most cases, this is enough, but sometimes it can be handy to sort by more than three columns of data. Here is how you can get around this limitation.

For this example, we will assume you have related data in columns A, B, C, D, and E, and you want to sort this data first by column A, then B, then C, then D, and then E. To do this, you need to be able to sort backward—in other words, sort by the last field first, and then work back to the first field.

Select columns A through E and then select Data → Sort. Select the sort order by specifying that column C be sorted first, then D, and then E. Click Sort. Now select columns A through E and select Data → Sort. This time, sort by column A and then by B. Click Sort, and everything will be in order. Excel will have sorted the columns by five fields instead of the usual three.

If you want to automate this task, you can use a macro that will sort the selection and guess whether your data has column headings based on the formatting of the first row in the selection. If headings are in bolded, Excel will know they are column headings and will not sort them. Instead, it will sort by the leftmost column first, through to the rightmost column, for any number of columns up to 256.

The macro code you need to use must be placed into a standard module. To get it there, select Tools → Macro → Visual Basic Editor (Alt/Option-F11), then select Insert → Module and enter this code:

```
Sub SortByX( )
Dim l As Long

For l = Selection.Columns.Count To 1 Step -1
    Selection.Sort Key1:=Selection.Cells(2, l), _
    Order1:=xlAscending, Header:=xlGuess, Orientation:=xlTopToBottom
Next l
End Sub
```

To return to Excel, either close the window or press Alt/⌘-Q. Once you have the hang of it, you will be able to perform much more complicated sorts than just the standard types on offer.

Random Sorting
#30

You can use Excel to pick three winners—1st, 2nd, and 3rd—chosen at random from a list in your spreadsheet. The easiest and fairest way to do this is to use Excel's RAND function in combination with its sorting capabilities.

Assume you have a three-column table in your spreadsheet, starting from column B and containing Name, Age, and ID No., in that order. You can place the RAND function in cell A2 and copy this down as many rows as needed, all the way to the end of your table. As soon as you do this, each cell in column A containing the RAND function will automatically return a random number by which you can sort the table. In other words, you can sort columns A, B, C, and D by column A in either ascending or descending order, and the three winners can be the top three names.

The RAND function is a volatile function that will recalculate automatically whenever an action takes place in Excel—e.g., entering data somewhere else, or forcing a recalculation of the worksheet by pressing F9. You'd better write down your winners quickly.

However, you can use this volatility to your benefit and record a macro that sorts data immediately after you recalculate and force the RAND function to return another set of random numbers. You then can attach this macro to a button so that each time you want to draw three winners, all you need to do is click the button and use the top three names.

For example, assume you have your data in columns B, C, and D and that row 1 is used for headings. First, place the heading **RAND** in cell A1. Enter **=RAND( )** in cell A2 and copy down as far as needed. Then select any single cell and select Tools → Macro → Record New Macro....

Select columns A, B, C, and D and press F9 (to force a recalculation). Select Data → Sort and sort the data by column A. Stop recording the macro.

Next, select View → Toolbars → Forms. Select a button from the Forms toolbar and place it anywhere on the worksheet. Assign the macro you just recorded to this button and click OK. (Change the text for the button from Button 1 to something more meaningful, if you want.) (You can select column A and hide it completely, as there is no need for a user to see the random numbers generated.) Each time you click the button, your data will be sorted randomly, and you can just read off the top three names to be the winners. See Figure 2-13.

> The RAND function in Excel 2003 has a major flaw. Although the Help clearly states the random number returned will be between 0 and 1, this is not always the case if the RAND function is used in many cells. Sometimes the RAND function will return a number less than 0. To read Microsoft's take on why they changed the algorithm, visit *http://support.microsoft.com/default.aspx?kbid=828795*.

	B	C	D	E	F	G
1	**Name**	**Age**	**ID No.**	**Place**	Pick Winner	
2	Dave	21	11256	1		
3	Paul	19	11257	2		
4	Anne	23	11135	3		
5	Gemma	30	11248			
6	Peter	52	11356			
7	Fred	30	11236			
8	Nigel	36	11237			
9	Bill	25	11234			
10	Jill	52	11245			

Figure 2-13. The end result of a random sort with column A hidden

HACK #31 Manipulate Data with the Advanced Filter

If you are familiar with Excel's AutoFilter tool, you also are familiar with its limitations. If you require extensive data manipulation, using Excel's Advanced Filter tool is the way to go.

Although limited, AutoFilters are a useful way to display only the data that meets particular criteria. Sometimes, however, you cannot glean the information you need using the standard options available in AutoFilters. Excel's versatile Advanced Filter tool enables you to further manipulate your data.

When you use Excel's Advanced Filter tool, your table must be set up in a classic table format as described at the start of Chapter 1.

When using Excel's Advanced Filter tool, you will need a copy of your table's column headings somewhere above your data. You should always leave at least three blank rows above your table of data. To ensure that your headings are exactly the same and will remain so regardless of whether you change your column headings, always reference the column headings with a simple reference formula such as =A4, where A4 contains a column heading. Copy this across for as many column headings as you have in your table. This will ensure that the criteria headings for the Advanced Filter are dynamic. Directly below these copied headings, place the criteria for the Advanced Filter to use. For more details on this process, see the Excel Help under Advanced Filters Criteria.

One point to keep in mind when using the Advanced Filter is that two or more criteria placed directly underneath the applicable heading use an OR statement. If you want to use an AND statement, the column headings and their criteria must appear twice, side by side. Figure 2-14 shows how to use the OR operator to filter your data, and Figure 2-15 shows how to use the AND operator.

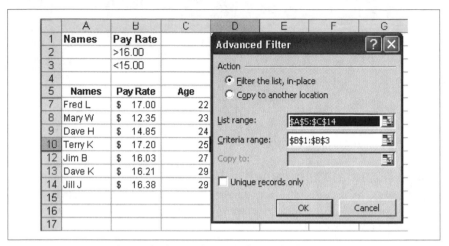

Figure 2-14. *Using Advanced Filter with OR to show only those people who have a pay rate greater than $16.00 OR less than $15.00*

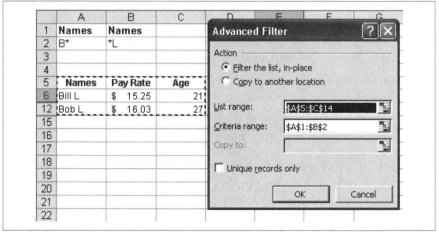

Figure 2-15. *Using Advanced Filter with AND to show only those people who have a name starting with B AND ending with L*

Both of the preceding examples show fairly simple uses of the Advanced Filter tool and can be accomplished via AutoFilter if needed. Next we'll provide some examples of the Advanced Filter in which the use of Auto-Filter would not be possible.

It's important to note that whenever you use a formula for your criteria, you must not use above the criteria a heading that is identical to the one within the table. For example, if you have a list of numeric data in column A and the list begins in cell A5 (with A4 being the heading), and you need to extract all the numbers in that list that are greater than the average, you would use criteria such as these:

    =A5>AVERAGE($A$5:$A$500)

If the criteria were placed in cell A2, the criteria range would be $A$1:$A$2, but $A$1 could not contain the same heading as the one the list uses. It must be either blank or a different heading altogether.

It also is important to note that any formula you use should return either TRUE or FALSE. The range for the average function is made absolute by the addition of dollar signs, while the reference to cell A5 is a relative reference. This is needed because when you apply the Advanced Filter, Excel will see that A5 is a relative reference and will move down the list one entry at a time and return either TRUE or FALSE. If it returns TRUE, it knows it needs to be extracted. If it returns FALSE, it does not meet the criteria; therefore, it will not be shown.

Also assume that many of the names are repeated in the range $A$5:A$500, with A4 being the headings. Also assume that many of the headings are repeated numerous times. You have been given the task of extracting from the list all the names that appear more than once. To do this you need to use the Advanced Filter and the following formula as your criteria:

    =COUNTIF($A$5:$A$500,A5)>1

Once you apply the Advanced Filter to this and use the Copy to Another Location: option, the newly created list will contain all the names that appeared more than once in the original list (see Figure 2-16). Many of these names will be repeated numerous times, but you can easily filter this new list again with the Advanced Filter, this time selecting Unique Records Only (see Figure 2-17). This will give you a list of names that appear in the list more than once.

Advanced Filter users commonly ask how they can force Excel to filter their data by the exact criteria they have provided. If your criterion is Dave and you perform an Advanced Filter on a long list of names, Excel would show not only the name Dave, but also names such as Davey, Dave J, Dave K, etc. In other words, any name that begins with the letters Dave, in that order, will be considered a match for the criteria. To force Excel to find exact matches— e.g., in this case find only the name Dave—enter your criteria as **="=Dave"**.

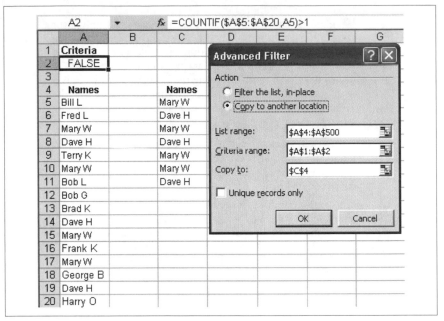

Figure 2-16. Using Advanced Filter to extract names from a list that appear more than once

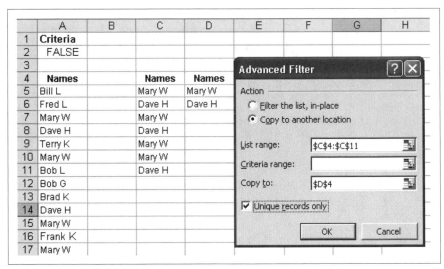

Figure 2-17. Using Advanced Filter on the extracted list of names to filter down to show each name only once (Unique Records Only)

HACK #32 Create Custom Number Formats

Excel comes with built-in number formats, but sometimes you need to use a number format that is not built into Excel. Using the hacks in this section, you can create number formats that you can customize to meet your needs.

Before you try these hacks, it helps if you understand how Excel sees cell formats. Excel sees a cell's format as having the following four sections (from left to right): *Positive Numbers, Negative Numbers, Zero Values, and Text Values.* Each section is separated by a semicolon (;).

When you create a custom number format, you do not have to specify all four sections. In other words, if you include only two sections, the first section will be used for both positive numbers and zero values, while the second section will be used for negative numbers. If you include only one section, all number types will use that one format. Text is affected by custom formats only when you use all four sections; the text will use the last section.

Don't interpret the word *number* to mean custom formats applying to numeric data only. Number formats apply to text as well.

The custom number format shown in Figure 2-18 is Excel's standard currency format, which shows negative currencies in red. We modified it by adding a separate format for zero values and another one for text. If you enter a positive number as a currency value, Excel will format it automatically so that it includes a comma for the thousands separator, followed by two decimal places. It will do the same for negative values, except they will show up in red. Any zero value will have no currency symbol and will show two decimal places. If you enter text into a cell, Excel will display the words "No Text Please," regardless of the true underlying text.

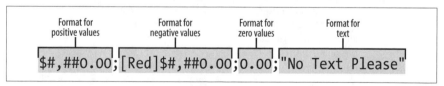

Figure 2-18. Custom number format sections

It is important to note that formatting a cell's value does not affect its underlying true value. For example, type any number into cell A1. Select Format → Cells → Number → Custom, and using any format as a starting point, type **"Hello"** (with the quotation marks). Then click OK.

Although the cell displays the word Hello, you can see its true value by selecting the cell and looking in the Formula bar, or by pressing F2. If you were to reference this cell in a formula—e.g., =A1+20—the result cell would take on the custom format. If you were to reference cell A1 along with many other cells that have any standard Excel format—e.g., =SUM(A1:A10)—the result cell would still take on the custom format of cell A1. Excel is taking an educated guess that you want the result cell formatted the same way as the referenced cell(s). If the referenced cells contain more than one type of format, any custom format will take precedence.

This means you must always remember that Excel uses a cell's true value for calculations, and not its displayed value. This can create surprises when Excel calculates based on cells that are formatted for no decimal places or for few decimal places, for instance. To see this in action, enter **1.4** in cell A1 and **1.4** in cell A2, format both cells to show zero decimal places, and then place **=A1+A2** into a cell. The result, of course, is 3, as Excel rounds.

> Excel does have an option called "Precision as Displayed," which you can find by selecting Tools → Options → Calculation, but you should be aware that this option will permanently change stored values in cells from full precision (15 digits) to whatever format, including decimal places, is displayed. In other words, once it's been checked and given the okay, there is no turning back. (You can try, but the extra precision information is gone for good.)

The default format for any cell is General. If you enter a number into a cell, Excel often will *guess* the number format that is most appropriate. For example, if you enter **10%** into a cell, Excel will format the cell as a percentage. Most of the time, Excel guesses correctly, but sometimes you need to change it.

> When using Format → Cells, resist the temptation to force a left, right, or center horizontal format! By default, numbers are right-aligned and text is left-aligned. If you leave this alone, you can tell at a glance whether a cell is text or numeric, as in the case of the earlier example in which cell A1 appears to hold text, when in fact, it holds a number.

Each section of a given format uses its own set of formatting codes. These codes force Excel to make data appear how you want it to appear. So, for instance, suppose you want negative numbers to appear inside parentheses, and all numbers, positive, negative, and zero, to show two decimal places. To do this, use this custom format:

    0.00_ ;(-0.00)

If you also want negatives to show up in red, use this custom format:

```
0.00_ ;[Red](-0.00)
```

Note the use of the square brackets in the preceding code. The formatting code tells Excel to make the number red.

You can use many different formatting codes within sections of a custom format. Tables 2-1 through 2-5, derived from Microsoft documentation, explain these codes.

Table 2-1. Formatting codes

Number code	Description
General	General number format.
0 (zero)	A digit placeholder that pads the value with zeros to fill the format.
#	A digit placeholder that does not require extra zeros to be displayed.
?	A digit placeholder that leaves a space for insignificant zeros but does not display them.
%	A percentage. Excel multiplies by 100 and displays the % character after the number.
, (comma)	A thousands separator. A comma followed by a placeholder scales the number by 1,000.
E+ E- e+ e-	Scientific notation.

Table 2-2. Text codes

Text code	Description
$ - + / ( ) : and blank space	These characters are displayed in the number. To display any other character, enclose the character in quotation marks or precede it with a backslash.
\character	This code displays the character you specify. Note that typing !, ^, &, ', ~, {, }, =, <, or > automatically places a backslash in front of the character.
"text"	This code displays the text between the quotes.
*	This code repeats the next character in the format to fill the column width. Only one asterisk per section of a format is allowed.
_ (underscore)	This code skips the width of the next character. This code is commonly used as _) to leave space for a closing parenthesis in a positive number format when the negative number format includes parentheses. This allows both positive and negative values to line up at the decimal point.
@	A placeholder for text.

Table 2-3. Date codes

Date code	Description
M	A month represented as a number without leading zeros (1–12)
Mm	A month represented as a number with leading zeros (01–12)
Mmm	A month given as an abbreviation (Jan–Dec)
Mmmm	An unabbreviated month (January–December)
D	A day represented without leading zeros (1–31)
Dd	A day represented with leading zeros (01–31)
Ddd	A weekday represented as an abbreviation (Sun–Sat)
Dddd	An unabbreviated weekday name (Sunday–Saturday)
Yy	A year given as a two-digit number (for example, 96)
Yyyy	A year given as a four-digit number (for example, 1996)

Table 2-4. Time codes

Time code	Description
H	Hours given as a number with no leading zeros (0–23)
Hh	Hours given as a number with leading zeros (00–23)
m	Minutes given as a number with no leading zeros (0–59)
mm	Minutes given as a number with leading zeros (00–59)
s	Seconds given as a number with no leading zeros (0–59)
ss	Seconds given as a number with leading zeros (00–59)
AM/PM am/pm	Time of day based on a 12-hour clock

Table 2-5. Miscellaneous codes

Miscellaneous Code	Description
[BLACK], [BLUE], [CYAN], [GREEN], [MAGENTA], [RED], [WHITE], [YELLOW], [COLOR n]	These codes display characters in the specified colors. Note that *n* is a value from 1 to 56 and refers to the nth color in the color palette.
[Condition value]	*Condition* can be <, >, =, >=, <=, or <>, while *value* can be any number. A number format can contain up to two conditions.

Note in particular the last kind of formatting codes in Table 2-5: the comparison operators. Assume you want the custom number format 0.00_ ;[Red](-0.00) to display negative numbers in a red font and in brackets only if the number is less than -100. To do this, use the following:

```
0.00_ ;[Red][<-100](-0.00);0.00
```

The formatting codes [Red][<-100](-0.00) placed in the section for negative numbers make this possible. Using this method in addition to conditional formatting you can double the number of conditional format conditions available from three to six.

Often, users want to display dollar values as words. To do this, use the following custom format:

```
0 "Dollars and" .00 "Cents"
```

This format will force a number entered as 55.25 to be displayed as 55 Dollars and .25 Cents. If you want to convert numbers to dollars and cents, consult these two custom functions from Microsoft: *http://www.ozgrid.com/VBA/ValueToWords.htm* and *http://www.ozgrid.com/VBA/CurrencyToWords.htm*.

You can also use a custom format to display the words Low, Average, or High, along with the number entered. Simply use this formatting code:

```
[<11]"Low"* 0;[>20]"High"* 0;"Average"* 0
```

Note the use of the *. This repeats the next character in the format to fill the column width, meaning that all the Low, Average, or High text will be forced to the right, while the number will be forced to the left.

Add More Levels of Undo to Excel for Windows

HACK #33 We all are familiar with Excel's fabulous Undo feature, which enables a user to undo his mistakes. Unfortunately, the default level for this is a mere 16 changes. With the hack in this section, you can change the registry so that you can undo up to 100 mistakes.

When you use Excel's Undo feature, and you reach undo number 16, the first undo is replaced by the 17th, and so on. Also, as soon as you save your workbook, the Undo Stack is wiped out, and the Undo History is lost. This is because when you press Save, you're actually telling Excel that you are happy with the changes you made, so it decides for you that your Undo History is no longer required.

You might have discovered that at times having only your last 16 changes retained in the Undo Stack is not enough. Instead of living with this, you can change this by editing the registry, something that works only in Windows. To do this, begin by quitting Excel completely. Select Start → Run, and in the Open box type **Regedit.exe**. Click OK. When regedit starts, expand the folder for HKEY_CURRENT_USER. Then expand the Software folder underneath it, then the Microsoft folder, the Office folder, and the 10.0 folder. (This last folder varies for different versions. 10.0 is for Excel 2002.) Expand the Excel folder, and finally, open the Options folder.

Select Edit → New → DWORD Value, enter the word **UndoHistory**, and press Enter. Double-click the UndoHistory you just created, and enter a value greater than 16 and less than 100.

Hopefully, 100 undos will be enough for even the most demanding users, though the issue with save clearing the undo stack persists.

HACK #34   Create Custom Lists

By adding a custom list to Excel, you can type the first item in the list, drag it down using the fill handle, and watch the list fill automatically.

One of Excel's most popular time-saving features is its ability to automatically increment not only numbers, but certain text as well. Excel has a couple of built-in lists, such as days of the week and months of the year. Currently when you use the fill handle, you type the first item, then use the fill handle to fill cells with the next item in the list, and so forth. You can easily create our own custom list for commonly used items.

The most flexible way to create a custom list is to enter the list contents into a range of cells. For example, say you have a list of 100 employee names. Enter each name, starting with cell A1 and ending with cell A100, and sort the list, if needed. Then select Tools → Options..., and on the Custom Lists page tab, click Import List from the Cells box. Using the mouse pointer, left-click in cell A1 and drag all the way down to A100. Then click the Import button. From this point on, the custom list will be available to all workbooks on the same computer.

Once you create a custom list, you can turn the list upside down. To do this, return to the column next to the custom list and place the last entry from the list in the top cell. In the cell beneath it, place the second-to-last entry. Select both cells and double-click the fill handle. The list you produced should be reversed. You can sort the original list by selecting Data → Sort → Options, nominate the list, and then sort it.

If your list is sorted and you want to turn it upside down, you might find it easier to sort from Z to A if the list originally was sorted from A to Z.

HACK #35   Boldface Excel Subtotals

Wouldn't it be great if you could identify the subtotals in your worksheets so that you can find them easily? With the hacks in this section, you can.

When you are working with a spreadsheet that has subtotals you created by selecting Data → Subtotals, the subtotals can be very hard to identify, making the spreadsheet hard to read. This is true especially if you applied subtotals to a table of data with many columns.

Typically, the resulting subtotals appear on the right, while their associated headings are often in the first column. As the subtotal values are not in boldface, it can be hard to visually align them with their row headings. You can make these subtotals much easier to read by applying bold formatting to the subtotal values.

To test the problem, set up some data similar to that shown in Figure 2-19.

	A	B	C
1	**Quarter**	**Cost**	
2	Quart1	$10.00	
3	Quart1	$20.00	
4	Quart2	$10.00	
5	Quart2	$10.00	
6	Quart2	$10.00	
7	Quart3	$15.00	
8	Quart3	$10.00	
9	Quart3	$25.00	
10			

Figure 2-19. Worksheet data before adding subtotals

Now add the subtotals by selecting Data → Subtotals, accepting the defaults in the Subtotals dialog, and clicking OK.

In Figure 2-20, the subtotal headings have been boldfaced but their associated results have not. As this table has only two columns, it is not that hard to read and pick out the subtotal amounts.

	A	B	C
1	**Quarter**	**Cost**	
2	Quart1	$10.00	
3	Quart1	$20.00	
4	**Quart1 Total**	$30.00	
5	Quart2	$10.00	
6	Quart2	$10.00	
7	Quart2	$10.00	
8	**Quart2 Total**	$30.00	
9	Quart3	$15.00	
10	Quart3	$10.00	
11	Quart3	$25.00	
12	**Quart3 Total**	$50.00	
13	**Grand Total**	$110.00	
14			
15			

Figure 2-20. Worksheet data after subtotals have been applied

The more columns a table has, however, the harder it is to visually pick out the subtotals. You can solve this problem by using Excel's conditional formatting. Using the table in Figure 2-19 as an example, try this before adding your Subtotals. Select cell A1:B9, ensuring that A1 is the active cell. Select Format → Conditional Formatting..., select Formula Is, and then add the following formula:

```
=RIGHT($A1,5)="Total"
```

Now click the Format button and then the Font tab, and select Bold as the Font Style. Click OK, then OK again.

The important part of the formula is the use of an absolute reference of the column ($A) and a relative reference of the row (1). As you started the selection from cell A1, Excel will automatically change the formula for each cell. For example, cells A2 and B2 will have the conditional format formula =RIGHT($A2,5)="Total", and cells A3 and B3 will have the conditional format formula =RIGHT($A3,5)="Total".

Add the subtotals, and they will look like those in Figure 2-21.

	A	B	C
1	Quarter	Cost	
2	Quart1	$10.00	
3	Quart1	$20.00	
4	**Quart1 Total**	**$30.00**	
5	Quart2	$10.00	
6	Quart2	$10.00	
7	Quart2	$10.00	
8	**Quart2 Total**	**$30.00**	
9	Quart3	$15.00	
10	Quart3	$10.00	
11	Quart3	$25.00	
12	**Quart3 Total**	**$50.00**	
13	**Grand Total**	**$110.00**	
14			

Figure 2-21. Worksheet data after subtotals have been formatted

One last thing to remember is that if you remove the subtotals, the boldfaced font will no longer apply.

Hacking the Hack

The only possible pitfall with this method is that the Grand Total appears in the same style as the Subtotals. It would be nice to see the Grand Total formatted in another way so that it stand outs from the Subtotals and is identified more easily. You can do this using the same example.

Starting with your raw data, select cell A1:B9, ensuring that A1 is the active cell. Now select Format → Conditional Formatting.... Select Formula Is and then add the following formula:

```
=$A1="Grand Total"
```

Click the Format button and then the Font tab, and select Bold as the Font Style. Click OK, and then click Add to add a second format condition. Select Formula Is and add the following formula:

```
=RIGHT($A1,5)="Total"
```

Click the Format button and then the Font tab. On this tab, select Bold Italic as the Font Style. Select Single from Underline, click OK, and then click OK again.

Next, select Data → Subtotals, accept the defaults, and click OK. Your worksheet data should now look like Figure 2-22.

1 2 3		A	B	C
	1	Quarter	Cost	
	2	Quart1	$10.00	
	3	Quart1	$20.00	
	4	*Quart1 Total*	*$30.00*	
	5	Quart2	$10.00	
	6	Quart2	$10.00	
	7	Quart2	$10.00	
	8	*Quart2 Total*	*$30.00*	
	9	Quart3	$15.00	
	10	Quart3	$10.00	
	11	Quart3	$25.00	
	12	*Quart3 Total*	*$50.00*	
	13	**Grand Total**	**$110.00**	
	14			

Figure 2-22. Worksheet data with more prominent grand total

You can use any format you want to make your subtotals easier to read.

Convert Excel Formulas and Functions to Values
HACK #36

Most Excel spreadsheets contain formulas. Sometimes you may want to force only the result of a formula to occupy a cell, instead of leaving the formula in place, where it will change if/when the data it references changes.

You can do this manually in a couple of ways, or you can use a macro that will make the job a breeze. Let's look at the manual methods first.

Using Paste Special

You can copy the formula results and still leave the original formulas in place using Excel's Paste Special tool. Assume you have formulas residing in cells A1:A100. Select this range, select Copy, and then select the starting cell for the mirror results. Select Edit → Paste Special → Values and click OK.

If you want to override the original formulas with their results, select the formula range and select Copy. With the formula range still selected, select Edit → Paste Special → Values and then click OK.

Using Copy Here as Values Only

You also can copy formula results and still leave the original formulas in place by using a pop-up menu that many users don't even know exists.

Select the formula range and right-click the right or left border of the selection (in other words, anywhere in the selection except for the fill handle). While holding down the right mouse button (or Ctrl-clicking on a Macintosh), drag to the destination, release the right mouse button, and click "Copy Here as Values Only" from the resulting pop-up shortcut menu.

You also can override the original formulas with their results. Select the formula range, then right-click the right or left border of the selection (again, anywhere in the selection except for the fill handle). While pressing the right mouse button (or Ctrl-clicking), drag over one column to the right or left and then back to the starting range, release the right mouse button, and click "Copy Here as Values Only" from the resulting pop-up shortcut, shown in Figure 2-23.

Using a Macro

If you frequently convert cells containing formulas and functions to their values, you can use this simple macro:

```
Sub ValuesOnly( )
Dim rRange As Range
    On Error Resume Next
        Set rRange = Application.InputBox(Prompt:="Select the formulas", _
                            Title:="VALUES ONLY", Type:=8)
        If rRange Is Nothing Then Exit Sub
    rRange = rRange.Value
End Sub
```

To use this macro, select Tools → Macro → Visual Basic Editor (Alt/Option-F11). While in the VBE, select Insert → Module to insert a standard module. Enter the preceding code directly into the module. Click the window's Close button, or press Alt/⌘-Q to get back to Excel. Select Tools → Macro → Macros (Alt/Option-F8), select ValuesOnly, and then click Options to assign a

Figure 2-23. Pop-up shortcut menu

shortcut key to the macro. When you use the macro you will be presented with an InputBox and asked to select a range that contains your formulas. The selected range address will show automatically in the InputBox, and all you need to do to make the conversion is click OK.

HACK #37 Automatically Add Data to a Validation List

The validation feature in Excel is great, but there is one key thing it cannot do (without the following hack): automatically add a new entry to the list being used as the source for the validation list.

If you have used validation, you know it's a neat feature. Perhaps most impressive is its ability to add a list to any cell from which the user can then select. Wouldn't it be nice if, when you enter a new name in a validated cell, Excel automatically adds it to the list? This is possible, thanks to the following hack.

Assume you have a list of names in the range A1:A10, as in Figure 2-24.

These names represent employees in a company. It is not uncommon for new employees to be added to such a list, but at present, the only way to achieve this is to add the new names to the end of the list and then select the new names from the list in the validated cell.

Figure 2-24. Workbook set up for validation list

To overcome this limitation, follow these steps. In cell A11, enter the following formula and copy it down to row 20, as in Figure 2-25 (note the relative reference of A10):

```
=IF(OR($D$1="",COUNTIF($A$1:A10,$D$1)),"x",$D$1)
```

Figure 2-25. List with formula added to rows A11:A20

Now select Insert → Name → Define, and in the Names in Workbook: box, type **MyNames**. In the Refers To: box, enter the following formula, as shown in Figure 2-26, then click Add, and then OK:

```
=OFFSET(Sheet1!$A$1,0,0,COUNTIF(Sheet1!$A:$A,"<>x"),1)
```

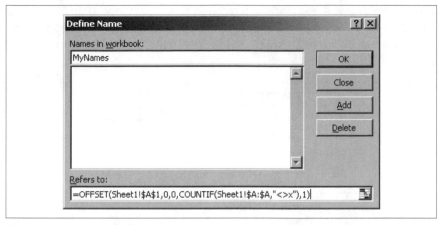

Figure 2-26. Making the list dynamic

Select cell D1 and then select Data → Validation. Select List from the Allow: box, and in the Source: box, type **=MyNames**, ensuring that the In-Cell drop-down box is checked. Click the Error Alert page tab and uncheck the "Show error alert after invalid data is entered" box. Now click OK. You'll see the result in Figure 2-27.

	A	B	C	D	E
1	Robyn Fenlon				
2	Joe Smith				
3	Bill Bloggs				
4	Fred Stone				
5	Neil Watts				
6	Judith Thurley				
7	Jacqui Jones				
8	Connie Eldon				
9	Kim Holmes				
10	Andrea Brooks				
11	x				
12	x				
13	x				

Figure 2-27. The list with validation added to cell D1

Right-click the Sheet Name tab and select View Code. Enter the following code:

```
Private Sub Worksheet_Calculate( )
On Error Resume Next
    Application.EnableEvents = False
    Range("MyNames") = Range("MyNames").Value
    Application.EnableEvents = True
On Error GoTo 0
End Sub
```

Close the window to get back to Excel and save your workbook. Now select cell D1, type in any name that is *not* part of the list, and press Enter. Select cell D1 again and look at the list. The new name should be part of it, as shown in Figure 2-28.

	A	B	C	D	E
1	Robyn Fenlon			Jim Jones ▼	
2	Joe Smith				
3	Bill Bloggs				
4	Fred Stone				
5	Neil Watts				
6	Judith Thurley				
7	Jacqui Jones				
8	Connie Eldon				
9	Kim Holmes				
10	Andrea Brooks				
11	Jim Jones				
12	x				
13	x				

Figure 2-28. The list after adding a new entry to cell D1

If you want to add more than 10 names to your list, just copy the formula down past row 20.

Hack Excel's Date and Time Features

#38   Excel's date and time feature is great if you're creating simple spreadsheets, but they can cause problems for more advanced projects. Fortunately, there are ways to get around Excel's assumptions when they don't meet your needs.

Excel (by default) uses the 1900 date system. This means the date 1 Jan 1900 has an underlying numeric value of 1, 2 Jan 1900 has a value of 2, and so forth. These values are called *serial values* in Excel, and they enable you to use dates in calculations.

Times are very similar, but Excel treats times as decimal fractions, with 1 being the time 24:00 or 00:00. 18:00 has a numeric value of 0.75 because it is three-quarters of 24 hours.

To see the numeric value of a date and/or a time, format the cell containing the value as *General*. For example, the date and time 3/July/2002 3:00:00 PM has a numeric value of 37440.625, with the number after the decimal representing the time, and the 37440 representing the serial value for 3/July/2002.

Adding Beyond 24 Hours

You can add times by using the SUM function (or a simple plus sign). Therefore, =SUM(A1:A5) would result in Total Hours if A1:A5 contained valid times. There is, however, a big "Gotcha!" Unless told otherwise, Excel will not add past 24 hours. This is because when a time value exceeds 24 hours (a true value of 1), it rolls into a new day and starts again. To force Excel not to default back to a new day after 24 hours, you can use a cell format of 37:30:55 or a custom format of [h]:mm:ss.

You can use a similar format to get the total minutes or seconds of a time. To get the total minutes of the time 24:00, for instance, format the cell as [m] and you will get 1440. To get the total seconds, use a custom format of [s] and you get 86400.

Time and Date Calculations

If you want to use these real time values in other calculations, keep the following "magic" numbers in mind:

60
> 60 minutes or 60 seconds

3600
> 60 secs * 60 mins

24
> 24 hours

1440
> 60 mins * 24 hours

86400
> 24 hours * 60 mins * 60 secs

Once you are armed with these magic numbers and the preceding information, you'll find it's much easier to manipulate times and dates. Take a look at the following examples to see what we mean (assume the time is in cell A1).

If you have the number 5.50 and you really want 5:30 or 5:30 a.m., use this:

    =A1/24

and format as needed.

If it should be 17:30 or 5:30 p.m., use this:

    =(A1/24)+0.5

To achieve the opposite—that is, a decimal time from a true time—use this:

    =A1*24

If a cell contains the true date and the true time (as in 22/Jan/03 15:36) and you want only the date, use this:

```
=INT(A1)
```

To get only the time, use this:

```
=A1-INT(A1)
```

or:

```
=MOD(A1,1)
```

and format as needed.

To find out the difference between two dates, use this:

```
=DATEDIF(A1,A2,"d")
```

where A1 is the earlier date.

This will produce the number of days between two dates. It also will accept "m" or "y" as the result to return—that is, Months or Years. (The DATEDIF function is undocumented in Excel 97 and is really a Lotus 123 function.)

If you do not know in advance which date or time is the earliest, the MIN and MAX functions can help. For example, to be assured of a meaningful result, you can use this:

```
=DATEDIF(MIN(A1,A2),MAX(A1,A2),"d")
```

Also, when working with times, you might need to account for start time and end time, with the start time being 8:50 p.m. in cell A1, and the end time being 9:50 a.m. in cell A2. If you subtract the start time from the end time (=A2-A1), you get ######, as Excel, by default, cannot work with negative times. See "Display Negative Time Values" **[Hack #74]** for more on how to work with negative times.

Alternatively, you can work around this in these two ways, ensuring a positive result:

```
=MAX(A1,A2)-MIN(A1:A2)
```

or:

```
=A1-A2+IF(A1>A2,1)
```

You can also tell Excel to add any number of days, months, or years to any date:

```
=DATE(YEAR(A1)+value1,MONTH(A1)+value2,DAY(A1)+value3)
```

To add one month to a date in cell A1, use this:

```
=DATE(YEAR(A1),MONTH(A1)+1,DAY(A1))
```

Excel also offers some additional functions that are part of the Analysis ToolPak. Click Add-Ins on the Tools menu. Click to select the Analysis ToolPak checkbox, and then click Yes if you are asked if you want to install it. Additional functions, such as EDATE, EOMONTH, NETWORKDAYS, and WEEKNUM, will be available to you.

You can find all of these functions under the Date & Time category of the Paste Function dialog in the Function Wizard. The functions are easy to use; the hard part is knowing they're available and turning them on.

Real Dates and Times

Sometimes spreadsheets with imported data (or data that was entered incorrectly) end up with dates and times being seen as text and not real numbers. You can spot this easily in Excel by widening the columns a bit, selecting a column, selecting Format → Cells → Alignment, and then changing the Horizontal alignment to General (the default format for cells). Click OK and examine your dates and times closely. If any are *not* right-aligned, Excel doesn't think they are dates.

To fix this, first copy any empty cell, and then select the column and format as any Date and/or Time format. While the column is still selected, select Edit → Paste Special → Value → Add. This will force Excel to convert any text dates and times to real dates and times. You might need to change the format again. Another simple method is to reference the cell(s) like this:

```
=A1+0 or A1*1
```

A Date Bug?

Excel incorrectly assumes that the year 1900 was a leap year. This means Excel's internal date system believes there was a 29 Feb 1900, when there wasn't! The most surprising part is that Microsoft did this intentionally, or so they say! More information is available at *http://support.microsoft.com/ default.aspx?scid=kb;EN-US;q181370*.

Here are some additional good links to information on dates and times:

HOW TO: Use Dates and Times in Excel 2000
    http://support.microsoft.com/default.aspx?scid=kb;en-us;Q214094#6

Text or Number Converted to Unintended Number Format
    http://support.microsoft.com/default.aspx?scid=kb;en-us;Q214233

Maximum Times in Microsoft Excel
    http://support.microsoft.com/default.aspx?scid=kb;en-us;Q214386

Dates and Times Displayed as Serial Numbers When Viewing Formulas
   http://support.microsoft.com/default.aspx?scid=kb;en-us;Q241072

Controlling and Understanding Settings in the Format Cells Dialog Box
   http://support.microsoft.com/default.aspx?scid=kb;en-us;Q264372

How to Use Dates and Times in Microsoft Excel
   http://support.microsoft.com/default.aspx?scid=kb;en-us;214094

Dates and times are probably one of the most confusing areas within Excel. Armed with this information, hopefully you will understand more about their many quirks and have an easier time dealing with them.

Naming Hacks
Hacks 39-44

Probably the biggest advantage to using named ranges is that formulas become a lot easier to read and understand, not only to you but also to others who need to work with your spreadsheets. Using named ranges (easily one of Excel's most useful features), you can reference a range of cells and give it a specific name. From that point on, you can reference the range via the name rather than its range address. Although named ranges are powerful, you can go beyond the standard range names in many ways.

HACK #39 Address Data by Name

Although cell numbers are at the foundation of everything Excel does, it's much easier to remember names, such as Item Number and Quantity, than it is to remember cell numbers, such as A1:A100. Excel makes this easy.

Excel uses the same technique for defining named cells and named ranges: the Name box at the left end of the Formula bar. To name a cell, select it, type the name you want into the Name box, as shown in Figure 3-1, and press Enter. To name a range of cells, select the range, type the name you want for that range in the Name box, and press Enter.

The drop-down list at the right side of the Name box enables you to find your named ranges and cells again. (See "Identify Named Ranges on a Worksheet" **[Hack #44]** at the end of this chapter for more ways to locate ranges.) If you happen to select a range precisely, its name will appear in the Name box instead of the usual cell references.

In formulas, you can use these names in place of cell identifiers or ranges. If you name cell E4 "date," for instance, you could write =date instead of =E4. Similarly, if you create a range called "quantity" in A3:A10 and want a total of the values in it, your formula could say =SUM(quantity) rather than =SUM(A3:A10).

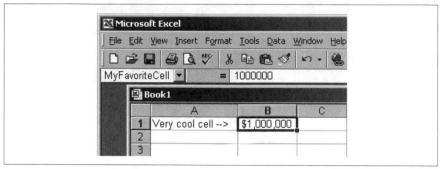

Figure 3-1. Naming a cell MyFavoriteCell

As spreadsheets grow larger and more intricate, named cells and ranges are crucial tools for keeping them manageable.

HACK #40 Use the Same Name for Ranges on Different Worksheets

Sometimes it would be convenient to use the same name for data in the same place on multiple worksheets within the same workbook. Excel requires a few extra steps to make this work.

Usually when you name a range, the name is at the workbook level, meaning that one name refers to a specified range on a specified worksheet wherever it is used in the workbook. Once the name has been used, it cannot be used again to represent a range on another worksheet. There is a way around this, however.

Assume you have a workbook with three worksheets. These three worksheets are simply named Sheet1, Sheet2, and Sheet3. You want to have a named range called MyRange (this can be any legitimate name) that will refer to the range Sheet1 A1:A10 when on Sheet1, Sheet2 A1:A10 when on Sheet2, and Sheet3 A1:A10 when on Sheet3.

To do this, activate Sheet1, select the range A1:A10, and then click in the Name box, as you did in "Address Data by Name" **[Hack #39]**. Type **Sheet1!MyRange** and then press Enter. Do the same for Sheet2 and Sheet3, typing **Sheet2!MyRange** and **Sheet3!MyRange**, respectively.

Now activate any sheet and click the drop arrow on the Name box. You should see only one occurrence of the name MyRange. Select this and you will be taken directly to the range A1:A10. Now activate any other sheet and do the same. You always will be taken to the range A1:A10 of that sheet.

You can do this because you preceded the name with the sheet name followed by ! (an exclamation mark). If you select Insert → Name → Define, you will see only one name: the one that refers to the currently active sheet.

If your worksheet name includes spaces, you cannot simply refer to the range Sheet1 A1:A10 as **Sheet1!MyRange**. Instead, you must call it **'Sheet 1'!MyRange**, putting a single apostrophe around the word Sheet1. In fact, you also can use single apostrophes with a worksheet name with no spaces, so it is a good idea to always use single apostrophes when referring to worksheet names to cover all your bases.

You can use a relative reference named range as well. By default, named ranges are absolute, but you do not have to leave them this way. Try the following.

Select cell A11 on any worksheet and then select Insert → Name → Define. In the Names in Workbook: box, type **MyNumbers**. In the Refers To: box, type **=A$1:A$10** and then click Add, then OK.

Now enter the number **1** in cell A1. Select cell A1, move your cursor to the fill handle, and press the left mouse button. While holding down the Ctrl key, drag down to cell A10. Holding down the Ctrl key with a single number will cause Excel to create a list incremented by 1.

Enter **1** in cell B1 and drag down to cell B10, without holding down the Ctrl key this time. Into cell A11, enter the following formula:

    =SUM(MyNumbers)

In cell B11, enter this formula:

    =SUM(MyNumbers)

You should get 55 and 10, respectively, because cell A11 was active when you selected Insert → Name → Define and referred the range name to A$1: A$10, which is a relative column and absolute row named range.

The dollar sign ($) forces any range to be absolute.

When you use the name **MyNumbers** in a formula, it always will refer to the 10 cells immediately above the formula. If you use =SUM(MyNumbers) in cell A11 of another worksheet, it still will refer to cells A1:A10 on the sheet that was active when you originally created the range name.

Suppose you want to simplify the summing of the 10 cells mentioned earlier. Select cell A11 on any worksheet. Select Insert → Name → Define and type **MySum** in the Name box. Then, in the Refers To: box, type the following:

    =SUM(A$1:A$10)

Click Add, then OK. Now enter the number **1** in cell A1. Select cell A1, move your cursor to the fill handle, and press the left mouse button. Hold down the Ctrl key and drag down to cell A10. Once you've done that, enter **1** in cell B1, and drag down to cell B10 without holding down the Ctrl key.

In cell A11, enter the following formula:

    =MySum

In cell B11, enter this formula:

    =MySum

You will get the same results you got before, but without requiring the SUM function. Mixing up the absolute and relative references and nesting a few functions together can be very handy and can save a lot of work.

HACK #41   Create Custom Functions Using Names

Although referencing data by name is convenient, it's sometimes more helpful to store a constant value or even a formula, especially if you've been creating custom functions in VBA.

Assume you have a tax rate of 10%, which you need to use throughout your workbook for various calculations. Instead of entering the value **10% (0.1)** into each formula that requires this tax rate, you can enter the word **TaxRate** and Excel automatically will know that TaxRate has a value of 0.1. Here is how to do this.

Select Insert → Name → Define, and in the Names in Workbook: box, type **TaxRate**. In the Refers To: box, enter **=0.1** and then click Add.

From this point on, you can enter any formula into any cell, and instead of adding 10% as part of the calculation, you can use the word TaxRate. Probably one of the biggest advantages to using this method is that if and when your tax rate increases or decreases, and your formulas need to reflect this new percentage, you can select Insert → Name → Define, then select the name TaxRate and just modify it to suit.

To take things a step further with this concept, you can use formulas as your Refers To: range rather than a cell address or constant value. Suppose you want to create a name that, when entered into a cell, automatically returns the SUM of the 10 cells immediately above it.

Select cell A11 on any worksheet and then select Insert → Name → Define. In the Names in Workbook: box, type the name **Total**. In the Refers To: box, type the following:

```
=SUM(A1:A10)
```

Click Add, then OK.

Enter any 10 numbers in any column starting from row 1. Now come down to row 11 of the same column and type the following:

```
=Total
```

The name Total automatically will return the SUM of the 10 cells you just entered in A1:A10.

If you want to create a similarly named formula that is not restricted to only 10 cells, but rather, includes all the cells directly above whatever row happens to contain =Total, follow these steps.

Select cell B11 and then select Insert → Name → Define. Click the name Total.

Examine the Refers To: box, which will say =SUM(B1:B10). This enables you to create named formulas. In other words, because you did not make the column references absolute for the original name Total, it always will reference the column you use it in.

Now, click the Refers To: box and change the formula to the following:

```
=SUM(B$1:B10)
```

Click Add, then OK.

Select any row in any column other than row 1 and enter **=Total**, and you automatically will get the SUM of all the cells above where you enter this, regardless of how many rows there are. This is because you anchored the row number 1 by making it an absolute reference, yet left the reference to cell B10 as a relative reference, meaning it always will end up being the cell immediately above where you entered the named formula =Total.

By combining this hack with one of Excel's standard, although little known, features—the intersect method—it's possible to create sophisticated lookup functions. If you are not aware of how the intersect method works, here is a small example to get you acquainted.

In cell A1, enter the heading **Name**, in cell B1, enter the heading **Pay**, and in cell C1, enter the heading **Title**. Enter **Bill** in cell A2 and **Fred** in cell A3.

Enter **10** in cell B2 and **20** in cell B3. Enter **Mr** in cell C2 and **Dr** in cell C3. Now, select the range A1:C3 and then select Insert → Name → Create.

Ensure that both the top row and left column checkboxes are checked, then click OK.

Select any cell outside your table and enter **=Fred Title**. You should get the correct title for the name Fred.

> The space between the words Fred and Title is important, as this is what Excel understands as the intersect operator.

Building on this concept, you can combine this capability with Excel's named formula capabilities to again make your spreadsheets not only easier to use, but also much easier to read and understand.

Assume that you have a table set up on a spreadsheet in a fashion similar to that shown in Figure 3-2, and that you are using this table to create your names in Excel.

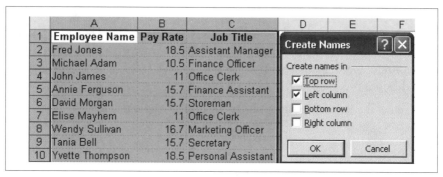

Figure 3-2. Shows Table and Create Names dialog

Once you create the names for the table, you will see that Excel automatically places an underscore in the spaces between two or more words. This is because the names of named ranges cannot contain a space.

Select Insert → Name → Define, and in the Names in Workbook: box, enter **FredsPayRate**. In the Refers To: box, type **=Fred_Jones Pay_Rate** and then click Add, as shown in Figure 3-3.

Now, in any cell outside your table, enter the following:

```
=FredsPayRate
```

The pay rate for Fred will be returned automatically.

You might want to experiment with intersections to see how they work best in your projects.

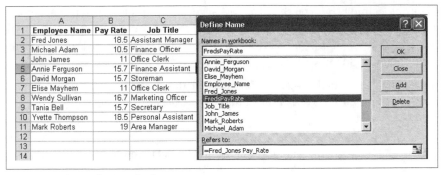

Figure 3-3. Created Name look-up

Create Ranges That Expand and Contract

If you need to constantly update and add to your data, or if you work with charts and PivotTables, you'll want to create dynamic named ranges, which expand and contract relative to your data.

To understand how dynamic named ranges function, first you should familiarize yourself with Excels OFFSET function (if you haven't already). The OFFSET function is one of Excel's Lookup and Reference functions.

We'll start off with the simplest of dynamic named ranges, one that will expand down a single column, but only as far as there are entries in that column. For example, if column A contains 10 continuous rows of data, your dynamic named range will incorporate the range A1:A10. Follow these steps to create a basic dynamic named range.

Select Insert → Name → Define, and in the Names in Workbook: box, type **MyRange**. In the Refers To: box, type the following:

```
=OFFSET($A$1,0,0,COUNTA($A$1:$A$100),1)
```

Now click Add, then OK.

> When defining the range for COUNTA, resist the temptation to include an entire column of data so that you do not force the COUNTA function to count potentially thousands of unnecessary cells.

Now, provided that you have some data in column A, this named range will incorporate all the data in continuous rows, starting from cell A1. If you want to check a dynamic named range, you can do so in a few ways.

Unfortunately, dynamic named ranges are not available via the standard Name box, immediately to the left of the Formula bar. Despite this, you can click the Name box, type the name **MyRange**, and press Enter. Excel automatically will select the range. Of course, you also can use the Go To... dialog by selecting Edit → Go To... (Ctrl/⌘-G) and typing **MyRange** in the Reference: box, then clicking OK.

The dynamic named range you created in the previous example nests the COUNTA function as the Height argument in the OFFSET function.

 Remember that COUNTA will count all nonblank cells. Be aware that this also will include formulas you have in those cells, which might be returning empty text ("").

If you have a list that contained numeric data only, and at the end of this list you want to store text, but don't want this text included as part of your dynamic named range, you could replace the COUNTA function with Excel's standard COUNT function. COUNT counts only cells containing numeric data.

In this next example, you will use the dynamic named range to define a table of data that you want to be dynamic. To do this, type the following function into the Refers To: box:

    =OFFSET($A$1,0,0,COUNTA($A$1:$A$100),COUNTA($1:$1))

Here, the dynamic named range will expand down as many entries as there are in column A, and across as many rows as there are headings in row 1. If you are sure the number of columns for your table of data will remain stable, you can replace the second COUNTA function with a fixed number such as 10.

The only problem with using a dynamic named range for a table of data is that it assumes column A will set the maximum length for the table. In most cases, this probably will be true; however, sometimes the longest column might be another column on the spreadsheet.

To overcome this potential problem, you can use Excel's MAX function, which returns the highest number in a range of cells. As an example, set up a table in a manner similar to the one shown in Figure 3-4.

Use row 1 to store a number of COUNTA functions that are referencing down the column and, thus, returning the number of entries in each column. Use the MAX function for the Height argument in the OFFSET function. This ensures that the dynamic named range for the table always will expand down as far as the longest column in the table. You can, of course, hide row 1, as there is no need for a user to see it.

In all these examples, you assumed your data will always be in continuous rows without blank cells in between. Although this is the correct way to set up a list or a table of data, sometimes you have no control over this.

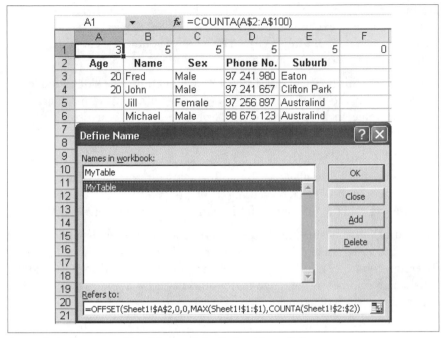

Figure 3-4. *Dynamic table of data and the Define Name dialog*

In the next example, the list of numbers in column A also contains blank cells. This means that if you try to use the COUNT or COUNTA function, the dynamic named range will fall short of the real last cell containing any data. For example, consider Figure 3-5.

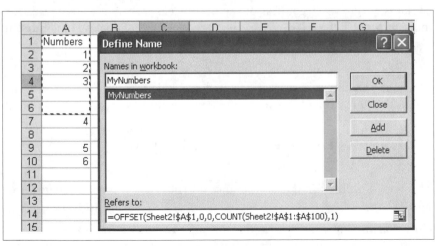

Figure 3-5. *Range of numbers and Define Name dialog*

In this case, although the last number in the range is actually in row 10, the dynamic range is expanding down to row 6. This is because you used the COUNT function to count from A1 to A100. Only six numeric entries are in the list, so the range expands down only six rows.

To overcome this problem, use Excel's MATCH function. The MATCH function is used to return the relative position of an item in an array that matches a specified value in a specified order. For example, if you use this MATCH function:

    =MATCH(6,$A$1:$A$100,0)

on the same set of numbers as shown in Figure 3-5, the MATCH function will return the number 10, representing row 10 in column A. It returns 10 because you told the function to find the number 6 in the range A1:A100.

Obviously, when using the MATCH function as part of a dynamic named range, the last number in the range probably is not known in advance. Therefore, you need to tell the MATCH function to try and locate a ridiculously high number in the range that would never exist and to swap the last argument for the MATCH function from 0 to 1.

In the previous example, you told MATCH to find the exact number 6, nothing less and nothing more. Replacing 0 with 1 tells MATCH to locate the largest value that is less than or equal to that value.

To do this, use this formula:

    =MATCH(1E+306,$A$1:$A$100,1)

To create a dynamic named range that will expand down to the last row that contains a number (regardless of the blank cells in between), type this formula into the Refers To: box of the Define Name dialog, as illustrated in Figure 3-6:

    =OFFSET(Sheet2!$A$1,0,0,MATCH(1E+306,Sheet2!$A$1:$A$100,1),1)

The next logical type of dynamic named range that would flow on from this is one that will expand down to the last text entry, regardless of any blank cells in the list or table.

To do this, replace the MATCH function with the following:

    MATCH("*",$A$1:$A$100,-1)

This always will return the row number for the last text entry in range $A$1: $A$100.

Now that you know how to do this for numeric entries and text entries, it is only logical that you need to somehow define a dynamic named range that will look past blank cells in a list that contains both text and numeric data.

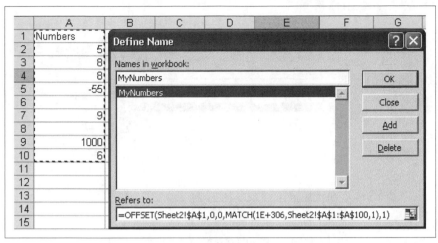

Figure 3-6. A dynamic range extending to the last numeric entry

To do this, first insert two blank rows above your list by selecting rows 1 and 2 and then selecting Insert → Row. In the first row (row 1), add this function:

```
=MAX(MATCH"*",$A$3:$A$100,-1),MATCH(1E+306,$A$3:$A$100,1))
```

In the cell immediately below this, place the number **1**. The cell below this must contain a text heading for your list. You added the number 1 so that the second MATCH function does not return #N/A when or if there are no numbers in A3:A100. The second MATCH function will always find text because you have a heading.

Name cell A1 **MaxRow** and select Insert → Name → Define, give the dynamic range a name, such as **MyList**, and in the Refers To: box, as shown in Figure 3-7, type the following:

```
=OFFSET(Sheet2!$A$3,0,0,MaxRow,1)
```

The following list outlines other types of dynamic named ranges you might find useful. For *all* of these examples, you will need to fill column A with a mix of text and numeric entries. To do this, select Insert → Name → Define, and in the Names in Workbook: box, type any one-word name (for instance, **MyRange**). The only part that will change is the formula you place in the Refers To: box.

Expand down as many rows as there are numeric entries
    In the Refers To: box, type the following:

```
    =OFFSET($A$1,0,0,COUNT($A:$A),1)
```

Expand down as many rows as there are numeric and text entries
    In the Refers To: box, type the following:

```
    =OFFSET($A$1,0,0,COUNTA($A:$A),1)
```

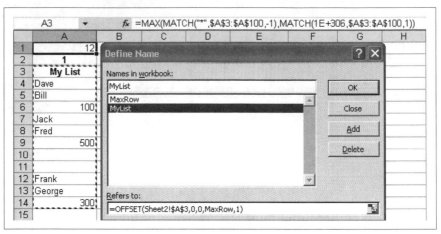

Figure 3-7. *Dynamic list for numeric and text entries containing blanks*

Expand down to the last numeric entry

In the Refers To: box, type the following:

```
=OFFSET($A$1,0,0,MA>TCH(1E+306,$A:$A))
```

If you expect a number larger than 1E+306 (a 1 with 306 zeros), change this to a larger number.

Expand down to the last text entry

In the Refers To: box, type the following:

```
=OFFSET($A$1,0,0,MATCH("*",$A:$A,-1))
```

Expand down based on another cell value

Enter the number **10** in cell B1, and then, in the Refers To: box, type the following:

```
=OFFSET($A$1,0,0,$B$1,1)
```

Now change the number in cell B1, and the range will change accordingly.

Expand down one row each month

In the Refers To: box, type the following:

```
=OFFSET($A$1,0,0,MONTH(TODAY()),1)
```

Expand down one row each week

In the Refers To: box, type the following:

```
=OFFSET($A$1,0,0,WEEKNUM(TODAY()),1)
```

This one requires that you have the Analysis ToolPak installed. You can add it by selecting Tools → Add-ins.

Nest Dynamic Ranges for Maximum Flexibility

A dynamic named range that resides within another dynamic named range can be very useful for things such as long lists of names.

For example, it's possible to create a named range called Jnames that refers to all the names in a sorted list beginning with the letter J.

Start with a list of names in column A, such as the ones shown in Figure 3-8, where cell A1 is a heading, and the list is sorted. Select Insert → Names → Define. In the Names in Workbook: box, type **Names**, and in the Refers To: box, enter the following formula:

```
=OFFSET($A$2,0,0,COUNTA($A$2:$A$1000),1)
```

Click Add. Now click back into the Names in Workbook: box and enter the name **Jnames** (**J** can be any desired letter). In the Refers To: box, enter the following:

```
=OFFSET(INDIRECT(ADDRESS(MATCH("J*",Names,0)+1,1)),0,0,COUNTIF(Names,"J*"),↵
1)
```

where "J*" is a match for the data you want—in this case, names beginning with J). Now click Add. When you click back into the Refers To: box where the function is, all the names beginning with the letter J will have a marquee around them, as shown in Figure 3-8.

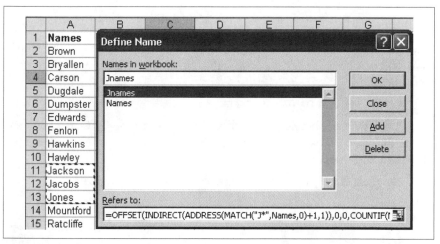

Figure 3-8. A dynamic named range within another dynamic named range

If you want, you can create one named range for each letter of the alphabet, but perhaps a better option is to have the named range change according to a letter that you type into a cell on a worksheet. To do this, simply enter any letter into any unused cell and then name that cell **Letter**.

Now, select Data → Validation, and select List from the Allow: box. Click into the Source: box and enter **A*,B*,C*,** etc., until all 26 letters of the alphabet are entered as shown in Figure 3-9. Click OK when you're done.

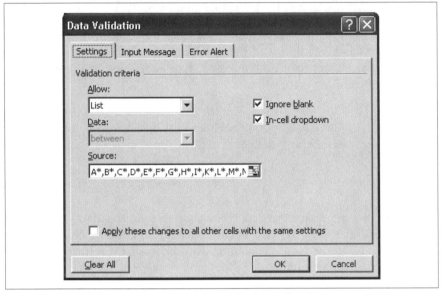

Figure 3-9. A validation list of letters, followed by the wildcard character

Select Insert → Names → Define, and enter the name **"Names"** in the Names in Workbook: box. Enter the following formula in the Refers To: box and then click Add:

```
=OFFSET($A$2,0,0,COUNTA($A$2:$A$1000),1)
```

Click back into the Names in Workbook: box and type **LetterNames**. Then, in the Refers To: box, enter the following formula, and when you're done, click Add and then OK:

```
=OFFSET(INDIRECT(ADDRESS(MATCH(Letter,Names,0)+1,1)),0,0,COUNTIF(Names,↵
    Letter),1)
```

The result will look like Figure 3-10.

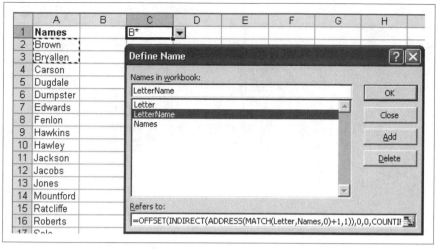

Figure 3-10. *A dynamic named range controlled by the content of another cell*

 You don't have to retype the formulas from scratch for the dynamic named ranges. Instead, while working in the Define Name dialog, click an existing dynamic named range, over-type the name that appears in the Names in Workbook: box, then move down to the Refers To: box, modify as needed, and click Add. This will not replace the original dynamic named range, but rather, add a totally new one with the different name you have given it.

To test this, enter any letter into the cell you named Letter, and you should see any data starting with the letter "L" with a marquee around it.

 ## Identify Named Ranges on a Worksheet

HACK
#44

Excel enables users to give meaningful names to specific ranges in their worksheets. As the number of different named ranges on a worksheet grows, you will need tools for identifying the areas referenced by your named ranges.

Here are two quick methods you can use to identify the referenced ranges for each named range.

Method 1

One very quick way to identify referenced ranges is to select Insert → Name → Paste, or press F3. In the Paste Name dialog, click OK, as shown in

Figure 3-11, and Excel will list all your names in rows, starting from your active cell, with the names' corresponding references in the opposite column.

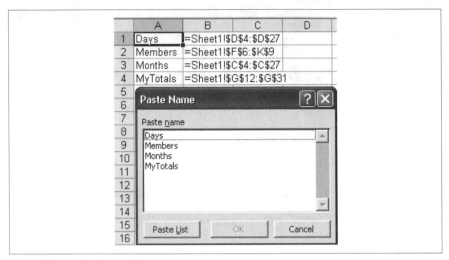

Figure 3-11. The Paste Name dialog

This will give you a list of all your names in the active workbook.

Although this can be handy to help you identify specific ranges, it still requires that you either manually select the specific named range, or perhaps use the Go To... dialog. However, once you have a list of named ranges, you can remove all the referenced cell addresses corresponding to the names and replace them with a simple hyperlink function.

This will enable you to create a list of all named ranges. Clicking any item on the list will take you to the specified range. For instance, assume your list of names resides in column A, starting from cell A1. In cell B1, enter this formula:

```
=HYPERLINK("[Book1.xls]"&A1,A1)
```

Copy this formula down as far as you need to and replace *Book1.xls* with your workbook's name.

Method 2

This method is very simple but not very well known. It was highlighted by one of the OzGrid Excel Forum members in the "Hey! That is Cool!" section of the OzGrid.com web site (*http://www.ozgrid.com/forum/forumdisplay. php?fid=14*).

All you need to do is set the zoom on your Excel worksheet to any percentage lower than 40—i.e., 39% or less. This will display all your named ranges on the sheet for easy identification, as shown in Figure 3-12.

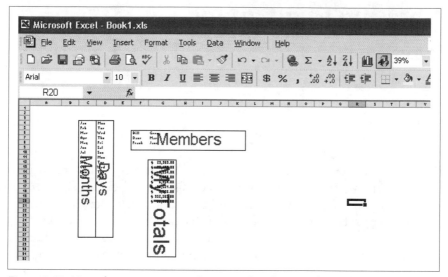

Figure 3-12. Named range zoom providing easy identification of named ranges

CHAPTER FOUR

Hacking PivotTables
Hacks 46-49

PivotTables are one of Excel's most powerful attractions, though many people don't know what they do. PivotTables display and extract a variety of information from a table of data that resides within either Microsoft Excel or another compatible database type. PivotTables are frequently used to extract statistical information from raw data. You can drag around the different fields within a PivotTable to view its data from different perspectives.

> The raw data for a PivotTable must be laid out in a classic table format. Row 1 of the table must be headings, with related data directly underneath. The data should not contain blank columns or blank rows. Even if you aren't planning to use PivotTables, keeping your raw data in this format makes it possible for other people to analyze your data with PivotTables.

If you have not yet delved into the world of PivotTables, you should consider doing so. As a starting point, visit *http://www.ozgrid.com/Excel/default.htm* and work your way through Microsoft's free online tutorial for Excel Pivot-Tables. To learn even more about the benefits of PivotTables as well as how you can create hacks that make PivotTables even more flexible and powerful, read on.

PivotTables: A Hack in Themselves

PivotTables are one of the wildest but most powerful features of Excel, an ingenious hack themselves that may take some experimentation to figure out.

We use PivotTables a lot when we develop spreadsheets for our clients. Once a client sees a PivotTable, they nearly always ask whether they can create one themselves. Although anyone can create a PivotTable, unfortunately many people tend to shy away from them, as they see them as too complex. Indeed, when you first use a PivotTable, the process can seem a bit daunting. Some persistence is definitely necessary.

You'll find that persistence will pay off once you experience the best feature of PivotTables: their ability to be manipulated using trial and error and immediately show the result of this manipulation. If the result is not what you expect, you can use Excel's Undo feature and have another go! Whatever you do, you are not changing the structure of your original table in any way, so you can do no harm.

Why Are They Called PivotTables?

PivotTables allow you to pivot data using drag-and-drop techniques and receive results immediately. PivotTables are interactive; once the table is complete, you very easily can see how your information will be affected when you move (or pivot) your data. This will become patently clear once you give PivotTables a try.

Even for experienced PivotTable developers, an element of trial and error is always involved in producing desired results. You will find yourself pivoting your table a lot!

What Are PivotTables Good For?

PivotTables can produce summary information from a table of information. Imagine you have a table of data that contains names, addresses, ages, occupations, phone numbers, and Zip Codes. With a PivotTable, you very easily and quickly can find out:

- How many people have the same name
- How many people share the same Zip Code
- How many people have the same occupation

You also can receive such information as:

- A list of people with the same occupation
- A list of addresses with the same Zip Code

If your data needs slicing, dicing, and reporting, PivotTables will be a critical part of your toolkit.

Why Use PivotTables When Spreadsheets Already Offer So Much Analysis Capability?

Perhaps the biggest advantage to using PivotTables is the fact that you can generate and extract meaningful information from a large table of data within a matter of minutes and without using up a lot of computer memory. In many cases, you could get the same results from a table of data by using Excel's built-in functions, but that would take more time and use far more memory.

Another advantage to using PivotTables is that if you want some new information, you can simply drag-and-drop (pivot). In addition, you can opt to have your information update each time you open the workbook or click Refresh.

PivotCharts Extend PivotTables

Microsoft introduced PivotCharts in Excel 2000. The table you create via the PivotTable Wizard produces a PivotChart (or, more accurately, a PivotTable and PivotChart Report). When you create a PivotTable, you also can create a PivotChart at the same time, with no extra effort. PivotCharts enable you to create interactive charts that previously were impossible without using either VBA or Excel Controls.

The PivotTable Wizard is discussed in more detail later in this chapter.

PivotCharts are not available in Excel for the Macintosh.

Creating Tables and Lists for Use in PivotTables

When you create a PivotTable, you must organize the dataset you're using in a table and/or a list. As the PivotTable will base all its data on this table or list, it is vital that you set up your tables and lists in a uniform way.

In this context, a table is no more than a list that has a title, has more than one column of data, and has a different heading for each column. A list often is referred to in the context of a table as well. The best practices that apply to setting up a list will help you greatly when you need to apply a PivotTable to your data.

When you extract data via the use of lookup or database functions, you can be a little less stringent in how you set up the table or list. This is because you can always compensate with the aid of a function and probably still get your result. Nonetheless, it's still easiest to set up the list or table as neatly as possible. Excel's built-in features assume a lot about the layout and setup up of your data. Although they offer a degree of flexibility, more often than not you will find it easier to adhere to the following guidelines when setting up your table or list:

- Headings are required, as a PivotTable uses them for field names. Headings should always appear in the row directly above the data. Also, never leave a blank row between the data and the headings. Furthermore, make the headings distinct in some way; for instance, boldface them.

- Leave at least three blank rows above the headings. You can use these for formulas, critical data, etc. You can hide the rows if you want.

- If you have more than one list or table on the same worksheet, leave at least one blank column between each list or table. This will help Excel recognize them as separate entities. However, if the lists and tables are related to each other, combine them into one large table.

- Avoid blank cells within your data. Instead of leaving blank cells for the same data in a column, repeat the data as many times as needed.

- Sort your list or data, preferably by the leftmost column. This will make the data easier to read and interpret.

If you follow these guidelines as closely as possible, using PivotTables will be a relatively easy task.

Figure 4-1 shows a well-laid out table of data, and a PivotTable in progress. Note that many of the same dates are repeated in the Date column. In front of this data is the Layout step for the data showing the optional Page, Row, and Column fields, as well as the mandatory Data field.

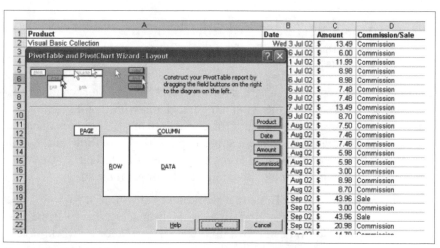

Figure 4-1. PivotTable generated from a well-laid out table of data

The PivotTable and PivotChart Wizard

As noted earlier, to help users create PivotTables, Excel offers a PivotTable and PivotChart Wizard. This Wizard guides you through the creation of a PivotTable using a four-step process, in which you tell Excel the following:

- How the data is set up and whether to create an associated PivotChart (if PivotCharts are available in that version of Excel)
- Where the data is stored—e.g., a range in the same workbook, a database, another workbook, etc.
- Which column of data is going into which field: the optional Page, Row, and Column fields, as well as the mandatory Data field
- Where to put your PivotTable (i.e., in a new worksheet or in an existing one)

You also can take many side steps along the way to manipulate the Pivot-Table, but most users find it easier to do this after telling Excel where to put it.

> Excel 2000 and later versions have a major advantage over Excel 97: they enable you to choose how to set up your data after the Wizard is finished.

Now that you know more about PivotTables and what they do, it's time to explore some handy hacks that can make this feature even more powerful.

HACK #46   Share PivotTables but Not Their Data

Create a snapshot of your PivotTable that no longer needs the underlying data structures.

You might need to send PivotTables for others to view, but for whatever reason you cannot send the underlying data associated with them. Perhaps you want others to see only certain data for confidentiality reasons, for instance. If this is the case, you can create a static copy of the PivotTable and enable the recipient to see only what he needs to see. Best of all, the file size of the static copy will be only a small percentage of the original file size.

Assuming you have a PivotTable in a workbook, all you need to do is select the entire PivotTable, copy it, and on a clean sheet select Edit → Paste Special... → Values. Now you can move this worksheet to another workbook or perhaps use it as is.

The one drawback to this method is that Excel does not paste the Pivot-Table's formats along with the values. This can make the static copy harder to read and perhaps less impressive. If you want to include the formatting as well, you can take a static picture (as opposed to a static copy) of your Pivot-Table and paste this onto a clean worksheet. This will give you a full-color, formatted snapshot of the original PivotTable to which you can apply any type of formatting you want, without having to worry about the formatting being lost when you refresh the original PivotTable. This is because the full-color, formatted snapshot is not linked in any way to the original PivotTable.

To create a static picture, format the PivotTable the way you want it and then select any cell within it. From the PivotTable toolbar, select PivotTable → Select → Entire Table. With the entire PivotTable selected, hold down the Shift key and select Edit → Copy → Picture. From the Copy Picture dialog box that pops up, make the selections shown in Figure 4-2, then click OK.

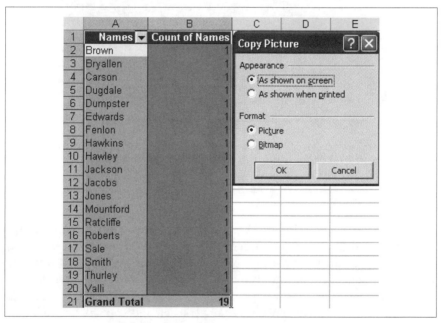

Figure 4-2. Copy Picture dialog in action

Finally, click anywhere outside the PivotTable and select Edit → Paste. You will end up with a fully colored and formatted snapshot of your PivotTable, as shown in Figure 4-3, complete with formatting. This can be very handy, especially if you have to email your PivotTable to other people for viewing. They will have the information they need, including all relevant formatting, but the file size will be small and they won't be able to manipulate your data. Also, they will be able to see only what you want them to see.

	A	B	C	D	E
1	Original Pivot Table		Picture Of Pivot Table		
2	Names ▼	Count of Names	Names ▼	Count of Names	
3	Brown	1	Brown	1	
4	Bryallen	1	Bryallen	1	
5	Carson	1	Carson	1	
6	Dugdale	1	Dugdale	1	
7	Dumpster	1	Dumpster	1	
8	Edwards	1	Edwards	1	
9	Fenlon	1	Fenlon	1	
10	Hawkins	1	Hawkins	1	
11	Hawley	1	Hawley	1	
12	Jackson	1	Jackson	1	
13	Jacobs	1	Jacobs	1	
14	Jones	1	Jones	1	
15	Mountford	1	Mountford	1	
16	Ratcliffe	1	Ratcliffe	1	
17	Roberts	1	Roberts	1	
18	Sale	1	Sale	1	
19	Smith	1	Smith	1	
20	Thurley	1	Thurley	1	
21	Valli	1	Valli	1	
22	Grand Total	19	Grand Total	19	

Figure 4-3. Original PivotTable contrasted with a picture of the PivotTable

You also can use this picture-taking method on a range of cells. You can follow the preceding steps, or you can use the little-noticed Camera tool on your toolbar.

To use this latter method, select View → Toolbars → Customize.... From the Customize dialog, click the Commands tab, from the Categories box, select Tools, and from the Commands box on the righthand side scroll down until you see Camera. Left-click and drag-and-drop this icon onto your toolbar where you want it to be displayed. Select a range of cells, click the Camera icon, and then click anywhere on the spreadsheet, and you will have a linked picture of the range you just took a picture of. Whatever data or formatting you applied to the original range will automatically be reflected in the picture of the range.

HACK #47 Automate PivotTable Creation

The steps you need to follow to create a PivotTable require some effort, and that effort often is redundant. With a small bit of VBA, you can create simple PivotTables automatically.

PivotTables are a very clever and potent feature to use on data that is stored in either a list or a table. Unfortunately, the mere thought of creating a

PivotTable is enough to prevent some people from even experimenting with them. Although some PivotTable setups can get very complicated, you can create most PivotTables easily and quickly. Two of the most commonly asked questions in Excel concern how to get a count of all items in a list, and how to create a list of unique items from a list that contains many duplicates. In this section, we'll show you how to create a PivotTable quickly and easily that accomplishes these tasks.

Assume you have a long list of names in column A, with cell A1 as your heading, and you want to know how many items are on the list, as well as generate a list of unique items. Select cell A1 (your heading) and then select Data → PivotTable and PivotChart Report (or Data → PivotTable Report on Macs) to start the PivotTable Wizard.

Make sure that either Microsoft Excel List or Database is selected, or that you have selected a single cell within your data. This will allow Excel to automatically detect the underlying data it is to use next. If you're using a Windows PC, select PivotTable under "What kind of report do you want to create?" (This question isn't asked on Macintoshes.) Click the Next button. The PivotTable Wizard should automatically have picked up the correct range for your data in column A and will highlight it in your sheet. If it is highlighted, click the Next button. Otherwise, use your mouse to select the range. Click the Layout button and drag to the Data area what will be your only field—you should see your title as it appears in cell A1 floating about. Drag the field again, this time into the Row area. Your screen should look something like Figure 4-4. Click OK.

> At this stage, if you want you can double-click the Field button in the Data area (this is labeled Count of Names in Figure 4-3) and change the Summarize by: option to a function of your choice—e.g., Sum, Average, etc. Excel will by default use the COUNT function if it's working with text and use the SUM function if it's working with numbers.

Finally, select New Worksheet as the destination of your PivotTable Report and click the Finish button. You should see your PivotTable on a new worksheet containing the unique items from your list along with a count of how many times each item (name) appears in your list.

What if you want to have a macro perform all those steps for you, creating a PivotTable from any column you feed it? If you simply record a macro, you'll find it often works only if your data has the same heading. To avoid this, you can create a simple macro stored in your workbook or in your personal macro workbook (described in Chapter 7) that you can use to create a

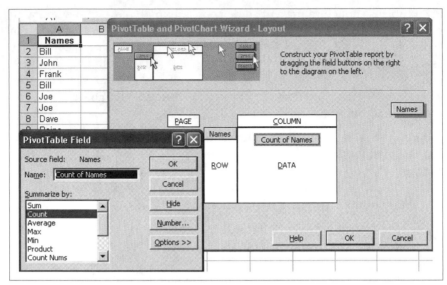

Figure 4-4. PivotTable Field and PivotTable Layout dialogs

PivotTable on any list of items. This requires that you write some generic VBA code and enter it into a standard module in your personal macro workbook or in any other workbook.

To start, select Tools → Macro → Visual Basic Editor (Alt/Option-F11) and then select Insert → Module. Enter the following code:

```
Sub GetCount( )
Dim Pt As PivotTable
Dim strField As String

    strField = Selection.Cells(1,1).Text
    Range(Selection, Selection.End(xlDown)).Name = "Items"

    ActiveWorkbook.PivotCaches.Add(SourceType:=xlDatabase, _
    SourceData:="=Items").CreatePivotTable TableDestination:="", _
    TableName:="ItemList"

    Set Pt = ActiveSheet.PivotTables("ItemList")
     ActiveSheet.PivotTableWizard TableDestination:=Cells(3, 1)
     Pt.AddFields RowFields:=strField
     Pt.PivotFields(strField).Orientation = xlDataField

End Sub
```

To return to Excel, close the Script window, or press Alt/⌘-Q, and save your workbook.

Before running this code, select the heading of your list and ensure that your list contains no blank cells.

Sorting your list will remove blank cells quickly.

The code will automatically create a named range of your list, called Items. It will then create the PivotTable based on this named range on a new worksheet.

The next time you have a long list of data, you can simply select its heading and run this macro. All the PivotTable setup work will be done in the blink of an eye.

HACK #48 Move PivotTable Grand Totals

One of the most annoying things about PivotTables is that the Grand Total that summarizes your data always ends up at the bottom of the table, meaning you have to scroll down just to see the figures. Move your Grand Total up to the top where it's easier to find.

Although PivotTables are a great way to summarize data and extract meaningful information, there is no built-in option to have the Grand Total float to the top for a quick bird's-eye view.

Before we describe a very generic method to move the Grand Total to the top, we'll explain how you can accomplish this with the GETPIVOTDATA function, which is designed specifically to extract data from a PivotTable.

You can use the function like this:

```
=GETPIVOTDATA("Sum of Amount",$B$5)
```

or like this:

```
=GETPIVOTDATA("Amount",$B$5)
```

Either function will extract the data and will track the Grand Total as it moves up, down, left, or right. We used the cell address $B$5, but as long as you use any cell within the PivotTable, you always will pick up the total.

The first function uses the Sum of Amount field, while the second one uses the Amount field. If your PivotTable has the Amount field in the Data area, you need to name the field **Amount**. If, however, the Amount field is being used two or more times in the Data area, you must specify the name you gave it, or the name you accepted by default (see Figure 4-5).

You can double-click these fields to change them. This issue can become confusing if you are not up to speed with PivotTables. Luckily in Excel 2002 and later, the process is much easier, as you can have a cell fill in the arguments and give the correct syntax by using the mouse pointer. In any cell,

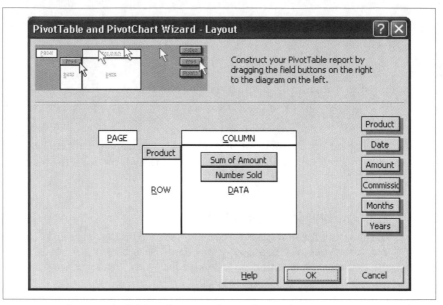

Figure 4-5. The Amount field used twice and named Sum of Amount in one case and Number Sold in the other

type = (an equals sign) and then use your mouse pointer to click in the cell currently housing the Grand Total. Excel will automatically fill in the arguments for you.

> Unfortunately, if you use the Function Wizard, or first type =GETPIVOTDATA( ) and then click in the cell currently housing the Grand Total, Excel makes a mess by trying to nest another GETPIVOTDATA function within that cell.

Probably the easiest, if least sophisticated, way to extract the Grand Total is to use the following function:

    =MAX(PivGTCol)

where the column currently housing the Grand Total is named PivGTCol.

You also can use the LARGE and SMALL functions to extract from a PivotTable a host of figures according to their size. The following formula, for instance, extracts the second largest figure from a PivotTable:

    =LARGE(PivGTCol,2)

You can add some extra rows immediately above the start of the PivotTable and place these formulas there so that you can see this type of information instantly, without having to scroll to the bottom of your PivotTable.

Efficiently Pivot Another Workbook's Data

Use data residing in another workbook as the source for your PivotTable.

When creating a PivotTable in Excel, you have lots of options for your data source. By far the easiest and most powerful approach is to use data that resides within the same workbook. Unfortunately, for whatever reason, this is not always possible or feasible. Perhaps the data that resides in another workbook is entered daily, for instance, and the users entering the data should not see the PivotTable.

Using a dynamic named range will greatly decrease the refresh time needed for your PivotTable to update. As you cannot reference a dynamic named range from another workbook, this also means you prevented the Pivot-Table from referencing perhaps thousands of blank rows and causing the file size to increase substantially. This way, you can pull in data from another workbook, and then base your PivotTable on the data in the same workbook rather than referencing it externally.

In the workbook that will contain your PivotTable, insert a new worksheet and call it **Data**. Open the workbook containing the data to be referenced, and ensure that the worksheet containing the data is the active sheet. In any spare cell on this worksheet, enter this formula:

```
=IF(A1="","",A1)
```

where A1 is the very first heading of your data table.

Select cell A1. Then cut it, activate your original workbook, and paste cell A1 in cell A1 on the Data sheet. This will give you the reference to the other workbook. Copy this cell across as many columns as there are headings in your data source. Then select Insert → Name → Define, and in the Names in Workbook: field, type **PivotData**. In the Refers to: box, type the following:

```
=OFFSET($A$1,0,0,COUNTA($A:$A),COUNTA($1:$1))
```

Click Add, then click OK. Next, to insert some code that will run each time the workbook is opened, right-click the Excel icon (located at the top left corner of the screen) and enter the following code:

```
Private Sub Workbook_Open()
  With Worksheets("Data")
    .Range("2:1000").Clear
    .Range("1:1").AutoFill .Range("1:1000")
    .Range("2:1000") = .Range("2:1000").Value
  End With
End Sub
```

This shortcut isn't available on a Mac. You'll have to open the VBE by pressing Option-F11, or by selecting Tools → Macro → Visual Basic Editor. Then Ctrl-click This Workbook in the Projects window.

To return to Excel, close the script window or press Alt/⌘-Q.

The preceding code includes only 1,000 rows of data. This figure should always be greater than the number of rows you believe you will need. In other words, if your table in the other workbook contains 500 rows, add a few hundred more to accommodate any growth in the original table.

Avoid using an extremely high row number (like 10,000, unless you actually have that much data), as this will greatly impact how quickly the code runs and the data updates.

Save the workbook, close it, and then reopen it, making certain that you enabled macros. The code you added will fire automatically and will copy the formulas in row 1 on the Data sheet, then automatically convert all but row 1 into values only. This will leave you with a copy of your original data source, which will update each time you open the workbook.

Now you can hide this sheet if you want by selecting Format → Sheet → Hide or by using the method described in "Hide Worksheets So That They Cannot Be Unhidden" [Hack #5].

Now, to base a PivotTable on this dynamic named range, select anywhere within the PivotTable, then select the Wizard option from the PivotTable toolbar. Click the Back button until you reach Step 1 of the Wizard. Select the first option, Microsoft Excel List or Database, click Next, and in Step 2, type **=PivotData** (the name of the dynamic named range). Then click Finish.

You will not experience the lag that often occurs when a PivotTable is referencing an external data source because now the data itself is stored within the same workbook. As an added bonus, because you can use a dynamic named range, the PivotTable is dynamic without having to reference heaps of blank rows, and the file is kept to a manageable size.

CHAPTER FIVE

Charting Hacks
Hacks 50-59

Charts are one of Excel's most popular features, giving spreadsheets visual power beyond mere calculations. Although Excel's chart capabilities are impressive, many times you'll want to go beyond the basic functionality provided by the software's built-in Chart Wizard to create charts that are more responsive to changes in data, or you simply will want to go beyond the range of options Excel most obviously provides. The hacks in this chapter enable you to do all of this and more.

Explode a Single Slice from a Pie Chart

Although pie charts are excellent visual aids, sometimes you want to emphasize a particular piece of the pie. Separating it from the rest gives it more attention.

The default option on an exploded pie chart is to explode all the slices simultaneously and for the same distance. With a couple of mouse clicks, you can explode one slice at a time.

To begin, set up a basic pie chart such as the one shown in Figure 5-1.

Next, click the pie chart and then slowly double-click the slice you want to explode. Drag the selected slice of pie away from the center of the chart, and you will see the exploded effect shown in Figure 5-2.

Dragging the single slice will leave the other slices unaffected. You can repeat this for other slices if you want. This technique also works just as well with a 3D pie. To make the pie 3D, click the chart, right-click and select Chart Type, and then select the 3D Pie icon.

If you want to explode all the slices at the same time, simply click the pie to select it, then drag away from the center, and all the slices will have the exploded effect shown in Figure 5-3. The further you drag the slices, the smaller they will get.

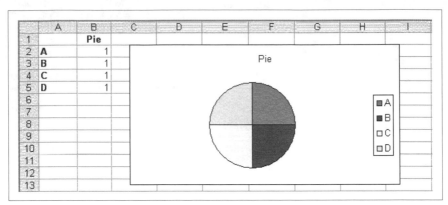

Figure 5-1. Simple pie chart set up from worksheet data

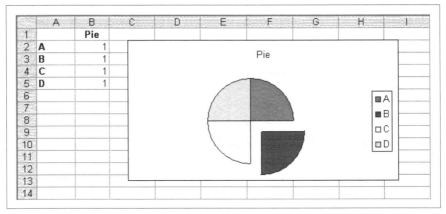

Figure 5-2. Simple pie chart with exploding slice

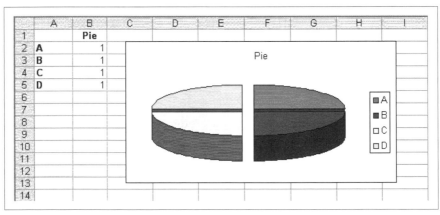

Figure 5-3. 3D pie chart with exploding slices

The reverse also works if you want to "unexplode" your pie. Simply click the piece of pie and drag toward the middle to put it all back together again.

—Andy Pope

Create Two Sets of Slices in One Pie Chart

Most people think pie charts are limited to a single set of values, but here is a way to create a pie chart based on two columns of values.

It is a bit tricky to see two series of values charted on separate axes within one chart, but the effect is well worth the effort. To see how this works, first create a basic pie chart. Put some data in the range B1:C5, and then select that range and click the Chart Wizard button in the toolbar. In Step 1 of the Wizard, under Chart Type, select the first pie chart. Now work your way through the Chart Wizard, making any changes you need. When you reach Step 4, make sure you place the chart as an object in the current worksheet.

Next, select the pie chart, right-click it, and select Format → Source Data → Series. Click Add to add another series. Select cell D1 for the Name and cells D2:D5 for the Values, then click OK. You'll get the chart shown in Figure 5-4.

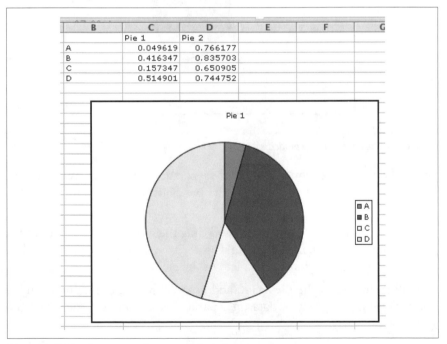

Figure 5-4. Pie chart set up from worksheet data

Double-click the pie itself again to select it, select Format Data Series, choose the Axis tab, and plot the series on the secondary axis. Click OK. The pie chart still looks the same on the surface, but it isn't the same underneath.

Select the pie, and while pressing the left mouse button, drag out from the center, then release the left mouse button. This will create the exploded effect you are looking for, as shown in Figure 5-5.

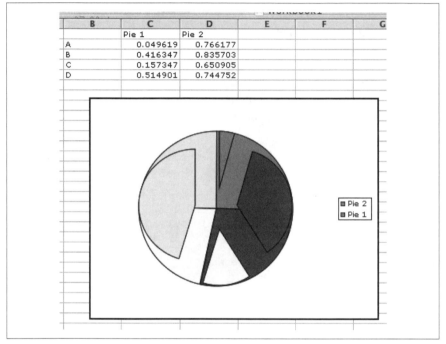

Figure 5-5. Pie chart with exploded secondary axis

By exploding the pie, you will not only separate the two axes, revealing the second pie chart, but also compress the pie chart plotted on the secondary axis, allowing you to see both charts.

Now, select each slice of pie in turn and drag them back to the center of the pie, producing the chart shown in Figure 5-6. Remember that two slow clicks will highlight an individual piece of the pie.

Join all the pieces of the pie again, and you will have a fully functional pie chart plotting two series of data on separate axes. Now you can color and format accordingly.

—Andy Pope

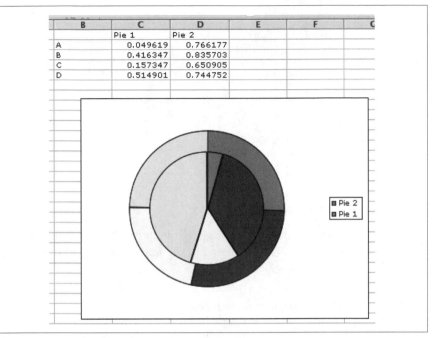

B	C	D	E	F	C
	Pie 1	Pie 2			
A	0.049619	0.766177			
B	0.416347	0.835703			
C	0.157347	0.650905			
D	0.514901	0.744752			

Figure 5-6. Completed pie chart containing two pies

HACK #52 Create Charts That Adjust to Data

Your charts can include and plot new data automatically, the moment you add the data to your spreadsheet.

If you use dynamic named ranges in lieu of range references, your chart will plot any new data the moment you add it to your worksheet. To see how this works, begin with a clean worksheet and set up some data similar to that shown in Figure 5-7.

To create the chart and make it dynamic, you need to add two named ranges. One of the named ranges is for the category labels (Dates) and the other is for the actual data points (Temperature).

> If you are unsure as to how to insert a dynamic named range, check out "Create Ranges That Expand and Contract" [**Hack #42**], which discusses this in full.

Create a dynamic named range called **TEMP_DATES** for the dates in column A by selecting Insert → Name → Define, and type this formula:

```
=OFFSET($A$1,1,0,COUNTA($A:$A)-1,1)
```

	A	B	C
1	**Dates**	**Temperature**	
2	1/10/2003	10	
3	2/10/2003	12	
4	3/10/2003	13	
5	4/10/2003	13	
6	5/10/2003	12	
7	6/10/2003	14	
8	7/10/2003	15	
9	8/10/2003	13	
10	9/10/2003	12	
11	10/10/2003	11	
12			

Figure 5-7. Data to be charted

Notice that you included a -1 immediately after the COUNTA argument. This ensures that the heading is not included in the named range for that particular series.

> In this example, you referenced the entire column A as the COUNTA argument ($A:$A). In older versions of Excel, it is often good practice to restrict this range to a much smaller group of cells, so as not to add unnecessary overhead to calculations. In other words, you could be forcing Excel to look in potentially thousands of cells unnecessarily. Some of Excel's functions are smart enough to know which cells are *dirty* (contain data), but some functions are not. However, this is slightly less necessary with more recent versions of Excel, as Excel has improved its handling of large ranges.

Next, for the Temperature readings in column B, set up another dynamic range called **TEMP_READINGS**, using this formula:

```
=OFFSET($B$2,0,0,COUNTA($B:$B)-1,1)
```

Now you can create the chart using the dynamic named ranges you created in lieu of cell references.

Highlight the data (range $A$1:$B$11), then select the Chart icon on the Standard toolbar. From Step 1 of the Wizard, select the chart type you want to use (for this example we will use a column), and click Next. In Step 2 of the Wizard, you will be presented with two tabs: Data Range and Series. Series is the one you want. Delete the formula that presently sits in the Value: box, and enter the following:

```
=Sheet1!TEMP_READINGS
```

It is very important to include the Sheet name of your workbook in your formula references. If you don't, you will not be able to enter the named range in your formula.

Finally, delete the formula that presently sits under Category X Labels: and enter the following:

```
=Sheet1!TEMP_DATES
```

Complete the rest of the Chart Wizard to finish your chart, making any changes required along the way. The result will look like Figure 5-8.

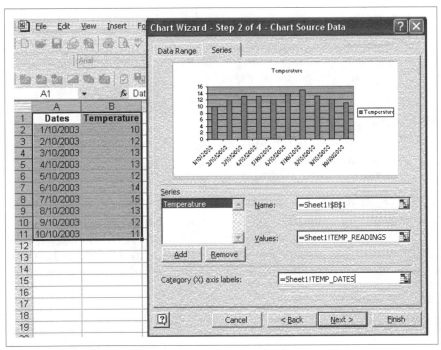

Figure 5-8. Dynamic named ranges in lieu of static range references

Once this chart is set up, every time you include another entry in either column A (Dates) or column B (Temperature), it will be added to your chart automatically.

Plotting the Last x Number of Readings

Another type of named range that you can use with charts is one that picks up only the last 10 readings (or whatever number you nominate) in a series of data. Try this using the same data you used in the first part of this hack.

For the dates in column A, set up a dynamic named range called **TEMP_DATES_ 10DAYS** that references the following:

```
=OFFSET($A$1,COUNTA($A:$A)-10,0,10,1)
```

For readings in column B, set up another dynamic named range called **TEMP_ READINGS_10DAYS** and enter the following:

```
=OFFSET(Sheet1!$A$1,COUNTA(Sheet15!$A:$A)-10,1,10,1)
```

If you want to vary the number of readings—to 20, for instance—change the last part of the formula so that it reads as follows:

```
=OFFSET(Sheet1!$A$1,COUNTA(Sheet15!$A:$A)-20,1,20,1)
```

Using dynamic named ranges with your charts gives you enormous flexibility and will save you loads of time tweaking your charts whenever you make an additional entry to your source data.

—*Andy Pope*

Interact with Your Charts Using Custom #53 Controls

To make your chart truly interactive, you can use one or more dynamic ranges in your chart and then use either a scrollbar or a drop-down list from the Forms toolbar to reveal the figures your readers want to peruse.

As you saw in the previous hack, you can use dynamic named ranges to add flexibility to your charts. But you also can use dynamic named ranges to create interfaces controlling which data the chart plots. By linking dynamic named ranges to custom controls, you enable users to change the chart data by using the control, which simultaneously will update the data in the worksheet or vice versa.

Using a Dynamic Named Range Linked to a Scrollbar

In this example, you will use a scrollbar to reveal monthly figures over a 12-month period. The scrollbar is used to alter the number of months reported. The scrollbar's value also is used in a dynamic range, which in turn is used as the data source of the chart.

To begin, set up some data similar to that shown in Figure 5-9.

Create a dynamic named range by selecting Insert → Name → Define and call it **SALES_PERIOD**. In the Refers To: box, type the following:

```
=OFFSET($B$5,0,0,$C$5,1)
```

By using the OFFSET function, you can use cell $C$5 to force the referenced range for SALES_PERIOD to expand both up and down as the number in

Month	Product XYZ Sales for 2003
4	
5 JAN	505
6 FEB	943
7 MAR	500
8 APR	624
9 MAY	894
10 JUN	612
11 JUL	526
12 AUG	629
13 SEP	665
14 OCT	954
15 NOV	893
16 DEC	954
17	

Figure 5-9. Worksheet data for dynamic chart linked to scrollbar

$C$5 changes. In other words, changing the number in $C$5 to the number 5 would force the range to incorporate B5:B10.

> If you do not want the user to see cell C5, you can take this a step further and hide the contents of $C$5 by right-clicking it and selecting Format Cells → Custom. Enter the format ;;;, and then click OK. In Figure 5-9, the contents of cell C5 are hidden.

Create a chart (a line chart or a column chart works best). When you get to Step 2 of the Chart Wizard, select the Series tab and change the Formula Reference in the Values: box so that it reads =<Workbook.xls>!SALES_PERIOD. Doing this will make your chart dynamic.

Once you have created your chart, you will need to insert a scrollbar from the Forms toolbar. The easiest way to do this is to right-click the gray area at the top of the screen (this is known as the Toolbar area) and select Forms. This will bring the Forms toolbar onto the screen.

Click the scrollbar icon to select it. Once you have inserted a scrollbar, select it and move it onto your chart. Now right-click it and select Format Control, change the minimum value to **1**, change the maximum value to 12, and set the cell link to **$C$5**. The resulting chart will look like that shown in Figure 5-10.

Using a Dynamic Named Range Linked to a Drop-Down List

Another variation is to link to a drop-down list. Starting with some data such as that shown in Figure 5-9, you will add a dynamic range that will be

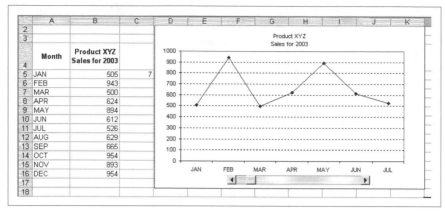

Figure 5-10. Dynamic chart linked to scrollbar

used as a data source for the chart. The dynamic range will be linked to a drop-down list you can use to view one student's test results from those of a group of students. You will use the drop-down list to select the name of the student whose results you want to view.

Use the formula **=AVERAGE(B6:B11)** in cell B12 and copy it across to cell F12, as shown in Figure 5-11.

	A	B	C	D	E	F
1						
2						
3						
4						
5		Exam A	Exam B	Exam C	Exam D	Exam E
6	Andy	45	52	69	62	47
7	Bernard	64	89	70	55	67
8	Charlie	72	72	90	60	41
9	Dave	57	39	67	74	64
10	Edward	57	93	43	85	56
11	Frank	46	58	42	68	47
12	Average	57	67	64	67	54
13						

Figure 5-11. Dynamic chart linked to a drop-down list

Create a dynamic range by selecting Insert → Name → Define, and call it **STUDENTS**. In the Refers To: box, type the following:

```
=OFFSET($A$5,$G$6,1,1,5)
```

Create another dynamic range called **STUDENT_NAME**, and in the Refers To: box, type the following:

```
=OFFSET($A$5,$G$6,0,1,1)
```

The use of the cell reference $G$6 in the OFFSET formula forces the referenced ranges for STUDENTS and STUDENT_NAME to expand both up and down as the number in $G$6 changes.

Now create a clustered column chart using the range A11:F12. When you get to Step 2 of the Chart Wizard, select the Series tab and change the Formula Reference in the Values: box for the first series (Frank) so that it reads **=<Workbook.xls>!STUDENTS**. In the Name: box, enter **<Workbook.xls>!STUDENT_ NAME**.

At this point, you need to insert a ComboBox from the Forms toolbar. Select the ComboBox, right-click it, enter **$A$6:A:11** for the input range and enter **$G$6** for the cell link.

To finish, place the CONCATENATE function in an empty cell, such as cell B4, like this:

```
=CONCATENATE("Test Result for ",INDEX(A6:A11,G6))
```

Clicking the downward-pointing arrow on the ComboBox shown in Figure 5-12 will change the name of the student and show his test results.

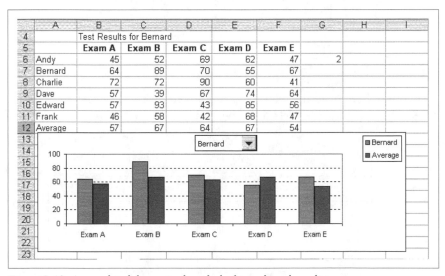

Figure 5-12. A completed dynamic chart linked to a drop down list

—*Andy Pope*

Three Quick Ways to Update Your Charts

Although creating new charts is wonderful, updating them to reflect new circumstances can take a lot of effort. You can reduce the amount of work needed to change the data used by a chart in a number of ways.

Using Drag-and-Drop

You can add data to an existing series or create a completely new data series by simply dragging and dropping data onto a chart. Excel will try to decide how to treat the data, which might mean adding to any existing data series when you really wanted a new series. You can, however, get Excel to display a dialog box, which lets you to determine which action you want to use.

Try setting up some data such as that shown in Figure 5-13.

	A	B	C	D
1		**2001**	**2002**	**2003**
2	January	7.43	7	3
3	February	1	3	10
4	March	21.3	2	4
5	April	11.6	1	9
6	May	10	3	4
7				

Figure 5-13. Data for clustered column chart

Using the Chart Wizard, create a clustered column chart for the range $A$1: $D$5 only, producing the result shown in Figure 5-14.

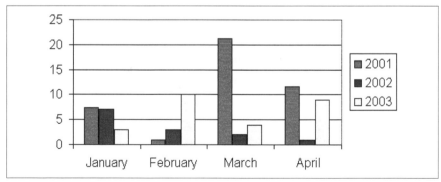

Figure 5-14. Clustered column chart created with range A1:D5 only

Highlight the range A6:D6, right-click the selection border, press the right mouse button, and drag onto the chart. When you release the mouse button, the Paste Special menu will pop up, as shown in Figure 5-15.

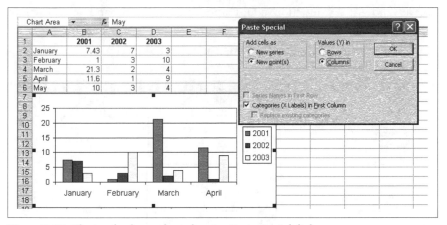

Figure 5-15. Clustered column chart showing Paste Special dialog

Select the Columns option and then click OK. This will add the May data series to the chart, as shown in Figure 5-16.

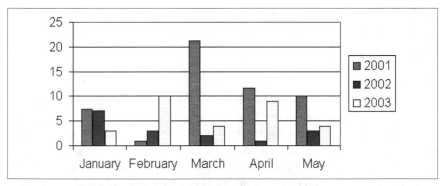

Figure 5-16. Clustered column chart with May data series added

The Paste Special dialog takes care of most of the actions you need in order to use this nifty trick.

Using the Formula Bar

You also can update your chart by using the Formula bar. When you select a chart and click a data series within it, look at the Formula bar and you will see the formula Excel uses for the data series.

Called a SERIES function, the formula generally uses four arguments, although a bubble chart requires an additional fifth argument for [Size].

The syntax (or order of structure) of the SERIES function is as follows:

```
=SERIES( [Name] , [X Values] , [Y Values] , [Plot Order] )
```

So, a valid SERIES function could appear as follows, and as shown in Figure 5-17:

```
=SERIES(Sheet1!$B$1,Sheet1!$A$2:$A$5,Sheet1!$B$2:$B$5,1)
```

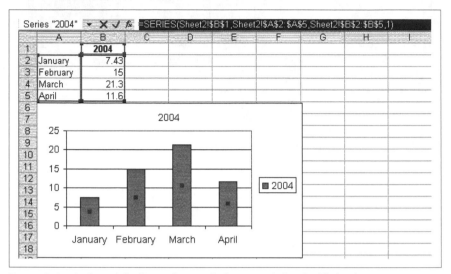

Figure 5-17. A clustered column chart with the Formula bar highlighted

In terms of Figure 5-17, the first part of the reference, Sheet1!$B$1, refers to the name, or the chart title, which is 2004. The second part of the reference, Sheet1!$A$2:$A$5, refers to the X values, which in this case are the Months. The third part of the reference, Sheet1!$B$2:$B$5, refers to the Y values, which are the values 7.43, 15, 21.3, and 11.6. Finally, the last part of the formula, the 1, refers to the plot order, or the order of the series. In this case, there is only one series, so this series can only take the value 1. If there were more than one series, the first series would take the number 1, the second series would take the number 2, and so forth.

To make changes to the chart, simply alter the cell references in the Formula bar.

Besides using cell references, you can enter explicit values, known as array constants, into your charts (see "About Array Formulas and Array Constants" in Excel Help for full details). To achieve this, add {} (curly brackets) around the X and Y values, as shown in the following formula:

```
=SERIES("My Bar",{"A","B","C","D"},{1,2,3,4},1)
```

In the previous SERIES formula, A, B, C, and D would be the X values, while 1, 2, 3, and 4 would be their corresponding Y values.

By using this method, you can create or update a chart without having to store data in cells.

Dragging the Bounding Area

If your chart data contains continuous cell references, you can easily extend or reduce the data in the series by dragging the bounding area to a desired point. Slowly click the data series you want to either extend or reduce. After two slow clicks, black square(s) (also called handles) will appear around the outside of the series (or in the middle if you're using a line chart). All you need to do is click a square and drag the bounding area in the direction required, as shown in Figure 5-18.

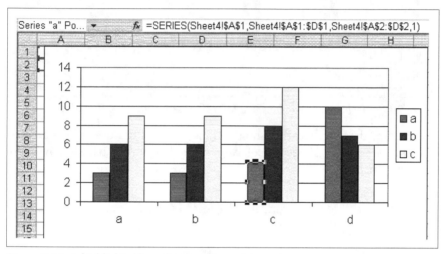

Figure 5-18. A highlighted bounding area for a chart series

If you either extend or reduce the series data, as shown in Figure 5-19, the original source data as well as the axis labels (if set to Auto) also will alter to reflect the changes you made.

This is great for testing scenarios, when you want to explore what the results of different data sets will be.

—Andy Pope

Hack Together a Simple Thermometer Chart

Excel doesn't provide a thermometer chart. If you want one, you'll have to construct it.

By using the Chart Wizard to create a basic clustered column chart that compares values across categories, and then manipulating the various chart elements, you can create a visual, workable thermometer chart with little effort.

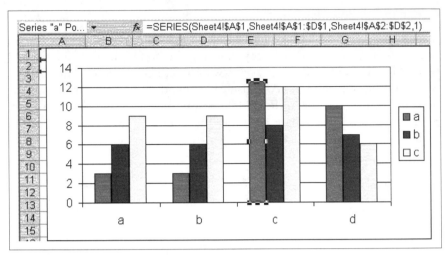

Figure 5-19. A highlighted bounding area for a chart series after it is expanded

Set up some data, such as that shown in Figure 5-20, and use the Chart Wizard to create a basic clustered column chart, charting the data in rows. We used the range B3:C4.

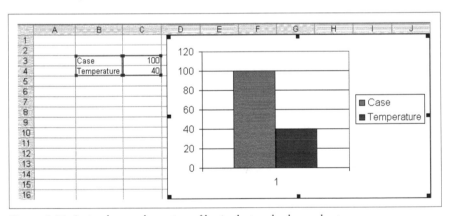

Figure 5-20. Series data and creation of basic clustered column chart

Remove the legend and the gridlines (click them to highlight them, then press Delete), and format the Temperature Data Series to the Y2 axis. Do this by selecting the series, right-clicking, selecting Format Data Series → Axis, and then selecting the Secondary Axis option, resulting in the chart in Figure 5-21.

Format both the Y1 (on the left) and Y2 (on the right) axes by highlighting each axis in turn, right-clicking, and selecting Format Axis → Scale. Set the Minimum to 0, the Maximum to 100, the Major Unit to 10, and the Minor Unit to 5. You'll see the chart shown in Figure 5-22.

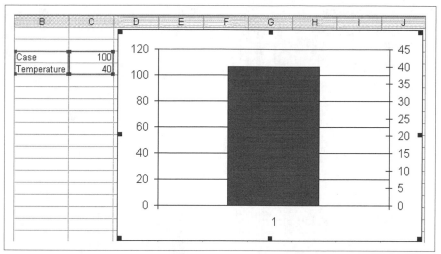

Figure 5-21. Two series plotted on the Y2 axis

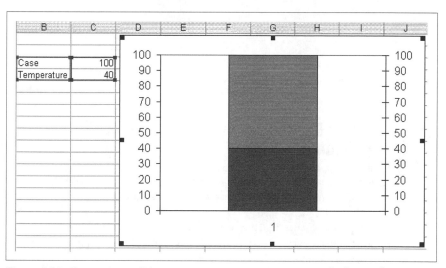

Figure 5-22. Case series on Y1 axis, temperature series on Y2 axis, both axes formatted identically

Format the Case data series to White, format the Temperature series to Red, and format the Plot Area to White. At this point, the thermometer chart should be taking shape.

Reduce the Gap Width property for both columns by right-clicking and selecting Format Data Series → Options. Finally, remove the X axis (highlight the axis and click Delete) and then size and position to suit.

As Figure 5-23 demonstrates, by fiddling around a bit with Excel's existing chart features, you can come up with a thermometer chart that looks great and works well.

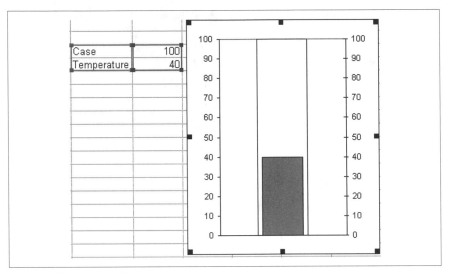

Figure 5-23. Completed thermometer chart

—*Andy Pope*

HACK #56 Create a Column Chart with Variable Widths and Heights

Wouldn't it be nice to create a column chart whose columns can vary in width and height? Then, as you plot your data into the columns, the columns' width and height cleverly adjust themselves simultaneously.

Excel doesn't provide this feature directly, but by hacking an XY scatter chart you can create a very effective variable width column chart. XY scatter charts are used to compare values; therefore, they provide a perfect base on which to start creating a variable width column chart.

Figure 5-24 shows a variable width column chart that charts the percent share versus cost for the following expenses: gas, electricity, water, food, travel, and other. The X axis (the axis along the bottom of the chart) shows the percentages (%), while the Y axis (the axis on the lefthand side) shows the cost ($).

To create this chart, set up some data such as that in Figure 5-24 and, using the Chart Wizard, highlight the range D2:E8. Then, in Step 1 of the Chart Wizard, select the XY Scatter Chart option. Accept the default scatter chart, which shows only points, and click Next to move to Step 2 of the Wizard.

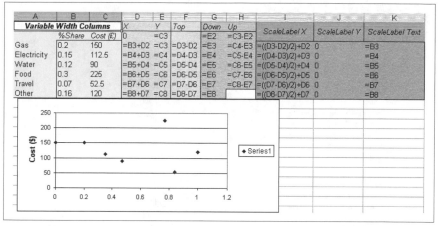

	A	B	C	D	E	F	G	H	I	J	K
	Variable Width Columns			X	Y	Top	Down	Up	ScaleLabel X	ScaleLabel Y	ScaleLabel Text
		%Share	Cost (£)	0	=C3		=E2	=C3-E2			
	Gas	0.2	150	=B3+D2	=C3	=D3-D2	=E3	=C4-E3	=((D3-D2)/2)+D2	0	=B3
	Electricity	0.15	112.5	=B4+D3	=C4	=D4-D3	=E4	=C5-E4	=((D4-D3)/2)+D3	0	=B4
	Water	0.12	90	=B5+D4	=C5	=D5-D4	=E5	=C6-E5	=((D5-D4)/2)+D4	0	=B5
	Food	0.3	225	=B6+D5	=C6	=D6-D5	=E6	=C7-E6	=((D6-D5)/2)+D5	0	=B6
	Travel	0.07	52.5	=B7+D6	=C7	=D7-D6	=E7	=C8-E7	=((D7-D6)/2)+D6	0	=B7
	Other	0.16	120	=B8+D7	=C8	=D8-D7	=E8		=((D8-D7)/2)+D7	0	=B8

Figure 5-24. XY scatter chart set up from range D2:E8

Ensure that Columns is selected. Click the Next button to move to Step 3 of the Wizard, and under Value (Y) Axis, type **Cost ($)**. Click the Next button and ensure that the chart will be produced as an object, not on a new sheet. Click Finish to see the scatter chart.

> You can use Ctrl-~ (which is the same on the Mac) to show you the correct formulas to place in the cells. You also could select Tools → Options... → View (Views under Excel → Preferences on Mac OS X) and check Formulas under Window options.

Now it's time to play around with the chart to create columns. First remove the legend and gridlines (highlight them, then click Delete) and format the plot area to no fill by clicking the gray background, right-clicking, and selecting Format Plot Area. Under Area, select None.

Highlight the X axis, then double-click it to get to the Format Axis dialog. Click Scale. Under Value Axis Scale, set the Minimum to 0 and the Maximum to 1. Click the Patterns tab and set the Major Tick Mark type to None and the Tick Mark Labels to None, then click OK. The scatter chart will look something like that shown in Figure 5-25.

The next step is to create the lines for the columns, so double-click the data points to bring up the Format Data Series dialog. Click the X Error Bars tab. In the Display section, select Minus, then select Custom - Range and highlight the range F2:F8. This produces the horizontal line at the top of the column.

Now click the Y Error Bars tab and select Both under Display. Set the Custom + Range to H2:H7 and the Custom - Range to G2:G8, then click OK. This will give you the vertical sides of the columns.

Create a Column Chart with Variable Widths and Heights

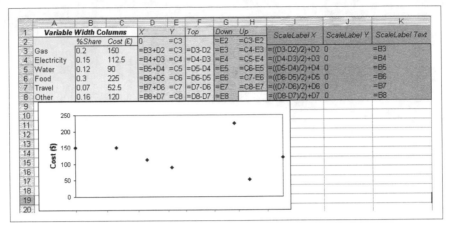

Figure 5-25. Modified scatter chart

Now that all the hard work is done, it's time to tidy up a bit and add some labels. First, under the Format Data Series dialog, select Patterns and then select None under Marker. The results are shown in Figure 5-26.

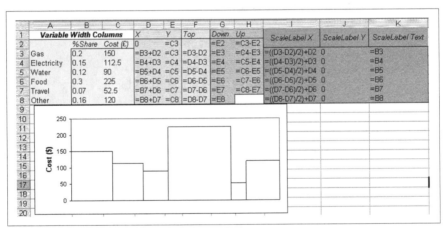

Figure 5-26. XY scatter chart manipulated to produce variable width column chart

If you want to use labels, you need to download John Walkenbach's Chart Tools, available from *http://j-walk.com/ss/excel/files/charttools.htm.* Part of this add-in is designed specifically for data labels. It enables you to specify a worksheet range for the data labels for a chart series. (Unfortunately, it doesn't seem to work on Excel for the Macintosh, even after extraction from its EXE distribution.)

Before you use Chart Tools, you must add a new data series to provide X-axis labels for the chart. So, highlight the chart, right-click, and select Source

Data and then Series. Select Add to add a new series. Under X Values, highlight the range I3:I8, and under Y Values, highlight the range J3:J8. Format the new data series so that it has no marker by going to the Format Data Series dialog, selecting Patterns, and then, under Marker, selecting None.

Now it's time to use an add-in. Make sure you have Series 2 selected, and then select Chart → JWalk Chart Tools. When the dialog box pops up, make the data label range **K3:K8**.

To add yet another new data series to provide column labels for the chart, highlight the chart, right-click, select Source Data, and then select Series. Select Add to add a new series. Under X Values, highlight the range I3:I8, and under Y Values, highlight the range C3:C8. Again, format the new data series to have no marker by selecting Pattern, then Marker, then None in the Format Data Series dialog.

Again, use your add-in. This time highlight Series 3 and link the data labels to A3:A8. The result will look like that shown in Figure 5-27.

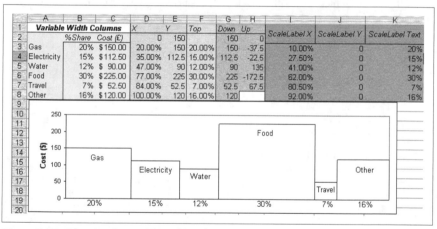

Figure 5-27. Completed variable width column chart

The fantastic thing about this type of chart is that the bars will either expand or contract up the Y axis and along the X axis when the entries in the % Share or the Cost ($) columns change. Pretty nifty.

—Andy Pope

Create a Speedometer Chart

You can create a really impressive, workable speedometer (or "speedo") chart, complete with moving needle, by using a combination of doughnuts and pie charts. The added touch is that you can control the speedometer via a scrollbar.

Excel's Chart Wizard offers many different types of charts, except, unfortunately, a speedometer chart. A speedometer chart provides a slick way to represent data. With the hacks in this section, you can create a speedometer chart as well as add a scrollbar from the Control Toolbox toolbar that will alter the chart and change the data in the worksheet simultaneously.

The first thing you need to do is to set up some data, such as that shown in Figure 5-28, and create a doughnut chart. Doughnut charts work a bit like pie charts, but they can contain multiple series, whereas a pie chart cannot.

	A	B	C	D	E	F
1	Bands	Dial	Dial Labels	Labels	Needle	
2	25	180	180	=$F$3 & "% Share"	200	Share
3	75	=(180/100)*A2	9	0	=((180/100)*F3)-1	0
4		=(180/100)*(A3-A2)	18	10	2	
5		=360-SUM(B2:B4)	18	20	=360-SUM(E2:E4)	
6			18	30		
7			18	40		
8			18	50		
9			18	60		
10			18	70		
11			18	80		
12			18	90		
13			9	100		
14						
15				Low		
16				Normal		
17				High		
18						

Figure 5-28. Data set up for speedometer chart

Press Alt/⌘-~ to show the actual formulas on the worksheet. You also can select Tools → Options... → View and check the Formulas option to see the formulas, though that's a longer process.

Now highlight the range B2:B5 and select the Chart Wizard. In Step 1 of the Chart Wizard, select the Standard Types tab (this should be the default anyway). Then, under Chart Type, select the first doughnut. Click the Next button to go to Step 2 of the Wizard and make sure your data is charted in rows. Click the Next button to take you to Step 3. You can make changes in Step 3 if you need to, but they aren't necessary for this hack. Click Next to go to Step 4, and make sure the chart ends up as an object in the current worksheet (again, this is the default). Placing the chart as an object will make it easier to work with as you are setting up the speedometer (see Figure 5-29).

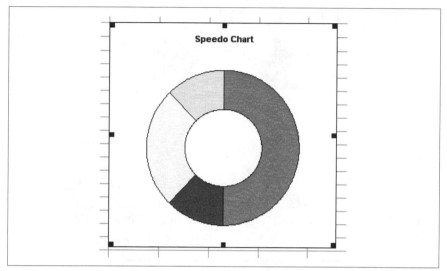

Figure 5-29. Basic doughnut chart

Highlight the doughnut chart, slowly double-click the largest slice to select it, and then select Format Data Series → Options. Set the angle of this slice to 90 degrees. Click the Patterns tab and set the area and border of this slice to None, then click OK. Slowly double-click to highlight each of the other slices in turn, then double-click to get back to the Format Data Series dialog and color the other three bands as required. The doughnut chart should look like the one in Figure 5-30.

You need to add another series (Series 2) of values to form the slots for the dial labels, so again highlight the chart, right-click, select Source Data, and then select the Series tab. Click the Add button, which will create a new series, and then, under Values, select the range C2:C13. Click the Add button again to add a third series (Series 3) to create the needle, and under Values, select the range E2:E5. Your result should look like Figure 5-31.

At this point, the speedometer is starting to take shape. If you want to add labels to the speedometer, you can download a tool for adding them for free from John Walkenbach's Chart Tools, at *http://j-walk.com/ss/excel/files/charttools.htm*.

Part of this add-in, which unfortunately works only on Windows, is designed specifically for data labels. It enables you to specify a worksheet range for the data labels for a chart series. John's add-in also contains the features described in the following list.

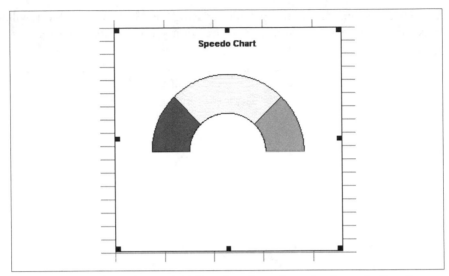

Figure 5-30. Doughnut chart with 90% angle and no color or border on the first slice

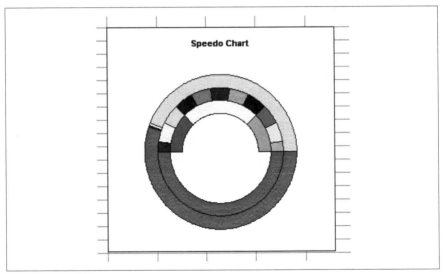

Figure 5-31. Doughnut chart with multiple series

Chart Size

Enables you to specify an exact size for a chart, or enables you to make all charts the same size.

Export

Enables you to save charts as *.gif*, *.jpg*, *.tif*, or *.png* files.

Picture

Converts a chart to a picture (color or grayscale).

Text Size

Freezes the size of all text items in a chart. When the chart is resized, the text elements will not change size.

Chart Report

Generates a summary report for all charts, or a detailed report for a single chart.

Use the add-in to format Series 2 to display data labels using the range D2: D13. Keep Series 2 highlighted, then double-click to bring up the Format Data Series dialog. Go to the Patterns tab, and select None for both the Border and Area. Your chart should look like that shown in Figure 5-32.

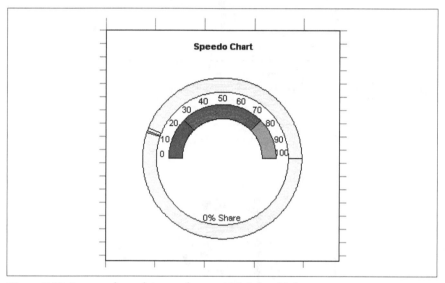

Figure 5-32. Improved speedometer chart, with labels added

Highlight Series 3, then right-click it and select Chart Type. Change this series to the default pie chart. Yes, it looks strange (see Figure 5-33). But rest assured, if the pie chart overlays the doughnut chart, you have done this correctly.

Next you need to reduce the size of the pie chart you just laid over the doughnut. To do this, explode it and reassemble the smaller slices. Select one section of the pie chart (two slow clicks on the desired slice will do this) and drag it outward. This will explode the pie and make it smaller, as shown in Figure 5-34.

Now select the whole pie, double-click it, and then select Format Data Series → Options. Change the Angle of the first slice to 90 degrees. Select each slice of pie in turn, then right-click, go to the Format Data Series dialog, then click the Patterns tab. Select None for the Border and the Area

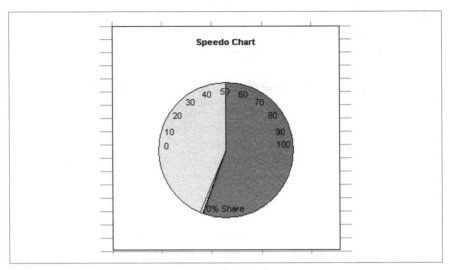

Figure 5-33. Speedometer chart overlaid with a pie chart

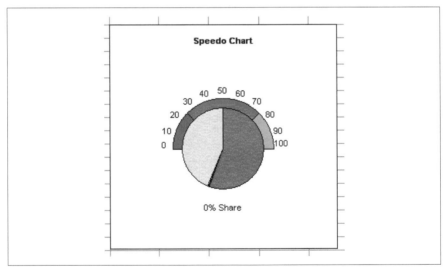

Figure 5-34. Pie chart exploded and resized

for all slices except the third slice, which needs to have a fill of Black. This will produce the chart shown in Figure 5-35.

If you want to add a legend, highlight the chart, then right-click and select Chart Options → Data Labels. Select Legend Key. This produces the speedometer in Figure 5-36. Now move, size, and edit the chart as required.

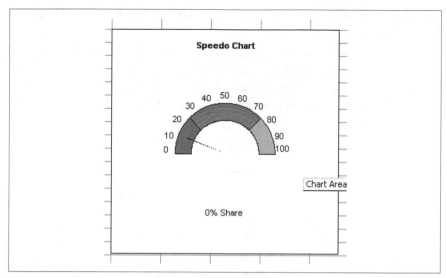

Figure 5-35. *Speedometer chart with only the third series of pie chart showing color*

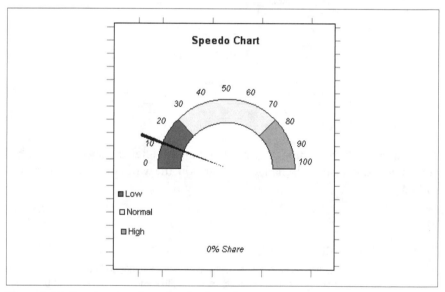

Figure 5-36. *Speedometer chart showing legend*

Now that the speedometer chart is built, you need to create a scrollbar from the Control Toolbox toolbar and make the scrollbar and chart talk to each other.

To do this, right-click the toolbar area of the screen (the top of the screen where the Standard and Formatting toolbars are located) and select Control

Toolbox. Now select the scrollbar tool and draw a scrollbar somewhere on the worksheet.

Select the scrollbar, right-click it, and select Properties. This will display the Properties dialog. Choose cell F3 as the linked cell, and set the Maximum value to 100 and the Minimum value to 0. When you close the Properties dialog and move the scrollbar onto the chart, you'll see something like that shown in Figure 5-37.

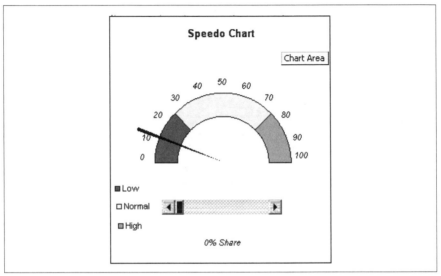

Figure 5-37. Final speedometer chart

Clicking the arrows or dragging the slide bar will alter the speedometer, but remember, this also will change the data on the worksheet to which it is linked.

—Andy Pope

HACK   Link Chart Text Elements to a Cell
#58

When creating and using charts repetitively, it can be handy to know how to link some of your chart text elements, such as titles and labels, directly to a cell. This means that if and when your underlying data changes, your chart data and its text elements will always be in harmony.

The chart text elements you can link to a cell are the chart title, the primary and secondary X-axis titles, the primary and secondary Y-axis titles, and the series data labels.

To see how this is done, you will link the title of a chart to a cell. So, to begin, set up some data such as that shown in Figure 5-38 and, using the Chart Wizard, create a basic clustered column chart. Now click cell A17 and type **Age of Employees**.

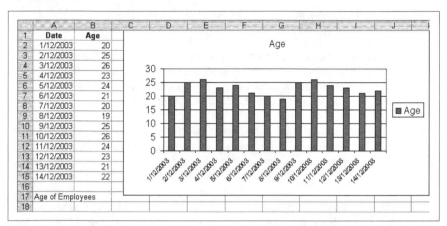

Figure 5-38. Clustered column chart with title created via Chart Wizard

The next step is to establish a link between the chart title and the cell. So, select the chart title (Age, in this case), then go to the Formula bar, type = (an equals sign), click cell A17, and press Enter. (Note that if you are referencing a cell on another sheet, you will have to type the sheet name followed by an exclamation mark [!], then the cell reference.)

The same process works for data labels, but you need to select an individual data label before linking it to a cell. Your results should look like Figure 5-39.

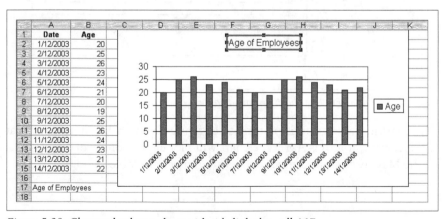

Figure 5-39. Clustered column chart with title linked to cell A17

This smart hack will make your chart text elements and chart data stay in harmony. Plus, it can save you time when creating charts.

—Andy Pope

HACK #59 Hack Chart Data So That Blank Cells Are Not Plotted

Excel treats blank cells as having a value of 0, which can result in some ugly charts. Your chart can suddenly drop off, leaving you with a chart that no longer accurately paints the picture you are trying to convey. With the hacks in this section, you can ensure that blank cells are not plotted.

You can prevent blank cells from being plotted in two very easy ways: by hiding rows or columns, and by having cells return a value of #N/A.

Hiding Rows or Columns

Set up some data as shown in Figure 5-40, create a line chart, and see what it looks like if you have 0 values plotted. Highlight the range A1:B12, then open the Chart Wizard and set up a line chart as an object in the current worksheet.

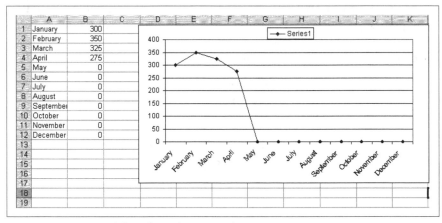

Figure 5-40. Data with line chart plotting 0 values

The chart in Figure 5-40 is plotting sales figures by month. This means that if the current month is April, the chart will plot eight months of empty cells, as the May through December figures are not yet available.

To avoid this, simply hide rows 5:12 (May:Dec). Excel will not plot hidden rows, and thereby will produce the result shown in Figure 5-41. To hide these rows, select them, and then select Format → Rows → Hide.

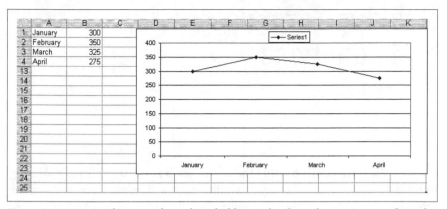

Figure 5-41. Data with rows 5 through 12 hidden, and a chart plotting January through April figures only

CHAPTER SIX

Hacking Formulas
and Functions
Hacks 60-80

Formulas and functions provide the logic that powers spreadsheets. Managing programming logic is always a challenge, but keeping track of programming logic across multiple cells, sheets, and workbooks can be particularly difficult, especially as spreadsheets grow and are reused. What's more, the formula and function capabilities built into Excel might not always be what you want, further complicating the situation. Fortunately, there are a lot of ways you can keep your formulas and functions sane.

 ### HACK #60 Add Descriptive Text to Your Formulas

Excel's named ranges and cell comments can help clarify formulas, but sometimes you want to put documentation into the formula itself. With the hacks in this section, you can add descriptive text to your formulas quickly and easily.

Even when you have written various formulas and functions yourself, coming back to them at a later date often requires that you follow cell references to try to figure out what the formulas are doing. It would be great if you could simply add to the end of your formula some text that wouldn't interfere with the result, but would give you the information you require at a later stage.

The problem, of course, is that the moment you add or incorporate text into part of a formula, the result will no longer be numeric and cannot be used in further calculations. Excel does, however, provide one often-overlooked function that you can use to add descriptive text to formulas or functions.

Say you have the following formula in cell A11:

    =SUM($A$1:$A$10)*$B$1

Assume $A$1:$A$10 houses various numeric results that represent totals for a particular month, and $B$1 contains a percentage value that represents a tax rate. You could add some descriptive text to the formula using Excel's N function:

```
=SUM($A$1:$A$10,N("Values for April"))*$B$1+N("Tax Rate for April")
```

Now you can determine what the formula is being used for simply by selecting this cell and looking in the Formula bar. The N function always will return a value of 0 for any text, and so does not interfere with the formula's result in any way.

Move Relative Formulas Without Changing References

In Excel, a formula reference can be either relative or absolute. Sometimes, however, you might want to reproduce the same formulas somewhere else in your worksheet or workbook, or on another sheet.

When a formula needs to be made absolute, type **$** (a dollar sign) in front of the column letter and/or row number of the cell reference, as in $A$1. Once you do this, no matter where you copy your formula, it will reference the same cells.

Sometimes, however, you might set up a lot of formulas that contain not absolute references, but relative references. You would usually do this so that when you copy the original cell formula down or across, the row and column references change accordingly.

Yet other times you might set up your formulas using a mix of relative and absolute references, and you want to reproduce the same formulas in another range on the same worksheet, another sheet in the same workbook, or perhaps another sheet in another workbook. You can do all these things without changing any range references inside the formulas.

Select the range of cells you want to copy. Select Edit → Replace..., and in the Find What: box, type = (an equals sign). In the Replace With: box, type @ (an at sign), or any other symbol you are sure is not being used in any of the formulas. Click Replace All.

All the formulas will appear on your worksheet with an @ in place of an =.

Now you can simply copy this range, paste it to the destination you desire, select the range, and select Edit → Replace.... This time, replace the @ with an =. Your formulas will reference the same cell references as your originals.

Compare Two Excel Ranges

Spotting the differences between two large tables of data can be a very time-consuming task. Fortunately, there are at least two ways in which you can automate what would otherwise be a very tedious manual process.

The two methods you will use are methods we have used in the past when we received an updated copy of a spreadsheet and we needed to identify which cells in the updated copy differed from the ones in the original copy. Both methods save hours of tedious manual checking and, more importantly, eliminate the possibility of mistakes.

For the following examples, we copied the newer data onto the same sheet as the older data beforehand. Figure 6-1 shows how the data is presented as two ranges. Note that for easier viewing, we boldfaced the cells in Table 2 that are not the same as their counterparts in Table 1.

	A	B	C
1	**Name**	**Age**	**Area**
2	Bill	22	1a
3	Joe	33	1a
4	Frank	55	2c
5	Brad	48	3d
6	Mary	29	3d
7	Anne	45	4a
8			
9	**Name**	**Age**	**Area**
10	Bill	22	**2c**
11	Joe	33	1a
12	Frank	55	**2d**
13	Brad	**43**	3d
14	**Dave**	29	3d
15	Anne	45	4a

Figure 6-1. Two ranges to be compared

Method 1: Using True or False

The first method involves entering a simple formula into another range of the same size and shape. The best part about this method is that you can add the formula in one step without having to copy and paste.

To compare the ranges shown in Figure 6-1, select the range E1:G7, starting from cell E1. This ensures that E1 is the active cell in the selection. With this range selected, click in the Formula bar and type the following:

```
=A1=A9
```

Enter the preceding formula by pressing Ctrl-Enter at the same time. In doing so, you are entering the relative reference formula into each cell of the selection. This is the standard method of entering a formula into an array of cells and having their references change appropriately.

The range E1:G7 should be filled with True (the same) and False (not the same) values.

If your two sets of data reside on different worksheets, you can use a third worksheet to store the True/False values simply by array-entering the formula. For example, assuming the second table of data is on Sheet2 and starts in cell A9, and the original table of data is on Sheet1 and starts in cell A1, on a third worksheet you can array-enter this formula:

```
=Sheet1!A1=Sheet2!A9
```

You might find it useful to adjust your zoom downward when working with large amounts of data.

To delete an array-entered formula, you must select and delete the whole range. You cannot delete part of it.

Method 2: Using Conditional Formatting

The second method is often preferred, as it is easier to make any needed changes once the comparison is made. However, with this method, both sets of data must reside on the same worksheet, which should entail only a simple copy and paste.

Again, assuming we're comparing the preceding two ranges, select the range A1:C7, starting from cell A1. This ensures that A1 is the active cell in the selection.

With this range selected, select Format → Conditional Formatting.... Select Formula Is and then type the following formula:

```
=NOT(A1=A9)
```

Click the Format button, shown in Figure 6-2, and choose the format with which you want to highlight the differences.

Click OK and all the differences will be formatted according to the format you chose.

When or if you make any changes to your data, the cells' format will automatically revert back to normal if the cell content is the same as the cell in the other table.

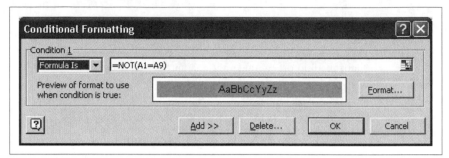

Figure 6-2. Conditional formatting dialog

HACK #63 Fill All Blank Cells in a List

Often, many people will leave a blank cell if the data for that cell is the same as the cell above it. Visually this makes lists easy to read, but structurally it is not a good idea. With the hacks in this section, you can fill all blank cells in a list quickly and easily.

Many of Excel's functions are designed to be used on lists. For most of these functions to work correctly, lists should not contain any blank cells, and column headings should be formatted differently from the data in the list.

When setting up data in Excel, it is good practice to ensure that all cells within a list are occupied. However, many lists are set up in a similar manner to the one shown in Figure 6-3.

◇	A	B
1	Fruits	Cost
2	Apple	$1.25
3		$1.25
4	Banana	$2.55
5		$2.55
6		$2.55
7	Orange	$1.55
8		$1.55
9		$1.55
10	Strawberry	$4.55
11		

Figure 6-3. Worksheet list set up with blank cells

Whereas prices are repeated in the Cost column, the types of fruits in the Fruits column are not. As discussed at the beginning of Chapter 1, this will create many problems when using features such as Subtotals and Pivot-Tables. In most cases, Excel expects your related data will be set up in a continuous list or table, with no blank cells.

There are two ways in which you can fill blank cells in a list: with a formula and with a macro.

Method 1: Filling Blanks Via a Formula

Say you have a list of entries in column A, similar to the previous example, and within the list you have many blank cells. Here is a quick and easy way to fill those blanks with the values of the cells above them.

Select all the data in column A, select Edit → Go To... (Ctrl-G), and then click Special. Check the Blanks option and click OK. At this point, you have selected only the empty cells within the list. Press = (the equals key), then the up arrow. Holding down the Ctrl key, press Enter.

You can quickly convert formulas to values only by selecting column A in its entirety. Select Edit → Copy (Ctrl-C), then select Edit → Paste Special..., check the Values checkbox, and then click OK.

Method 2: Filling Blanks Via a Macro

If you will be filling in blank cells frequently, you should consider handling this via a macro. The following macro makes this a breeze. To use it, select Tools → Macro → Visual Basic Editor (Alt/Option-F11), then select Insert → Module and enter the following code:

```
Sub FillBlanks( )
Dim rRange1 As Range, rRange2 As Range
Dim lReply As Integer

    If Selection.Cells.Count = 1 Then
        MsgBox "You must select your list and include the blank cells", _
        vbInformation, "OzGrid.com"
        Exit Sub
    ElseIf Selection.Columns.Count > 1 Then
        MsgBox "You must select only one column", _
        vbInformation, "OzGrid.com"
        Exit Sub
    End If

    Set rRange1 = Selection

    On Error Resume Next
    Set rRange2 = rRange1.SpecialCells(xlCellTypeBlanks)
    On Error GoTo 0

    If rRange2 Is Nothing Then
        MsgBox "No blank cells Found", _
                vbInformation, "OzGrid.com"
        Exit Sub
    End If

    rRange2.FormulaR1C1 = "=R[-1]C"
```

```
        lReply = MsgBox("Convert to Values", vbYesNo + vbQuestion, "OzGrid.com")
        If lReply = vbYes Then rRange1 = rRange1.Value
    End Sub
```

After entering this code, close the window to get back to Excel, and then save your workbook. Now select Tools → Macro → Macros (Alt/Option-F8), select Fill Blanks, and click Run, or use Options to assign a shortcut key.

HACK #64 Make Your Formulas Increment by Rows When You Copy Across Columns

Excel's automatic incrementing of cell references works well most of the time, but sometimes you might want to override how it works.

You might want to reference a single cell, such as cell A1, and then copy this reference across columns to the right. Naturally, this results in the formula reference changing to =B1, =C1, =D1, etc., which is not the result you want. You want the formula to increment by rows rather than columns—that is, =A1, =A2, =A3, etc.

Unfortunately, there is no option in Excel that lets you do this. However, you can get around this by using the INDIRECT function with the ADDRESS function nested inside.

Perhaps the best way to explain how to create the required function is to use an example with predictable results. In cells A1:A10, enter the numbers **1** through **10** in numerical order. Select cell D1, and in this cell enter the following:

```
=INDIRECT(ADDRESS(COLUMN( )-3,1))
```

As soon as you enter this, the number 1 should appear in cell D1. This is because the formula references cell A1.

If you copy this formula across the column to the right, cell E1 will contain the number 2. In other words, although you are copying across columns, the formula reference is incrementing by rows, as shown in Figure 6-4.

This method is especially useful when a spreadsheet has headings going down rows in one column, and you want to create a dynamic reference to these row headings across other columns.

If you keep copying this to the right, cell F1 will contain the number 3, cell G1 will contain the number 4, etc. This is a fairly straightforward process if you are referencing only a single cell. Many times, however, you will need to reference a range of cells that is being used in the argument for a function.

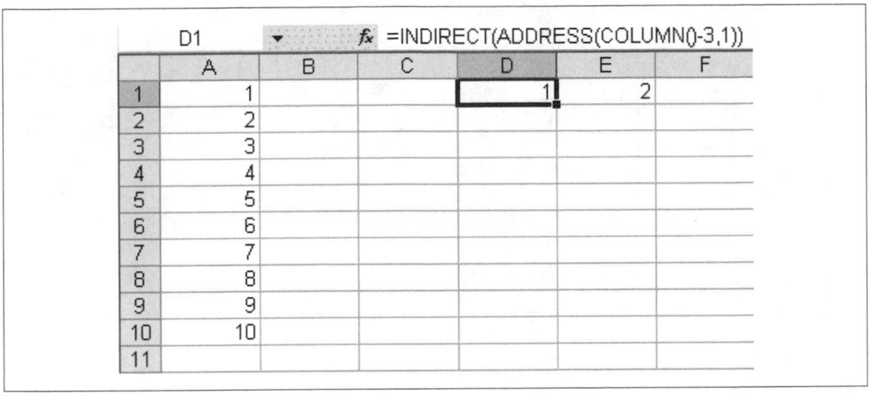

Figure 6-4. The result of copying cell D1 to cell E1

We'll use the ever-popular SUM function to demonstrate what we mean. Assume you receive a long list of numbers, and your job is to sum the column of numbers in a running total fashion, like this:

```
=SUM($A$1:$A$2), =SUM($A$1:$A$3), =SUM($A$1:$A$4)
```

The problem occurs because the results need to be dynamic and to span across 100 columns on row 1 only, not down 100 rows in another column (as often would be the case).

Naturally, you could manually type such functions into each individual cell, but this would be very time-consuming. Instead, you can use the same principle as the one that you used when referencing a single cell.

Fill the range A1:A100 with the numbers **1** through **100** in numeric order. Enter **1** into cell A1, select cell A1, hold down the Ctrl key, left-click, and drag down 100 rows with the fill handle.

Select cell D1 and enter this formula:

```
=SUM(INDIRECT(ADDRESS(1,1)&":"&ADDRESS(COLUMN( )-2,1)))
```

This will give you a result of 3, which is the sum of cells A1:A2. Copy this formula across to cell E1 and you will get a result of 6, which is the sum of cells A1:A3. Copy to cell F1 and you will get a result of 10, which is the sum of cells A1:A4 (see Figure 6-5).

The volatile COLUMN function caused the last cell reference to increment by 1 each time you copied it across to a new column. This is because the COLUMN function always returns the column number (not letter) of the cell that houses it unless you reference a different cell.

Alternatively, you can use the Paste Special... → Transpose feature in Excel. Add the formula **=SUM($A$1:$A2)** to cell B1 (note the relative row absolute column reference to $A2), and then copy this formula down to cell B100.

D1	▼	*fx*	=SUM(INDIRECT(ADDRESS(1,1)&":"&ADDRESS(COLUMN()-2,1)))					
	A	B	C	D	E	F	G	H	I
1	1			3	6	10		
2	2							
3	3							
4	4							
5	5							
6	6							
7	7							
8	8							
9	9							
10	10							
11	11							
12	12							
13	13							
14	14							
15	15							

Figure 6-5. The result of copying cell D1 to cell F1

With B2:B100 selected, copy, select cell D1 (or any cell that has 100 or more columns to the right), and then select Edit → Paste Special... → Transpose. If you like, you can delete the formulas in B2:B100.

Convert Dates to Excel Formatted Dates

HACK
#65

Dates imported from other programs frequently cause problems in Excel. Many people manually retype them, but there are easier ways to solve the problem.

Let's look at some of the date formats you might encounter and how to convert them to standard Excel dates.

As Figure 6-6 shows, the formulas in column B convert the data in column A to three results in column C, all of which follow the U.S. date format of mm/dd/yy.

◇	A	B	C
1	Old Date	Formula Used	Formula Result
2	112303	=VALUE(LEFT(A2,2)&"/"&MID(A2,3,2)&"/"&RIGHT(A2,2))	11/23/03
3	031123	=VALUE(MID(A3,3,2)&"/"&RIGHT(A3,2)&"/"&LEFT(A3,2))	11/23/03
4	231103	=VALUE(MID(A4,3,2)&"/"&LEFT(A4,2)&"/"&RIGHT(A4,2))	11/23/03
5			

Figure 6-6. Date formats converted to valid dates (U.S. format)

Figure 6-7 shows the same approach at work, except that the cells in column C were formatted with the European date format of dd/mm/yy.

Hopefully, these nifty formulas will take some of the stress out of working with imported dates.

	A	B	C
1	**Old Date**	**Formula Used**	**Formula Result**
2	112303	=VALUE(MID(A2,3,2)&"/"&LEFT(A2,2)&"/"&RIGHT(A2,2))	23/11/2003
3	31123	=VALUE(RIGHT(A3,2)&"/"&MID(A3,3,2)&"/"&LEFT(A3,2))	23/11/2003
4	231103	=VALUE(LEFT(A4,2)&"/"&MID(A4,3,2)&"/"&RIGHT(A4,2))	23/11/2003

Figure 6-7. Date formats converted to valid dates (European format)

HACK #66 Sum or Counting Cells While Avoiding Error Values

Error values are useful warnings, but sometimes you need to do calculations despite the errors. Choosing functions that tolerate errors will let you do this.

When a range of cells contains one or more error values, most formulas that reference that range of cells also will return an error. You can overcome this frustration by using the DSUM function.

Assume you have a long list of numbers for which you need to get the sum total. However, one of the cells, for whatever reason, is returning the #N/A error.

Set up some data such as that shown in Figure 6-8.

	A	B
1	**Numbers1**	**Numbers2**
2	#N/A	#N/A
3	1	1
4	2	2
5	3	3
6	4	4
7	5	5
8	6	6
9	7	7
10	8	8
11	9	9
12		

Figure 6-8. Data set up to generate #N/A error message

To generate the #N/A error, enter the formula **=#N/A( )** in cells A2 and B2. Cell A12 uses a standard SUM function that sums cells A2:A11, and because cell A2 has the #N/A error, the SUM function also returns #N/A. The range D1:D2 has been named Criteria and is used as the last argument in the DSUM function, which resides in cell B12.

The syntax for the DSUM function (and all the database functions) is as follows:

```
=DSUM(database,field,criteria)
```

The *database* argument identifies the range of cells that comprise the list or database. Within the database range, rows of related information are treated as records, while columns of data are treated as fields. The first row contains labels for all the columns.

The *field* argument indicates which column is used in the function. The column can be identified by name using the labels at the top of the column, or it can be identified by position. The first column is 1, the fourth column is 4, and so on.

The *criteria* argument identifies a range of cells containing conditions. The range used for the criteria must include at least one column label plus at least one cell below the column label that specifies a condition for the column.

If the data you want to sum will likely contain a variety of different kinds of errors, you might need to consider using the DSUM function with a wide range of criteria to accommodate the possible errors. However, it is always best to address the error at the source and eliminate it whenever possible rather than work around it.

To work around it, you again use the DSUM function, but this time you need to set up criteria that span four columns, expanding the named range criteria to include D1:G2 via Insert → Name → Define, as shown in Figure 6-9.

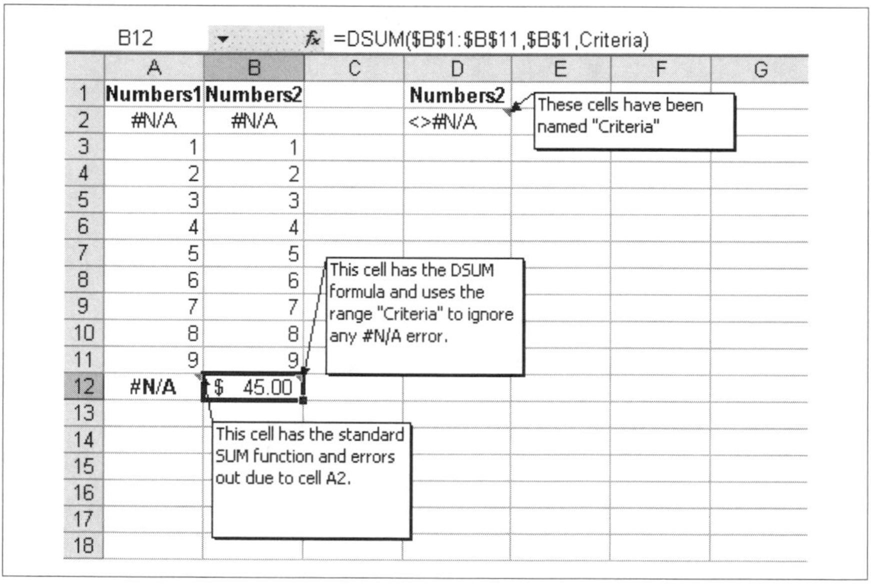

Figure 6-9. The DSUM function used to ignore a number of different errors

Excel has a rich set of database functions, and you can use any one of them in the same way. Consider using the same method for DCOUNT, DCOUNTA, DMAX, DMIN, DPRODUCT, etc.

Reduce the Impact of Volatile Functions on Recalculation

Volatile functions, which must be recalculated almost every time the user performs an action in Excel, can waste an enormous amount of time. Although volatile functions are too useful to discard entirely, there are ways to reduce the delays they create.

A *volatile function* is simply a function that will recalculate each time any action is performed in Excel, such as entering data, changing column widths, etc. (One of the few actions that will not trigger a recalculation of a volatile function is changing a cell's formatting, unless you do this via Paste Special... → Formats.)

Probably the most well-known of all volatile functions are the TODAY and the NOW functions. Because the TODAY function returns the current date, and the NOW function returns the current date and time, it is vital that both of them recalculate often. If you have a worksheet that contains many volatile functions, however, you could be forcing Excel to perform many unnecessary recalculations on a continuous basis. This problem can worsen when you have volatile functions nested within nonvolatile functions, as the formula as a whole will become volatile.

To see what we mean, assume you have a worksheet that is using the TODAY function in a 20-column-by-500-row table. This will mean you have 10,000 volatile functions in your workbook when a single one could accomplish the same job.

Rather than nesting 10,000 TODAY functions within each cell of your table, in most cases you can simply enter the TODAY function into an out-of-the-way cell, name it **TodaysDate** (or just use the cell identifier) or another applicable name, and then reference TodaysDate in all your functions.

> A quick and easy way to do this is to select the entire table and then select Edit → Replace... to replace TODAY( ) with TodaysDate in all your formulas.

You will now have one TODAY function in place of the 10,000 you would have had otherwise.

As another example, say the first 500 rows of column B are filled with a relative formula such as =TODAY( )-A1, and the first 500 rows of column A have different dates that are less than today's date. You are forcing Excel to recalculate the volatile TODAY function 499 times more than necessary each time you do something in Excel! By placing the TODAY function in any cell and naming the cell TodaysDate (or something similar), you can use = TodaysDate-A1. Now Excel needs to recalculate only the one occurrence of the TODAY function, resulting in a much tidier performance hit.

HACK #68 Count Only One Instance of Each Entry in a List

When you have a large list of items, you might want to perform a count on the items without counting entries that appear multiple times. With this hack, you can count each unique entry only once.

Consider the list in Figure 6-10, which has been sorted so that you can see multiple entries easily.

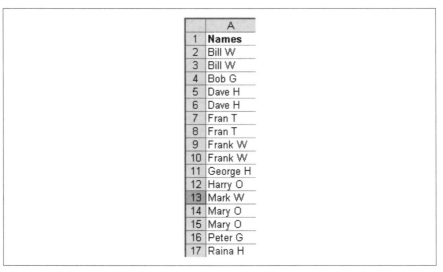

	A
1	**Names**
2	Bill W
3	Bill W
4	Bob G
5	Dave H
6	Dave H
7	Fran T
8	Fran T
9	Frank W
10	Frank W
11	George H
12	Harry O
13	Mark W
14	Mary O
15	Mary O
16	Peter G
17	Raina H

Figure 6-10. Range of sorted names

A normal count on this list (using COUNTA) would result in the names Bill W, Dave H, Fran T, Frank W, and Mary O being counted more that once. The DCOUNTA function offers an alternative that is very efficient and easy to modify.

The syntax of the DCOUNTA function is as follows:

```
DCOUNTA(database,field,criteria),
```

The arguments for this function are the same as those for the DSUM function described in "Convert Dates to Excel Formatted Dates" [Hack #65])

Building on the preceding list, in cell D1 enter the word **Criteria** (or any heading that is *not* the same as the field or column heading). Below this, in cell D2, enter this formula:

```
=COUNTIF($A$2:A2,A2)=1
```

Note the combination of relative (A2) references and absolute ($A$2) references! These are vital to the criteria working.

Now, in the cell where you want your result shown, enter this function:

```
=DCOUNTA($A$1:$A$100,1,$D$1:$D$2)
```

This will use the criteria to exclude duplicates and give you the result you need, which is 11, as there are 11 unique names.

HACK #69 Sum Every Second, Third, or nth Row or Cell

Every now and then you might want to sum every second, third, fourth, etc., cell in a spreadsheet. Now you can, with the following hack.

Excel has no standard function that will sum every *nth* cell or row. However, you can accomplish this in a number of different ways. All these approaches use the ROW function and the MOD function.

The ROW function returns the row number of a single cell reference:

```
ROW(reference)
```

The MOD function returns the remainder after *number* is divided by *divisor*:

```
MOD(number,divisor)
```

Nest the ROW function within the MOD function (to supply the number argument), divide it by 2 (to sum every second cell), and check to see whether the result is 0 (zero). If it is, the cell is summed.

You can use these functions in numerous ways—some of them producing better results than others. For instance, an array formula to SUM every second cell in the range $A$1:$A$100 could look like this:

```
=SUM(IF(MOD(ROW($A$1:$A$500),2)=0,$A$1:$A$500,0))
```

> Because this is an array formula, you must enter it by pressing Ctrl-Shift-Enter. Excel will add the curly brackets so that it looks like this:
>
> ```
> {=SUM(IF(MOD(ROW($A$1:$A$500),2)=0,$A$1:$A$500,0))}
> ```
>
> You must let Excel add these brackets, as adding them yourself will cause the array formula to fail.

Although this will do the job, it is not good spreadsheet design to use this method. It is an unnecessary use of an array formula. To make matters worse, it has the volatile ROW function nested within it, making the whole array formula volatile. This means the formula would constantly recalculate whenever you are working in the workbook. This is a bad way to go!

Here's another formula you can use, which is a slightly better choice:

```
=SUMPRODUCT((MOD(ROW($A$1:$A$500),2)=0)*($A$1:$A$500))
```

You should, however, be aware that this formula will return #VALUE! if any cells in the range contain text rather than numbers. This formula, although not a true array, also will slow down Excel if too many instances of it are used, or if those instances reference a large range.

Fortunately, there is a much better way that is not only more efficient, but also far more flexible. This requires using the DSUM function. For this example, we used the range A1:A500 as the range for which we need to sum every *nth* cell.

Enter the word **Criteria** in cell E1. In cell E2, enter this formula:

```
=MOD(ROW(A2)-$C$2-1,$C$2)=0
```

Select cell C2 and then select Data → Validation. Select List from the Allow: box, and in the Source: box, type: **1,2,3,4,5,6,7,8,9,10**. Ensure that the In-Cell drop-down box is checked and click OK. In cell C1, enter **SUM every....**. In any cell after row 1, enter this formula:

```
=DSUM($A:$A,1,$E$1:$E$2)
```

In the cell directly above where you entered the DSUM function, enter this:

```
="Summing Every " & $C$2 &
CHOOSE($C$2,"st","nd","rd","th","th","th","th","th","th","th") & " Cell"
```

Now all you need to do is choose the desired number from cell C2 and the DSUM function will do the rest.

As you can see from Figure 6-11, you can use one DSUM function to sum each cell at the interval you specify. The DSUM function is a far more efficient formula than an array formula or the SUMPRODUCT function. Although setup can take a little more time, it's really a case of a little pain for a lot of gain.

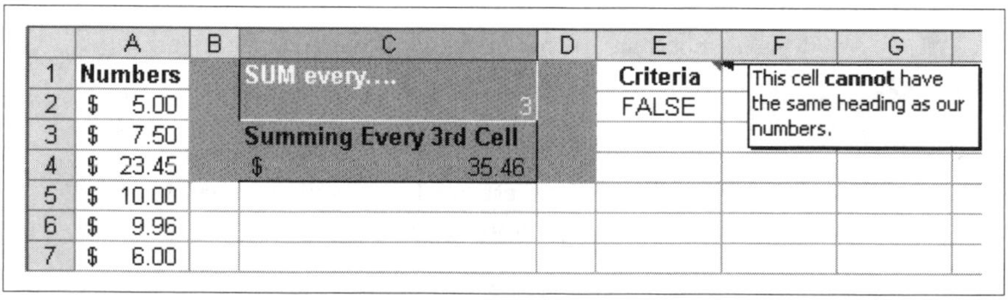

	A	B	C	D	E	F	G
1	**Numbers**		SUM every....		**Criteria**	This cell **cannot** have the same heading as our numbers.	
2	$ 5.00			3	FALSE		
3	$ 7.50		**Summing Every 3rd Cell**				
4	$ 23.45		$	35.46			
5	$ 10.00						
6	$ 9.96						
7	$ 6.00						

Figure 6-11. Possible end result with formatting

Find the nth Occurrence of a Value

HACK #70

Excel's built-in lookup functions can do some pretty clever stuff, but unfortunately Excel has no single function that will return the *nth* occurrence of specified data. Fortunately, there are ways to make Excel do this.

You can use Excel's lookup and reference functions on a table of data to extract details corresponding to a specified value. Perhaps the most popular of these Excel functions is VLOOKUP. Although VLOOKUP is great for finding a specified value in the leftmost column of a table, you cannot use it to find the *nth* occurrence in the leftmost column.

You can, however, use a very simple method to find any specified occurrence you choose when using VLOOKUP, or one of the other lookup functions.

For this example, we will assume you have a two-column table of data, with column A housing first names and column B their corresponding ages, as shown in Figure 6-12.

	A	B
1	**Names**	**Ages**
2	Fred	20
3	Joe	25
4	Dave	18
5	James	22
6	Dave	13
7	Reece	15
8	Jill	19
9	Robyn	18
10	Marlene	17
11	Dave	25
12	Tania	23
13	Bob	24
14	Wendy	22
15	Aleisha	20
16	Kate	18
17	Dave	19
18	Jack	21
19	Bill	23

Figure 6-12. Data setup for VLOOKUP

You can use a VLOOKUP function to extract a person's age based on his name. Unfortunately, some names occur more than once. You want to be able to look up the name Dave and have the VLOOKUP function find not the first occurrence, but rather, subsequent occurrences of the name. Here is how you can do this (remember, in this example, data is in columns A and B).

First, select column A in its entirety by clicking the letter A at the column head, and then select Insert → Columns to insert a blank column (which will become column A). Click in cell A2 (skipping A1 because B1 is a heading), and enter this formula:

```
=B2&COUNTIF($B$2:B2,B2)
```

Copy this down as many rows as you have data in column B (click back in cell A2 and double-click the fill handle). You will end up with names such as Dave1, Dave2, Dave3, etc., as shown in Figure 6-13. Note the absolute reference to $B$2 in the COUNTIF function and the use of a relative reference for all references. This is vital to the function working correctly.

	A	B	C
1		**Names**	**Ages**
2	Fred1	Fred	20
3	Joe1	Joe	25
4	Dave1	Dave	18
5	James1	James	22
6	Dave2	Dave	13
7	Reece1	Reece	15
8	Jill1	Jill	19
9	Robyn1	Robyn	18
10	Marlene1	Marlene	17
11	Dave3	Dave	25
12	Tania1	Tania	23
13	Bob1	Bob	24
14	Wendy1	Wendy	22
15	Aleisha1	Aleisha	20
16	Kate1	Kate	18
17	Dave4	Dave	19
18	Jack1	Jack	21
19	Bill1	Bill	23

Figure 6-13. Data with VLOOKUP formula added to column A

If you haven't guessed already, now you can use column A as the column to find the *nth* occurrence of any name.

Click in cell D2 and enter in the following formula:

```
=VLOOKUP("Dave3",$A$1:$C$100,3,FALSE)
```

The formula will return the age for the third occurrence of the name Dave, as shown in Figure 6-14.

You can, of course, hide column A from view, as you do not need to see it.

You also can use the names in column A as the Source range for a list in another cell by selecting Data → Validation → List. Then reference the cell housing this list in your VLOOKUP function.

	A	B	C	D
1		**Names**	**Ages**	
2	Fred1	Fred	20	25
3	Joe1	Joe	25	
4	Dave1	Dave	18	
5	James1	James	22	
6	Dave2	Dave	13	
7	Reece1	Reece	15	
8	Jill1	Jill	19	
9	Robyn1	Robyn	18	
10	Marlene1	Marlene	17	
11	Dave3	Dave	25	
12	Tania1	Tania	23	
13	Bob1	Bob	24	
14	Wendy1	Wendy	22	
15	Aleisha1	Aleisha	20	
16	Kate1	Kate	18	
17	Dave4	Dave	19	
18	Jack1	Jack	21	
19	Bill1	Bill	23	

Figure 6-14. Data with second VLOOKUP formula added to column D

HACK #71   Make the Excel Subtotal Function Dynamic

Although SUBTOTAL is one of Excel's most convenient functions, you sometimes want to choose the function it uses, or apply it to data that can expand and contract.

You use the SUBTOTAL function in Excel to perform a specified function on a range of cells that have had AutoFilters applied to them. When the Auto-Filter has been applied, the SUBTOTAL function will use only the visible cells; all hidden rows are ignored. The operation it performs depends solely on the number (between 1 and 11) that you supply to its first argument, Function_num. For example:

    =SUBTOTAL(1,A1:A100)

will average all visible cells in the range A1:A100 after AutoFilters have been applied. If all rows in A1:A100 are visible, it will simply average them all and give the same result as:

    =AVERAGE(A1:A100)

The number for the first SUBTOTAL argument, Function_num, and its corresponding functions are as shown in Table 6-1.

Table 6-1. SUBTOTAL function numbers and their corresponding functions

Function_Num	Function
1	AVERAGE
2	COUNT
3	COUNTA
4	MAX
5	MIN
6	PRODUCT
7	STDEV
8	STDEVP
9	SUM
10	VAR
11	VARP

Because you need to use only a number between 1 and 11, you can have one SUBTOTAL function perform whatever function you choose. You even can choose from a drop-down list that resides in any cell. Here is how to do this.

Add all the function names, in the same order as in Table 6-1, to a range of cells. For this example, we will use D1:D11. With this range selected, click the Name box (the white box on the left of the Formula bar) and type the name **Subs**. Then click Enter.

Select column D in its entirety and then select Format → Column → Hide. Now select View → Toolbars → Forms, click the ComboBox control, and then click cell C2.

Use the size handles to size the ComboBox so that it can display the longest function name—i.e., AVERAGE.

> To have your ComboBox automatically snap to the size of the column and row it resides in, hold down your Alt key at the same time as you size the ComboBox.

Right-click the ComboBox and choose Format Control, then the Control tab. In the Input range, type **Subs**. In the Cell-Link box, type **$C$2**. Now change the drop-down lines to **11**. In cell C3, enter this formula:

```
=IF($C$2="","","Result of "&INDEX(Subs,$C$2))
```

In cell C4, enter this formula:

```
=IF($C$2="","",SUBTOTAL($C$2,$A$4:$A$100))
```

where $A$4:$A$100 is the range on which the SUBTOTAL should act.

Now all you need to do is select the required SUBTOTAL function from the ComboBox and the correct result will be displayed, as shown in Figure 6-15.

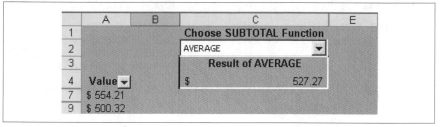

Figure 6-15. An adjustable SUBTOTAL

Add Date Extensions

HACK #72

Excel's date formats consist of many different formats that you can use to display a date. However, one format that has always been lacking in Excel— and still does not exist—is the ability to display a date as 15th October 2003. You can make Excel do this if you need it.

The use of the "th" after the digits 15 is the one format Excel does not have. To make matters even worse, as far as we are aware, it is not possible to set a custom format to display the date in this manner. Although most people simply accept that this is not possible, here is a way you can accomplish it.

On a clean worksheet, starting in cell A1, make the following entries: A1=**st**, A2=**nd**, A3=**rd**, A4:A20=**th**, A21=**st**, A22=**nd**, A23=**rd**, A24:A30=**th**, A31=**st**.

Name this range **Extensions**, then select Insert → Name → Define, and in the Names in Workbook: box, type **MyToday**. In the Refers To: box, enter the following formula:

```
=TEXT(TODAY(),"dddd d")&INDEX(Extensions,DAY(TODAY()),1) & TEXT(TODAY(),"
mmmm yyyy")
```

Click Add, then OK.

Now, in any cell, simply enter **=MyToday**, and the current date always will display with the format Thursday 16th October 2003, or whatever date it happens to be.

If you would rather not use cells on a worksheet to store date extensions— that is, th, st, rd, nd—you can use the CHOOSE function to house them. To do this, select Insert → Name → Define, and in the Names in Workbook: box, enter the word **Day**.

In the Refers To: box, enter this formula:

```
=DAY(TODAY())
```

Click Add. Go back to the Names in Workbook: box and enter the word **MyToday**.

In the Refers To: box, enter the following formula, and click Add:

```
=TEXT(TODAY( ),"dddd
d")&IF(Day=31,"st",IF(Day=30,"th",CHOOSE(Day,"st","nd","rd","th","th","th","
th","th","th","th","th","th","th","th","th","th","th","th","th","th","st","n
d","rd","th","th","th","th","th","th")))& TEXT(TODAY( )," mmmm yyyy").
```

After you click OK, you can enter **=MyToday** into any cell in which you want to display this format of date.

> The date returned by the use of either of these functions will not be a true numeric date as far as Excel is concerned; it will simply be a text entry, meaning you will not be able to reference the cell housing it in any formula that expects numeric data.

HACK #73   Convert Numbers with the Negative Sign on the Right to Excel Numbers

Have you ever had to work with imported negative numbers that have the negative sign on the right? SAP is one such program that does this with negative numbers—e.g., 200- instead of -200. Changing these by hand so that Excel understands them can be a hassle, but it doesn't need to be.

Say you have a long list of numbers you just imported and some of them are those so-called negative numbers. Your job is to convert these to valid negatives that Excel will recognize. For the purposes of this exercise, you will use the range A1:A100. In cell B1, enter this formula:

```
=SUBSTITUTE(IF(RIGHT(TRIM(A1))="-",RIGHT(TRIM(A1))&A1,A1),"-","",2)+0
```

Enter this as many cells down the column as needed and then copy them and select cell A1. Select Edit → Paste Special... → Values to remove the formula and retain the values only. Figure 6-16 shows a before-and-after example (A1:A7 represents before).

	A	B
1	200-	-200
2	150	150
3	356-	-356
4	200	200
5	526	526
6	301-	-301
7	258	258

Figure 6-16. Before and after moving the negative sign

To give you an idea of how the formula works, enter the following formula in any cell where A1 has the text 200-:

```
=RIGHT(TRIM(A1),1)&A1
```

You will end up with -200-.

The TRIM function simply ensures that there are no space characters in the cell. As you end up with -200-, you need to remove the second occurrence of the negative sign. This is what the SUBSTITUTE function is doing. You told it to substitute the second occurrence of - with "" (empty text). The result returned is actually text (as that is what the SUBSTITUTE function returns), so you simply use +0, and Excel will convert it to a number.

If you need to do this frequently, you should consider a macro to make the job easier. Here is one that will do the task at hand. It has been optimized for speed.

```
Sub ConvertMirrorNegatives()
Dim rCell As Range
Dim rRange As Range
Dim lCount As Long
Dim lLoop As Long

'Ensure they have the data selected and display a message if they _
 don't, then exit the macro.
If Selection.Cells.Count = 1 Then
  MsgBox "Please select the range to convert", vbInformation
  Exit Sub
End If

'Set a variable to ONLY text cells, e.g., 200-
On Error Resume Next
Set rRange = Selection.SpecialCells(xlCellTypeConstants, xlTextValues)

'If our variable returns Nothing, there are no incorrect negatives _
 so display a message, then exit the macro
If rRange Is Nothing Then
   MsgBox "No mirror negatives found", vbInformation
   On Error GoTo 0
   Exit Sub
End If

'Count just how many cells are like 200- and pass this number _
 to a variable to control how many loops are needed.
lCount = WorksheetFunction.CountIf(Selection, "*-")
'Set a variable to the first cell in the selection
Set rCell = Selection.Cells(1, 1)

    'Loop only as many times as there are incorrect negatives
    For lLoop = 1 To lCount
       'At each loop set a variable to the cell housing *-
```

```
              'The asterisk is a wildcard character
              Set rCell = rRange.Find(What:="*-", After:=rCell, _
                      LookIn:=xlValues, LookAt:=xlPart, _
                      SearchOrder:=xlByRows, SearchDirection:= _
                      xlNext, MatchCase:=False)
              'Use the standard Replace feature to replace the negative sign _
              with nothing. In other words, we remove it.
              rCell.Replace What:="-", Replacement:=""
              'Multiply the cell by -1 to convert it to a negative number
              rCell = rCell * -1
          Next lLoop

      On Error GoTo 0
      End Sub
```

To use this macro, select Tools → Macro → Visual Basic Editor (or Alt/
Option-F11). Now select Insert → Module and paste in the preceding code.
Close the window to return to Excel and select Tools → Macro → Macros,
and then select Convert Mirror Negatives. Click Options and assign a shortcut key. Now when you have to convert those imported negatives to true
negatives that Excel will recognize, simply select the figures and use your
shortcut key.

H A C K   Display Negative Time Values
#74
Sometimes you want to display negative time values, but Excel will only
display ######. There are several ways to escape this problem.

If you enter the time **12::00::00** (midday) into any cell and then format it as
General, you will see that it has a numeric value of 0.5. Similarly, enter the
time **24::00::00** in any cell. Look in the Formula bar and you will see that
Excel shows 1/1/1900 12::00::00 AM.

Excel sees dates and times as nothing more than numbers. In the case of a
date, by default Excel considers 1 January 1900 to have a numeric value of
1; 2 January 1900 a numeric value of 2; and so forth. Times are seen as deci-
mals, with the exception of midnight, which has a numeric value of 1. (See
"Hack Excel's Date and Time Features" [Hack #38] for full details.) Because of
this, Excel has real trouble coping with the notion of negative time.

Here are three methods to get Excel to display negative time values.

Method 1: Changing Excel's Default Date System

One quick and easy way to display negative values is to simply select Tools →
Options → Calculation and check the 1904 date system checkbox. (The 1904
date system is also called Macintosh dates and times.)

Be aware that doing this will cause Excel to change the starting dates from which all cells are calculated from 1 January
1900 to 2 January 1904. Changing this option will affect
only the workbook in which you make the change.

Now you will be able to subtract times from each other and have the result
displayed as a negative time value.

Try it. Select Tools → Options → Calculation and check the 1904 date system checkbox. Enter **5::00::00 AM** in cell A2. In cell A3, enter **6::00::00**
AM. In cell A4, type **=A2-A3**.

You will get the result of **-1:00**, but only if you checked the 1904 date system checkbox as described earlier.

If changing Excel's default date system to the 1904 date system is likely to
cause problems within the workbook for other time calculations, you need
to use another method that will change the appearance of a cell housing a
negative value.

Method 2: Using the TEXT Function

The second method requires the use of the TEXT function. To begin, enter **5:**
:00::00 AM in cell A2. In cell A3, enter **6::00::00 AM**. In cell A4, type the
following:

```
=TEXT(MAX($A$2:$A$3)-MIN($A$2:$A$3),"-H::MM")
```

With this nested formula, you are subtracting A3 from A2 to give a positive
time value. Then you are formatting the cell using the TEXT function so that
it shows a negative time. Using the combination of the MAX and MIN functions ensures that you are always subtracting the earlier time from the later
time.

You need to be aware that the result returned is actually a
text value, not a numeric value, in case you intend to use the
result in another formula.

Method 3: Using a Custom Format

One final way you can display negative times, without changing to the 1904
date system and still returning a true numeric value, is to select Format
→ Cells → Custom and use a Custom format of -h:mm.

This method works *only* if you always want a negative time value displayed.
It also requires that you always subtract the earlier time from the later time.

This means *all* times returned really will be positive and will only appear negative.

So, by using any one of these three methods, you will be able to display negative times. Just remember that there are pitfalls to each of them, so always use them with these pitfalls in mind.

HACK #75 Use the VLOOKUP Function Across Multiple Tables

Although VLOOKUP itself is very handy, it is restricted to looking in a specified table to return a result, which sometimes is not enough. You can escape this limitation with the INDIRECT function.

Sometimes you might need to use a single VLOOKUP formula to look in different tables of data set out in spreadsheets. One way in which you can do this is to nest several VLOOKUP functions together, telling them to look into a specified table depending on a number that you enter into another cell. For instance:

```
=IF(A1=1,VLOOKUP(B1,Table1,2,FALSE),IF(A1=2,VLOOKUP(B1,Table2,2,FALSE),""))
```

In this formula, you tell the VLOOKUP function to look in the named range Table1 if A1 contains the number 1 (IF(A1=1, VLOOKUP(B1,Table1,2,FALSE)), and to look in the named range Table2 if A1 contains the number 2 (IF(A1=2,VLOOKUP(B1,Table2,2,FALSE)).

As you can imagine, the formula will become very large and unwieldy if you use more than two nested IF functions. The following formula, for instance, uses only five nested functions, but it is very daunting!

```
=IF(A1=1,VLOOKUP(B1,Table1,2,FALSE),IF(A1=2,VLOOKUP(B1,Table2,2,FALSE),IF(A1
=3,VLOOKUP(B1,Table2,3,FALSE),IF(A1=4,VLOOKUP(B1,Table4,2,FALSE),IF
(A1=5,VLOOKUP(B1,Table5,2,FALSE),"")))))
```

Although the formula will return the desired results, you can make the formula a lot shorter, add more than five conditions, and end up with a formula that is very easy to manage.

Assume you have 12 different tables set up on a spreadsheet, each representing a different month of the year. Each table is two columns wide and contains the names of five employees and five corresponding amounts. Each table has been named according to the month that it represents—i.e., January's data has a named range of January, February's data has a named range of February, and so on, as shown in Figure 6-17.

Select cell A1. Then select Data → Validation, and on the Settings tab select List from the Allow: box. In the Source: box, type each month of the year, separating each with a comma. It is vital that your named ranges for each table are the same as the month names you used in the validation list. Click OK.

C	D	E	F	G	H	I	J
January		**February**		**March**		**April**	
Name	**Amount**	**Name**	**Amount**	**Name**	**Amount**	**Name**	**Amount**
Fred	20	Fred	35	Fred	35	Fred	19
Bill	21	Bill	32	Bill	32	Bill	15
Jack	22	Jack	36	Jack	36	Jack	22
Joe	23	Joe	31	Joe	31	Joe	23
Phil	20	Phil	35	Phil	35	Phil	25
May		**June**		**July**		**August**	
Name	**Amount**	**Name**	**Amount**	**Name**	**Amount**	**Name**	**Amount**
Braden	25	Braden	28	Braden	15	Braden	56
Ashley	26	Ashley	13	Ashley	22	Ashley	84
Liam	28	Liam	22	Liam	33	Liam	52
Marlene	27	Marlene	45	Marlene	65	Marlene	31
Mark	31	Mark	85	Mark	98	Mark	31
September		**October**		**November**		**December**	
Name	**Amount**	**Name**	**Amount**	**Name**	**Amount**	**Name**	**Amount**
Braden	25	Braden	25	Braden	25	Braden	25
Ashley	26	Ashley	26	Ashley	26	Ashley	26
Liam	28	Liam	28	Liam	28	Liam	28
Marlene	27	Marlene	27	Marlene	27	Marlene	27
Mark	31	Mark	31	Mark	31	Mark	31

Figure 6-17. Twelve tables, each representing a month of the year

Select cell B1 and set up a validation list as explained earlier, this time using the names of each employee. If the employee names are too large to type, simply reference a range of cells containing them for the source. Click OK.

In cell A2, enter this formula:

```
=VLOOKUP($B$1,INDIRECT($A$1),2,FALSE)
```

Select the required month from the list in cell A1 and the required employee name in the list in cell B1, and the formula in cell A2 will return the corresponding amount for that person for that month.

There are a few advantages to using this approach. If you are not familiar with the INDIRECT function, it is used to read the contents of a cell as a range address rather than as text. As you named 12 different ranges, each representing a month of the year, the formula using the INDIRECT function reads the word January as a range reference rather than as a text string.

Another advantage to using a formula with the INDIRECT function is that you can escape Excel's restriction of having only seven levels of nested functions.

HACK #76 Show Total Time as Days, Hours, and Minutes

When you add hours in Excel, you can have the result return as total hours and minutes, but unfortunately, not as days, hours, and minutes. Displaying that will take some extra work.

For example, if the total time was equal to 75 hours, 45 minutes, and 00 seconds, the total generally would be displayed as 75::45::00, proving the result cell is custom-formatted as [h]:mm:ss, which then allows for hours greater than 24. Although this is certainly the correct result, it means you must manually calculate how many days, hours, and minutes the total represents. This can be time-consuming and error-prone.

Assume you have a list of valid times in cells A1:A10. In cell A11, you have a regular SUM function that is summing up the total hours—i.e., =SUM($A$1:$A$10). If the total of this sum is to exceed 24 hours, the result cell housing the SUM function should be formatted as [h]:mm. Assume the result of this total is 306:26:00, which, of course, represents 306 hours and 26 minutes. However, this does tell you how many days/hours/minutes this total represents.

To have the result shown in days, hours, and minutes, use this formula:

```
=INT(A11) &" Days " & INT(MOD(A11,INT(A11))*24) & " Hours and " &
MINUTE(A11) & " Minutes"
```

Providing that cell A11 has the value of 306:26:00, the result of this is 12 days, 18 hours, and 26 minutes.

Let's look at how this works. If you are not familiar with how Excel stores and uses dates and time, you should first read and understand "Hack Excel's Date and Time Features" [Hack #38].

Select the formula result cell and then click the fx sign to the left of the Formula bar (this is the equals sign in older and in Macintosh versions of Excel). Click the first occurrence of INT from the Formula bar. This function will return the whole number 12 from the value 12.76805556. This is how many days there are.

Next you need to determine how many hours remain after taking off 12 days. Click the second INT function from the Formula bar. Here you are using MOD(A11,INT(A11) to return the remainder of 12.76805556 divided by 12, which is 0.76805556 (the number of minutes represented as a decimal number). Now you need to multiply that by 24 (which is 18.433333) to return a number that will represent the minutes. As you want only the whole number (18), we have nested the formula MOD(A11,INT(A11))*24 into the INT function.

Click the MINUTE function from within the Formula bar. The function will return 26 from the serial number 12.76805556.

As the result returned from the MINUTE function will never be a numeric value, it is wise to at least keep the original SUM function, which returns the total as hours in a cell, so that it can be referenced and used in further calculations if needed. The row that houses the total as hours can, of course, be hidden.

HACK #77 Determine the Number of Specified Days in Any Month

When you're creating calendar-related applications, especially payroll applications, you sometimes need to know how many times a given day of the week appears in a particular month.

Although Excel has many date and time functions, at the time of this writing, it does not have a date and time function that will, for example, tell you how many Mondays are in the month of January in the year 2005. You could use a very deeply nested variety of Excel's date and time functions to figure this out, but unfortunately, as you can imagine, this would be very cumbersome and awkward to reproduce.

This is a case in which VBA can simplify a complicated task. Instead of fumbling with complex functions, you can write a custom function that will do the same thing, and all you need to do is input the day and date for which you want a count.

You can use the following function to determine how may days are in any specified month. For example:

```
=HowManyDaysInMonth("1/12/03","wed")
```

will return 5, as there were five Wednesdays in the month of December in 2003. (Note that the date format should match your local settings—12/1/03 in the United States, for instance. The date format in the example is from Australia.)

Similarly, the following function:

```
=HowManyDaysInMonth("1/12/03","thu")
```

will return 4, as there were four Thursdays in the month of December in 2003.

To use this custom function in a workbook, you must first place the following code into a standard module, so open the workbook into which you

want to place the code and select Tools → Macro → Visual Basic Editor (Alt/
Option-F11). Then select Insert → Module and paste in the following code:

```
'The Code
Function HowManyDaysInMonth(FullDate As String, sDay As String) As Integer
Dim i As Integer
Dim iDay As Integer, iMatchDay As Integer
Dim iDaysInMonth As Integer
Dim FullDateNew As Date

iMatchDay = Weekday(FullDate)
    Select Case UCase(sDay)
        Case "SUN"
         iDay = 1
        Case "MON"
         iDay = 2
        Case "TUE"
         iDay = 3
        Case "WED"
         iDay = 4
        Case "THU"
         iDay = 5
        Case "FRI"
         iDay = 6
        Case "SAT"
         iDay = 7
    End Select
  iDaysInMonth = Day(DateAdd("d", -1, DateSerial _
          (Year(FullDate), Month(FullDate) + 1, 1)))
  FullDateNew = DateSerial(Year(FullDate), Month(FullDate), iDaysInMonth)
      For i = iDaysInMonth - 1 To 0 Step -1
          If Weekday(FullDateNew - i) = iDay Then
              HowManyDaysInMonth = HowManyDaysInMonth + 1
          End If
      Next i
End Function
```

Close the window to return to Excel.

Now simply enter the function into any cell as shown earlier, and Excel will
return a number that represents how many times the specified day occurred
in the specified month.

Construct Mega-Formulas

HACK #78

Mega-formulas—a formula within a formula within a formula—are enough
to send even the most seasoned Excel veteran running for the hills. With a
little forethought and by working step by step toward the formula you need,
however, you can tame those complex mega-formulas without fear.

Does the very thought of having to make sense of, let alone construct,
nested formulas fill you with dread? Some of those cells, so chock-full of

complex functional gobbledygook, make us feel a little faint too. But with a little forethought and a step-by-step approach, you'll be creating mega-formulas without fear. And maybe, just maybe, you'll even be able to read and understand them again later.

The trick is to build up your formulas, bit by bit, using Excel's standard functions. Use one function per cell, obtaining individually manageable results, and then nest them together to yield the result you need. Here's an example of such a process in action.

Say you've been given a long list of people's names, each consisting of first, middle, and last names—one full name per cell. Your job is to write a formula in the adjacent column to extract only the person's last name.

What you're after, then, is the start of the last name—the third word—in the cell. Actually, what you'll be looking for is the position of the second space character in the cell. Excel has no standard built-in function to automatically locate the second space character in a cell, but you can bring the FIND function to bear in such a way that it does what you need it to do.

Type the name **David John Hawley** (or any three-word name) into cell A1. In cell C1, enter this function:

    =FIND(" ",A1)

The FIND function finds one text string (find_text) within another text string (within_text), and returns the number of the starting position of find_text from the first character of within_text.

Here is the syntax:

    =find(*find_text, within_text, start_num*)

This will find the starting position of the first space character in cell A1 as you have told it to find " " (a space) in cell A1. In the case of David John Hawley, it will return a value of 6. But it's the second space you're after, not the first. What you'll do is use the number returned by the formula in C1 as the starting point for another FIND function in search for the second space character. So, in cell C2, enter the following:

    =FIND(" ",A1,C1+1)

Notice you've passed the FIND function a third argument this time, the initial position found by C1 (6, in this example), plus 1; this will serve as the starting point for the FIND function to find a space. The value returned will be the position of the second space character.

With that in hand, you want the next function to grab all characters thereafter until the end of the string of text. Use the MID function, which is designed to extract a range of characters from a string. In cell C3, enter the following:

```
=MID(A1,C2+1,256)
```

The MID function returns a specific number of characters from a text string, starting at the position you specify, based on the number of characters you specify. Here is its syntax:

```
MID(text, start_num, num_chars)
```

This tells the MID function to extract 256 characters from cell A1, starting with the first character after the second space in the string of text. You used 256 simply to ensure that regardless of the length (assuming it's less than 256 characters, that is), you get the person's entire last name.

With all the parts in hand, it's time to build out the whole: a nested formula you'd have cringed at just a few minutes ago. Basically, all you do is replace all cell references (except A1) within the functions with the formula in those cells. You do this via the use of cut and paste working within the Formula bar.

Click cell C2, and in the Formula bar, highlight the function and copy the entire FIND function except for the =, like this:

```
FIND(" ",A1,C1+1)
```

Press Enter to leave the cell, which will place you into cell C3. With cell C3 selected, in the Formula bar, highlight the reference to cell C2 and paste the FIND function (Ctrl-V) that you just copied in its place. Press Enter. Your function in cell C3 should now be as follows:

```
=MID(A1,FIND(" ",A1,C1+1)+1,256)
```

Now you need to replace the reference to cell C1 with the function that resides in cell C1. Select cell C1, highlight the formula from the Formula bar, omitting the =, click Copy, then press Enter twice to get back to cell C3. While in cell C3, highlight C1 in the Formula bar and paste the FIND function you just copied. Press Enter.

Now all you need to do is cut cell C3 and paste it into cell B1, then delete the formulas left over in cells C1 and C2. You should now end up with a final formula looking like below:

```
=MID(A1,FIND(" ",A1,FIND(" ",A1)+1)+1,256)
```

Following this concept, you should be able to see how you can build mega-formulas using a variety of Excel's functions. All you need to do is first plan a way that you will achieve it and then use individual cells to obtain the results needed. Finally, replace all cell references with the functions that are housed within them.

If you have more than seven levels of nested functions, you'll also want to use the INDIRECT function, described in "Display Negative Time Values" [Hack #74].

Hack Mega-Formulas that Reference Other Workbooks

Excel formulas get pretty complicated when a mega-formula references another workbook. Not only do you need to include cell references, but also you must include workbook names or sheet names, and even the full path if the referenced workbook is closed. There are several ways to simplfiy what can be a complex process.

Writing such formulas from scratch can become unwieldy quickly. In this hack, we will show you a quick and easy way that enables you to construct these formulas without the need for workbook names and file paths. The method is so simple it is often overlooked.

Let's first ensure that you use the correct means to reference cells and worksheets. When writing a formula, it is always a good idea to never type cell references, sheet names, or workbook names because this can introduce incorrect syntax and/or typos. Most people at an intermediate level should be using only their mouse pointer to reference cells, sheets, and workbooks. This certainly goes a long way toward preventing syntax errors and typos, but if you have ever done this with a nested function, you know the formula quickly becomes unwieldy and is very difficult to follow.

For instance, take a look at this formula:

```
=INT(SUM('C:\Ozgrid Likom\Finance\SoftwareSales\[Regnow.xls]Product
Sales'!C2:C2924))
```

It is a pretty straightforward SUM function nested with the INT function. As it references cells from a closed workbook, the entire path is included along with the cell references, worksheet name, and workbook name. However, if you need to nest some additional functions within this one, it will soon become very difficult to write.

Here is a quick way to write mega functions that reference external workbooks. The trick is to simply write the function in the workbook that you will be referencing in any spare cell. If you are going to be referencing only one worksheet in this workbook, it is best to use a cell on this worksheet.

First, using the method shown in "Determine the Number of Specified Days in Any Month" [Hack #77] that explained an easy way to nest functions, simply develop the formula in any spare cell in the workbook that it will end up referencing. Once you have the desired result, cut the formula from the cell, activate the workbook in which the result should reside, select the appropriate cell, and paste.

Excel does all the hard work for you by including the workbook names and any sheet names. When/if you need to add or modify the formula, simply open the referenced workbook, cut the formula from the original workbook, and paste it into the referenced workbook. Then make your changes and cut and paste back to where it came from.

HACK #80 Hack One of Excel's Database Functions to Take the Place of Many Functions

Excel's database functions—DSUM, DCOUNT, etc.—can take the place of potentially thousands of functions, thereby reducing both recalculation time and workbook space.

When using Excel's database functions, you can specify up to 256 different criteria. You might, for example, want to sum amounts in column A where the corresponding amount in column B is greater than 100 and the corresponding age in column C is less than 40. If, however, you want to sum amounts where corresponding amounts in column B are less than 50, you need to use another function and a different range of criteria. It would much easier if you had a single function and could easily and quickly change the criteria! If you have never used Excel's database functions before, we strongly recommend that you familiarize yourself with them, as they are very good for extracting statistical information from an Excel database or table.

To see how this works, set up your data as shown in Figure 6-18. Keep the column headings the same, but the data that resides in it can be any fictitious data. Name this table of data, including all column headings, **AllData**. Name the sheet Data.

Insert another worksheet and call this worksheet **Results**. In cell A2, enter the following formula:

    =Data!A1

Copy this across to cell F2 so that you have a mirror image of your table headings. In cell A3, enter any name that exists in your table on the data sheet, such as **John D**. Then, in cell B3, enter the following formula:

    =DGET(AllData,B2,$A$2:$A$3)

Copy this formula across to cell F3 and format cells C3:F3 in the required format.

	A	B	C	D	E	F
1	Name	Dates	Full Cost	Amount Paid	Percent Paid	Cost Remaining
2	Bill J	2/15/01	$ 25.00	$ 10.00	40%	$ 15.00
3	John J	2/16/01	$ 35.00	$ 12.00	34%	$ 23.00
4	Fred B	2/19/01	$ 25.00	$ 20.00	80%	$ 5.00
5	Joe H	2/20/01	$ 65.00	$ 65.00	100%	$ -
6	Mary K	2/21/01	$ 88.00	$ 80.00	91%	$ 8.00
7	Lisa G	2/22/01	$ 45.00	$ 25.00	56%	$ 20.00
8	Dave H	2/23/01	$ 60.00	$ 55.00	92%	$ 5.00
9	Edward F	2/26/01	$ 21.00	$ 21.00	100%	$ -
10	Keith B	2/27/01	$ 33.00	$ 10.00	30%	$ 23.00
11	Aleisha H	2/28/01	$ 22.00	$ 22.00	100%	$ -
12	Kylie M	3/1/01	$ 25.00	$ 20.00	80%	$ 5.00
13	Jonn D	3/2/01	$ 44.00	$ 15.00	34%	$ 29.00
14	Bill W	3/5/01	$ 88.00	$ 45.00	51%	$ 43.00
15	Harry B	3/6/01	$ 77.00	$ 28.00	36%	$ 49.00

Figure 6-18. Proposed data

To quickly copy cells such as this without formatting, select the cell, right-click the fill handle, and, holding down the right mouse button, drag across as far as needed. Then select Fill Without Formatting.

The corresponding data should be extracted out of the table for the name you entered into cell A3. This is just a simple example of how you can use the DGET function to extract relevant information.

If you get the #NUM! error, it means you have two or more identical names in your Name column.

At this point, most people would follow the same concept for all names for which they need information extracted from the table. However, this effort is unnecessary.

As you are always referencing cell A3 for the name, it would make a lot more sense in most cases if you could simply have a drop-down list in cell A3 containing all the names that are in the table. You can use Excel's standard validation feature to create such a list. However, as the original list of names resides on another worksheet, you cannot reference the list in the same way as you would a list residing on the same sheet—i.e., a standard range reference. You can overcome this easily by naming the Name column in the original table, then using that name as the list source for the validation.

As most tables are not static—in other words, data is usually continuously added and removed—you should consider
using a dynamic named range for the Names column. See
"Create Ranges That Expand and Contract" **[Hack #42]** for
more details on this.

Click back onto the Data sheet and, with any cell selected, select Insert →
Name → Define. In the Names in Workbook: box, enter **Names**. In the Refers
To: box, type the following formula, and click Add:

    =OFFSET($A$2,0,0,COUNTA($A$2:$A$1000),1)

Click the Results worksheet, select cell A3, and then select Data → Validation. Select List from the Allow: box, and in the Source: box, type the
following:

    =Name

Ensure that the In-Cell drop-down checkbox is checked and then click OK.
Now you can select any name from the list in cell A3, and your data to the
right will display the appropriate information automatically.

You can take this to another level and use the DCOUNT function to extract a
count of people that have a full cost greater than a number you specify, and
a percent paid less than a number you specify.

To do this, first you need to create a dynamic named range for both the Full
Cost column and the Percent Paid column. In the Names in Workbook:
box, enter **FullCost**. In the Refers To: box, type the following formula, and
click Add:

    =OFFSET($C$2,0,0,COUNTA($C$2:$C$1000),1)

This time, in the Names in Workbook: box, enter **PercentPaid**. In the Refers
To: box, type the following formula and click Add:

    =OFFSET($E$2,0,0,COUNTA($E$2:$E$1000),1)

Activate the Results sheet, select cell A11, and then select Data → Validation. Select List from the Allow: box and enter **=Full_Cost** in the Source:
box. Click OK.

Select cell B11, then select Data → Validation. Select List from the Allow:
box and enter **=Percent_Paid** in the Source: box. Click OK.

In cell A12, enter the following:

    =Data!C1

Select cell B12, and enter the following:

    =Data!E1

Select cell A13, and enter the following:

```
=">"&A11
```

Select cell B13, and enter the following:

```
="<"&TEXT(B11,"0%")
```

In cell A15, enter the following:

```
=DCOUNT(AllData,$A$12,$A$12:$B$13)
```

Select any Full Cost amount from cell A11 and any percent paid amount from cell B11, and the DCOUNT function will give you a count of all the people who meet that criteria. For instance, if you select 65 and 100%, you will be extracting a count of people that have a Full Cost greater than 65 and a Percent Paid less than 100.

As you can see, you can use this one DCOUNT function to extract any combination of criteria for the Full Cost and Percent Paid columns. With a little more work, you can take this to yet another level and make the comparison operators used in the criteria interchangeable.

The first thing you need to do is create a list of comparison operators that you can use in a validation list. Scroll across to an out-of-the-way column on the Results sheet, and on any row in that column, enter the heading **Operators**. Below this and moving down one cell at a time, enter =, >=, >, <, and <=, as shown in Figure 6-19.

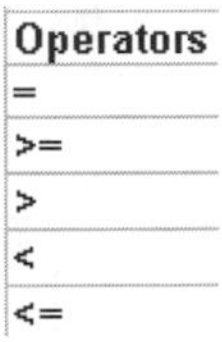

Operators
=
>=
>
<
<=

Figure 6-19. Comparison operators

To name this range, select the heading and all operators below it and then select Insert → Name → Create. Ensure that Top Row Only is selected, and click OK. Excel automatically will name the range based on the heading—in this case, Operators.

Select cell G7 and enter the heading **Select a Criteria**.

With cells G7 and H7 selected, center this across by selecting Format → Cells → Alignment, and from the Horizontal Text Alignment box, select Center Across Selection.

Select cells G8 and H8, select Data → Validation, and then select List from the Allow: box. In the Source: box, type =Operators. Ensure that the In-Cell drop-down box is checked and click OK.

Go back to the Data sheet and create a dynamic named range for the Dates column. Select Insert → Name → Define, and in the Names in Workbook: box, type **Dates**; in the Refers To: box, type the following formula and click Add:

```
=OFFSET($B$2,0,0,COUNTA($B$2:$B$1000),1)
```

Select cell G7, copy it, and paste it into cell G9. Change the word Criteria to **Date**. Select cells G10:H10, select Data → Validation, and then select List from the Allow: box. In the Source: box, enter =Dates. Ensure that the In-Cell drop-down box is checked and click OK. Select cell G11, and enter the following:

```
=Data!$B$1
```

Copy this across to cell H11. Select cell G12, enter the following formula (you should use the date format applicable to your particular region), and copy it across to cell H12:

```
=G8&TEXT(G10,"dd/mm/yy")
```

In cell F13, enter the word **Result** and center it across the selection, with F13 and G13 selected. In cell H13, enter the following function:

```
=DSUM(AllData,Data!$C$1,$G$11:$H$12)
```

The end result should look like Figure 6-20, which, for the sake of demonstration, has all formulas displayed.

G	H	I	J
Select a criteria			
>=	<=		
Select a Date			
19/02/01	20/02/01		
Dates	Dates		
=G8&TEXT(G10,"dd/mm/yy")	=H8&TEXT(H10,"dd/mm/yy")		
Result	=DSUM(AllData,Data!$C$1,$G$11:$H$12)		

Figure 6-20. Worksheet showing correct formulas and headings

Hide rows 11 and 12, as you do not need to see them. You will end up with a simple-to-use table that looks like Figure 6-21, which has had formatting applied for ease of reading.

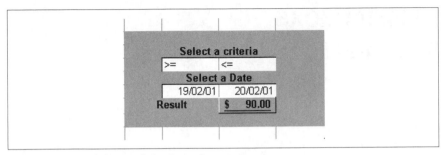

Figure 6-21. Worksheet with final interface

By using this principle, you can easily have either one or a few database functions doing the work of what usually would require hundreds.

For a working example of this exercise, as well as similar examples, visit *http:// www.ozgrid.com/download/default.htm* and click the heading DFunctions-WithValidation.zip.

CHAPTER SEVEN

Macro Hacks

Hacks 81-94

Macros make it wonderfully easy to automate repetitive tasks in Excel, but the way they're created and the facilities for using them are sometimes problematic. Fortunately, Excel is flexible enough that you can fix those problems and create new features with a minimum of effort.

Speed Up Code While Halting Screen Flicker

When you record macros from within Excel, the code it generates often produces screen flicker, which not only slows down your macro, but also makes the macro's activity look very disorganized. Fortunately, you can eliminate screen flicker while at the same time speeding up your code.

One drawback with recorded macros in Excel is that the code produced is often very inefficient. This can mean macros that should take a matter of seconds to complete often take a lot longer and look very unsightly. Also, when you write macros using the macro recorder, all keystrokes are recorded, whether they are meant to be or not. This means that if you make an error and then correct it, the keystrokes required to complete those actions also will be recorded in your macro code.

If you have played around a bit with macros or dabbled in VBA code, you might have heard of the `Application.ScreenUpdating` property. By setting ScreenUpdating to False at the start of a macro, you will not only stop the constant screen flicker associated with a recorded macro, but also speed up the macro's execution. The reason this method speeds up code is because Excel no longer needs to repaint the screen whenever it encounters commands such as `Select`, `Activate`, `LargeScroll`, `SmallScroll`, and many others.

To include `Application.ScreenUpdating = False` at the beginning of your existing macro, select Tools → Macro → Macros, select your macro, click the Edit button, and enter the following code:

```
'
' a Macro
' Macro recorded 1/12/2003 by OzGrid.com
'


'
Application.ScreenUpdating = False
'YOUR CODE
Application.ScreenUpdating = True
End Sub
```

Note how you set ScreenUpdating back to True on completion. Although Excel will set this back to True whenever focus is passed back to Excel (in other words, when your macro finishes), in most cases it pays to play it safe and include the code at the end.

In some cases, you might find that ScreenUpdating is set back to True before your recorded macro completes. This can happen with recorded macros that use the Select command frequently. If this does happen, you might need to repeat the line Application.ScreenUpdating = False in other parts of your macro.

HACK #82 Run a Macro at a Set Time

Many times it would be great to run a macro at a predetermined time or at specified intervals. Fortunately, Excel provides a VBA method that makes this possible.

The Application.OnTime method can make macros run automatically, once you've done some setup. Suppose you have a macro that you want to run each day at 15:00 (3:00 p.m.). First you need to determine how to kick off the OnTime method. You can do this using the Workbook_Open event in the private module of the Workbook object.

On Windows, the fastest way to get to the private module of the Workbook object (ThisWorkbook) is to right-click the Excel icon next to File and select View Code. (On a Macintosh, open the VBE and then open the module for the Workbook object from the Project window.) Enter the following code:

```
Private Sub Workbook_Open( )
    Application.OnTime TimeValue("15:00:00"), "MyMacro"
End Sub
```

MyMacro should be the name of the macro you want to run. It should reside in a standard module and contain the OnTime method, as follows:

```
Sub MyMacro( )
    Application.OnTime TimeValue("15:00:00"), "MyMacro"
'YOUR CODE

End Sub
```

This will run the procedure MyMacro at 15:00 each day, so long as Excel is open.

Now suppose you want to run MyMacro at 15-minute intervals after opening your workbook. Again you will kick it off as soon as the workbook opens, so right-click the Excel icon next to File, select View Code, and enter the following code:

```
Private Sub Workbook_BeforeClose(Cancel As Boolean)
    Application.OnTime dTime, "MyMacro", , False
End Sub

Private Sub Workbook_Open( )
    Application.OnTime Now + TimeValue("00:15:00"), "MyMacro"
End Sub
```

In any standard module (accessed by selecting Insert → Module), enter the following code:

```
Public dTime As Date
Sub MyMacro( )
dTime = Now + TimeValue("00:15:00")
Application.OnTime dTime, "MyMacro"

'YOUR CODE
End Sub
```

Note how you pass the time of 15 minutes to the public variable dTime. This is so that you can have the OnTime method cancelled in the Workbook_ BeforeClose event by setting the optional Schedule argument to False. The Schedule argument is True by default, so by setting it to False, you are telling Excel to cancel the OnTime method that is set to run at a specified time.

If you didn't pass the time to a variable, Excel would not know which OnTime method to cancel, as Now + TimeValue("00:15:00") is *not* static, but becomes static when passed to a variable. If you didn't set the optional Schedule argument to False, the workbook would open automatically every 15 minutes after you close it and run MyMacro.

HACK #83   Use CodeName to Reference Sheets in Excel Workbooks

Sometimes you need to create a macro that will work even if the sheet names it references change.

If you have recorded a macro in Excel that references a specific sheet in your workbook, you know the code will continue to work only if the sheet name(s) remain the same. For example, if your worksheet is named Budget, and the code in your macro reads Sheets("Budget").Select and then you change the worksheet name, the macro will no longer work. This is because the macro recorder generates code based on the sheet's tab name or on the name you see when working in Excel.

To overcome this limitation, you have two options, the first of which is to use index numbers. A sheet's index number is determined by its position in the workbook. The leftmost sheet will always have an index number of 1, the next worksheet immediately to the right will always have an index number of 2, and so on. Excel VBA enables you to specify any sheet by using its index number, but unfortunately Excel does not use this method when you record a macro.

Also, although using an index number such as Sheets(3).Select is a better option than using Sheets("Budget").Select, the sheet's position in the workbook could change if you add, remove, or move sheets.

Instead of using index numbers, savvy VBA coders use CodeNames. Each sheet in a workbook is given a unique CodeName that does not change even when that sheet is moved or renamed, or when any other sheets are added. You can see a sheet's CodeName only by going into the VBE (select Tools → Macro → Visual Basic Editor, or press Alt/Option-F11) and then displaying the Project window if necessary (select View → Project Explorer or press Ctrl-R).

In Figure 7-1, the CodeName for the sheet with a tab name of Budget is Sheet3. A sheet's CodeName is always the name that appears outside the parentheses when you look in the Project Explorer. You can reference this sheet with VBA code in the workbook by using Sheet3.Select, as opposed to Sheets("Budget").Select or Sheets(3).Select.

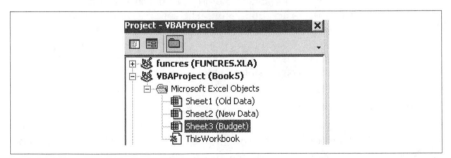

Figure 7-1. CodeNames and sheet names in the VBE Project window

If your workbook is already full of VBA code, recorded or written, that does not use a CodeName, you can change the code at the project level (all code in all modules in the workbook) by selecting Edit → Replace... while in the VBE.

The only time you *cannot* use a sheet's CodeName is when you reference a sheet that is in a workbook different from the one in which the code resides.

  Connect Buttons to Macros Easily

#84   Instead of giving every button its own macro, it's sometimes more convenient to create a single macro that manages all the buttons.

Users generally prefer to run macros via either a shortcut key or a button they can simply click, instead of having to hunt through menus and dialog boxes. The most popular way to access a button is from the Forms toolbar, available by selecting View → Toolbars → Forms. These buttons, in our opinion, are the best choice for running macros, especially recorded macros, because recorded macros often require the user to be on a specific worksheet when the macro is run. Simply put, recorded macros always use ActiveSheet if you recorded the macro without changing sheets. This means that if the user is not on the required worksheet (in other words, the same one you were on when recording), the recorded macro will often "bug out" and/or make changes on the wrong sheet. By using a button on a worksheet, you can force the user to navigate to that worksheet button to set the right conditions for the macro before clicking it.

Why a button from the Forms toolbar and not the Control Toolbox toolbar? Buttons are almost always used to detect a mouse click and then run a specified macro. You should use a command button from the Control Toolbox toolbar only when you need to determine other events such as a double-click, a right-click, and so on. The controls on the Control Toolbox toolbar are known as ActiveX controls, and using them to only run a macro adds unnecessary overhead to Excel, especially if you use a lot of buttons. It is akin to using a sledgehammer to bang in a nail.

When you have a lot of buttons in a workbook and each button is used to run a specified macro, you can attach the macros to the buttons by right-clicking the button border and choosing Assign Macro. Then find the correct macro in the Assign Macro dialog, as shown in Figure 7-2.

Because each button is usually used to run a different macro, often you must scroll through the entire macro list to find the correct one. There is a really simple way you can assign all the buttons to the same macro but still have each button run a different macro.

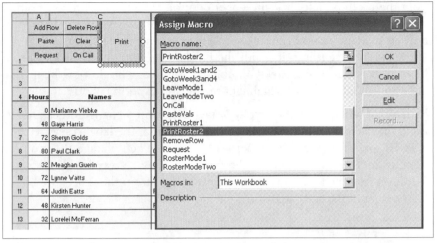

Figure 7-2. Print button highlighted and Assign Macro dialog active, with macro highlighted

Place the following code into any standard module. Select Tools → Macro → Visual Basic Editor (Alt/Option-F11) and create a new module by selecting Insert → Module and then entering the following code:

```
Sub WhichButton( )
    Run Application.Caller
End Sub
```

Now you need to give each button the same name as the macro it should run. To name a button from the Forms toolbar, simply left-click it, then replace the name shown in the Name box (at the left of the Formula bar) with the name of the macro the button should run. Do the same for all buttons. Now, if you named a button Macro1 and then assigned it to the macro WhichButton, when clicked it will run the macro Macro1.

HACK #85 Create a Workbook Splash Screen

Splash screens provide that extra bit of polish to an application—not to mention that they keep you entertained while the application loads. Why shouldn't a spreadsheet do the same?

You can use Excel's VBA capabilities to create a splash screen for any workbook; you'll find the process is easier than you might imagine it would be.

To create a splash screen that shows for 5 to 10 seconds when a workbook opens, then closes itself automatically, start by pressing Alt/Option-F11, or select Tools → Macro → Visual Basic Editor to open the VBE. Then select Insert → UserForm. If the Control toolbox is not showing, select View → Toolbox to view it.

From the toolbox, left-click the Label control. (Hover your mouse pointer over each control to display its name.) Left-click anywhere on the UserForm to insert the label. Using the size handles, drag out the label so that you can type some brief text into it. With the label still selected, left-click again. If the label is not selected, slowly double-click it. You should now be in Edit mode and should be able to highlight the default caption Label1.

Within that label, enter the text **My Splash Screen**. To change other properties of the label (its font size, color, etc.), ensure that the label is selected and press F4, or select View → Properties Window. Then change the required property in the Label Controls Property window. Now double-click the UserForm (not the label) and then select Initialize from the Procedure box at the top right of the screen, as shown in Figure 7-3.

Figure 7-3. Procedure drop-down box for the various events of the UserForm object

Within this procedure, enter the following:

```
Application.OnTime Now + TimeValue("00:00:05"), "KillForm"
```

Your code for the UserForm should look like this:

```
Private Sub UserForm_Initialize()
    Application.OnTime Now + TimeValue("00:00:05"), "KillForm"
End Sub
```

Next, select Insert → Module, and enter the following code exactly as shown:

```
Sub KillForm()
Unload UserForm1
End Sub
```

Now all you need is some code in the private module of the Workbook object (ThisWorkbook). In the Project Explorer, you should see the name of your workbook. Expand the folders branching off the bottom of the workbook until you see ThisWorkbook under Microsoft Excel Objects. Double-click ThisWorkbook to expose its private module.

In the private module of the ThisWorkbook object, enter the following:

```
Private Sub Workbook_Open( )
    UserForm1.Show
End Sub
```

Close the window to get back to Excel. Save and close the workbook, and reopen it to see your splash screen in action. Figure 7-4 shows an example.

Figure 7-4. Example splash screen in action

Just remember that the splash screen should show for only a short period of time and should contain brief but relevant text. Showing it for longer than 10 seconds might annoy users.

HACK #86 Display a "Please Wait" Message

Have you ever had one of those macros that seem to take forever to complete? If this is a problem with your macro, you can have Excel display a "Please Wait" message to the user.

Most users expect code to run and complete almost instantaneously. Sadly, this doesn't always happen. Recorded macros in particular generally take much longer to complete than well-written VBA code. To add to the problem, Excel VBA code is generally slower than a lot of other types of code.

Fortunately, you can use a bit of extra code to create a "Please Wait" message so that users know the code is running and Excel has not locked up on them! Unfortunately, one of the more popular ways to let users know code is running is via the use of an Excel progress meter.

There are two problems with this method. First, the progress meter can slow down your code even more, compounding the issue. Second, your slow code must be caused by a loop, and you cannot use the macro recorder to create a loop.

We prefer using VBA code, such as the following DoIt macro, which uses a rectangle from the Drawing toolbar.

```
Sub DoIt( )
Application.ScreenUpdating = True
    With Sheet1.Shapes("Rectangle1")
        .Visible = msoTrue = (Not Sheet1.Shapes("Rectangle1").Visible)
    End With
'Toggling sheets Forces Rectangle1 to show while code is running
Sheet2.Select
Sheet1.Select
End Sub
```

To use this code, add a rectangle from the Drawing toolbar to any sheet in the appropriate workbook. While the rectangle is selected, click in the Name box and name the rectangle **Rectangle1** (if it's not already called that).

Enter the text you want displayed while your code is running, and format, position, and size the rectangle as desired. Enter the preceding DoIt macro into a standard module of your workbook. If necessary, change Sheet1 in the code to the CodeName of the sheet on which you placed Rectangle1. (For more information on CodeNames, see "Use CodeName to Reference Sheets in Excel Workbooks" **[Hack #83]**.) Then select Tools → Macro → Macros and run DoIt from within Excel. This will hide Rectangle1 completely.

At the very start of the slow code, place the following:

```
Run "DoIt"
Application.ScreenUpdating = False
```

The use of Application.ScreenUpdating = False stops screen flicker and speeds up macros. At the very end of the slow code, simply place **Run "DoIt"**. Then run your macro as usual.

HACK #87 Have a Cell Ticked or Unticked upon Selection

Sometimes it's difficult to make choices with checkboxes. Fortunately, you can simplify this process using a basic bit of code.

You can use Excel workbooks to collect data for surveys. Usually you do this by offering users a number of answers to choose from and placing a checkbox next to each choice. Users then check the appropriate checkboxes. The problem with using this method, though, is that your workbook soon can end up with hundreds of checkboxes.

Instead, you can use some very simple VBA code to tick any cell within a specified range as soon as it's selected. If the cell within the specified range is ticked already, the code will remove it. The trick to the code is the use of the letter "a" in a cell whose font is set to Marlett. When it's time to add up the results, simply use the COUNTIF function to count the occurrences of the letter "a", like this:

```
=COUNITIF($A$1:A$100,"a")
```

The following code examples work only on the range A1:A100, but you can modify them easily to suit any range. To use the code, activate the worksheet on which the ticks should be displayed, right-click the Sheet Name tab, and select View Code. Paste in either CODE 1 (if you want the cell ticked when it's selected) or CODE 2 (if you want the cell ticked when it's double-clicked):

```
'CODE 1 - tick cell with selection

Private Sub Worksheet_SelectionChange(ByVal Target As Range)
 If Target.Cells.Count > 1 Then Exit Sub
    If Not Intersect(Target, Range("A1:A100")) Is Nothing Then
        Target.Font.Name = "Marlett"
        If Target = vbNullString Then
            Target = "a"
        Else
            Target = vbNullString
        End If
    End If
End Sub


'CODE 2 - tick cell with double-click

Private Sub Worksheet_BeforeDoubleClick(ByVal Target As Range, Cancel As
Boolean)
    If Not Intersect(Target, Range("A1:A100")) Is Nothing Then
     Cancel = True 'Prevent going into Edit Mode
        Target.Font.Name = "Marlett"
        If Target = vbNullString Then
            Target = "a"
        Else
            Target = vbNullString
        End If
    End If
End Sub
```

Once the desired code is in place, simply close the window to get back to Excel and save your workbook. If you need to see whether the cell is checked, just examine its contents.

HACK #88 Count or Sum Cells That Have a Specified Fill Color

Using a bit of code, you can easily SUM or COUNT cells whose fill color was specified manually.

Every now and then, it's convenient to SUM or COUNT cells that have a specified fill color that you or another user have set manually, as users often understand paint colors more readily than named ranges. To do this, first open the workbook where you want to COUNT or SUM cells by a fill color. Go into the VBE by selecting Tools → Macro → Visual Basic Editor (Alt/Option-F11) and then select Insert → Module to insert a standard module. In this module, type the following code:

```
Function ColorFunction(rColor As Range, rRange As Range, Optional SUM As
Boolean)
Dim rCell As Range
Dim lCol As Long
Dim vResult

lCol = rColor.Interior.ColorIndex

    If SUM = True Then
       For Each rCell In rRange
        If rCell.Interior.ColorIndex = lCol Then
                vResult = WorksheetFunction.SUM(rCell) + vResult
        End If
       Next rCell
    Else
        For Each rCell In rRange
        If rCell.Interior.ColorIndex = lCol Then
                vResult = 1 + vResult
        End If
       Next rCell
    End If

    ColorFunction = vResult
    End Function
```

Now you can use the custom function ColorFunction in formulas such as this:

```
=ColorFunction($C$1,$A$1:$A$12,TRUE)
```

to sum the values in the range of cells $A$1:$A$12 that have the same fill color as cell $C$1. The function will sum in this example because you used TRUE as the last argument for the custom function.

To count the cells that have the same fill color as cell $C$1, you can use this:

```
=ColorFunction($C$1,$A$1:$A$12,FALSE)
```

or:

```
=ColorFunction($C$1,$A$1:$A$12)
```

By omitting the last argument, the function automatically defaults to using FALSE as the last argument. Now you easily can SUM or COUNT cells that have a specified fill color, as shown in Figure 7-5.

	A	B	C	D	E
1	20				
2	22				
3	23				
4	25				
5	26				
6	27				
7	29				
8	30				
9	31				
10	32				
11	54				
12	21				
13	78	=ColorFunction($C$1,$A$1:$A$12,TRUE)			
14	3	=ColorFunction($C$1,$A$1:$A$12)			
15					

Figure 7-5. Using the custom ColorFunction to count by fill color

HACK #89 Add the Microsoft Excel Calendar Control to Any Excel Workbook

If you want to ensure that users enter dates correctly, the Excel Calendar Control can make things easier for both you and the users of the spreadsheet. With this hack, you can add the Calendar Control to any Excel workbook.

Unless a date is entered correctly, Excel won't recognize it as valid. This sometimes means you cannot perform calculations with figures that look like dates but aren't. It also means any charts or PivotTables based on these dates will not be valid. Although the use of Excel's very versatile validation feature (described in Chapter 2) can help with this, it is far from bulletproof.

With this hack, you can add the Calendar Control to any Excel workbook. To start, open the workbook for the calendar. It is a good idea to use your *Personal.xls* file for this, in which case you should first select Window → Unhide. If this option is grayed out, it means you do not have a *Personal.xls* file yet. You can create one easily by recording a dummy macro. Select Tools → Macro → Record New Macro and choose Personal Macro Workbook from the Store Macro In: box. Then click OK, select any cell, and stop recording. Excel will have created your *Personal.xls* file automatically.

Next, select Tools → Macro → Visual Basic Editor (Alt/Option-F11) and then select Insert → UserForm from within the VBE. This should display the Control toolbox. (If it doesn't, select View → Toolbox.)

Right-click the Control toolbox and select Additional Controls. Scroll through the list until you see the Calendar Control 10.0 checkbox (the number will differ depending on the version of Excel you are using). Check the checkbox and click OK. Click the calendar that is now part of the tool-box and then click the UserForm you inserted earlier.

Using the size handles on both the UserForm and the Calendar Control, size the UserForm and Calendar Control to a reasonable size, as shown in Figure 7-6.

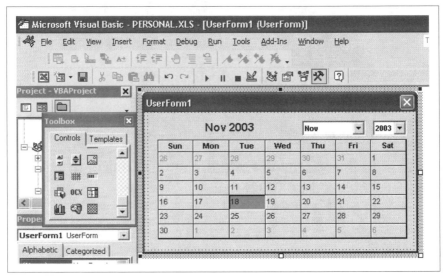

Figure 7-6. Inserted Calendar Control

Make sure the UserForm is selected (as shown in Figure 7-6) and then select View → Properties Window (F4). Select Caption from the Properties window and replace UserForm1 with the word **Calendar**. Now select View → Code (F7), and in the private module, add the following code:

```
Private Sub Calendar1_Click( )
 ActiveCell = Calendar1.Value
End Sub

Private Sub UserForm_Activate( )
 Me.Calendar1.Value = Date
End Sub
```

Select Insert → Module, and in the public module, place this code:

```
Sub ShowIt( )
    UserForm1.Show
End Sub
```

Close the window to return to Excel. Select Tools → Macro → Macros (Alt-F8) and then select ShowIt. Click Options, assign a shortcut key, and you're done. Just press your shortcut key, and the calendar will show with today's date as the default. Click any date and it will be inserted into the active cell.

Password-Protect and Unprotect All Excel Worksheets in One Fell Swoop

Sadly, there is no standard feature in Excel that will enable you to protect and unprotect all worksheets in one go; however, some simple code can make it happen.

Excel provides protection that you can add to an Excel worksheet by selecting Tools → Protection → Protect Sheet. You also can supply a password so that another user cannot unprotect the worksheet and gain access unless he knows the password.

Sometimes, though, you want to password-protect and unprotect all worksheets in a workbook in one step because protecting and unprotecting each worksheet individually is a huge nuisance. Here is how you can simplify this task.

Open the workbook to which you want to apply the code. Or, select Window → Unhide and unhide your *Personal.xls* file to make it available to any workbook. If this is grayed out, it means you do not have a *Personal.xls* file yet. You can create one easily by recording a dummy macro. Select Tools → Macro → Record New Macro and choose Personal Macro Workbook from the Store Macro In: box. Then click OK, select any cell, and stop recording. Excel will have created your *Personal.xls* file automatically.

Next, select Tools → Macro → Visual Basic Editor (Alt/Option-F11) and then select Insert → UserForm. This should display the Control toolbox. If it doesn't, select View → Toolbox.

From the toolbox, select a TextBox (indicated as ab|). Click onto the User-Form to add the TextBox to the UserForm. Position it in the top left of your form and size it to your preference.

Ensure that the textbox is still selected and then select View → Properties (F4). From the Properties window of the textbox, scroll down until you see PasswordChar, and in the white box on the right, enter an asterisk (*). From the toolbox, select a CommandButton and then click the UserForm and position it in the top right of your form.

With the CommandButton still selected, select View → Properties (F4). From the Properties window of the CommandButton, scroll down until you see Caption, and in the white box on the right, enter the caption **OK**. If you are using Excel 97, also scroll down until you see TakeFocusOnClick, and set this to False.

Now select the UserForm and, from its Properties window, find Caption and change it to **Protect/Unprotect all sheets**. Your form should look like that shown in Figure 7-7.

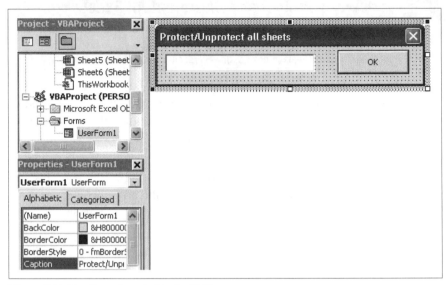

Figure 7-7. UserForm inserted in the VBE

Select View → Code (F7) and enter the following code exactly as shown:

```
Private Sub CommandButton1_Click( )
Dim wSheet As Worksheet
    For Each wSheet In Worksheets
        If wSheet.ProtectContents = True Then
            wSheet.Unprotect Password:=TextBox1.Text
        Else
            wSheet.Protect Password:=TextBox1.Text
        End If
    Next wSheet
    Unload me
End Sub
```

The code loops through all worksheets in the active workbook. If one is protected, it unprotects it using the password entered into the text box. If the worksheet is already unprotected, it protects it using the password entered into the text box.

Now select Insert → Module and enter this code:

```
Sub ShowPass( )
    UserForm1.Show
End Sub
```

This is used to launch the UserForm. Close the window to get back to Excel.

Select Tools → Macro → Macros (Alt/Option-F8). Select ShowPass and then click Options and assign a shortcut key. This will unprotect all worksheets that are protected and protect all worksheets that are unprotected.

> As this macro does not ask you to confirm your password, you should be very sure of what you type. Otherwise, you may find that typos lock you out of your spreadsheets.

If you're protecting the contents only from yourself, the following macro lets you perform the same tasks with a blank password instead:

```
Option Explicit

Sub Protect_Unprotect( )
Dim wSheet As Worksheet

For Each wSheet In Worksheets
    With wSheet
        If .ProtectContents = True Then
            .Unprotect Password:=""
        Else
            .Protect Password:=""
        End If
    End With
Next wSheet

End Sub
```

Although it's not very secure, it's definitely convenient.

HACK #91 Retrieve a Workbook's Name and Path

Every now and then you might want a cell to return the name of a workbook, or even the workbook's filename and path. With this hack, it's easy to retrieve a workbook's name and path.

The three user-defined functions we explain in this section place the name of a workbook into a cell, or the workbook's filename and path into a cell. The first two examples, MyName and MyFullName, do not take any arguments. The last one, SheetName, is used in place of nesting the MID and other functions inside the CELL function to get the sheet name, a process that commonly would require the following unwieldy formula:

```
=MID(CELL("filename",$A$1),FIND("]",CELL("filename",$A$1))+1,255)
```

As you can see, this requires quite a bit of typing for such a simple result, which is why we initially developed the SheetName custom function.

To use this user-defined function, press Alt/Option-F11, select Insert →
Module, and paste in the following code:

```
Function MyName( ) As String
  MyName = ThisWorkbook.Name
End Function
Function MyFullName( ) As String
  MyFullName = ThisWorkbook.FullName
End Function
Function SheetName(rAnyCell)
    Application.Volatile
    SheetName = rAnyCell.Parent.Name
End Function
```

Save the function and close the window. The function will appear under
User Defined in the Paste Function dialog (Shift-F3).

You can use the functions as shown in Figure 7-8. They take no arguments.
The formulas in column A are shown for demonstration purposes only and
have no effect on the result.

	A	B
1	Formula	Result
2	=MyName()	Workbook Path.xls
3	=MyFullName()	C:\OzGrid\Learning\Workbook Path.xls
4	=CELL("filename")	C:\OzGrid\Learning\[Workbook Path.xls]Sheet1
5	=sheetname(A1)	Sheet1

Figure 7-8. Functions and their result

In cell A4 in Figure 7-8, we also placed the standard CELL
function that returns a workbook's name, file path, and
active sheet name. The CELL function is a standard function
that will return information about the current operating system—in other words, information on formatting, location,
and contents of a workbook.

HACK #92 Get Around Excel's Three-Criteria Limit for Conditional Formatting

You can use VBA to hack conditional formatting to use more than three
criteria on your data. In fact, you can use the code to apply virtually an
unlimited number of criteria.

Excel has a very useful feature named conditional formatting (described in
Chapter 2). You can find it by selecting Format → Conditional Formatting...
on the worksheet menu bar. Conditional formatting enables you to format a
cell based on its content. For example, you can change to a red background
all cells whose value is greater than 5 but less than 10. Although this is

handy, Excel supports only up to three conditions, which sometimes is not enough.

If you want to set more than three conditions, you can use Excel VBA code that is fired automatically whenever a user changes a specified range. To see how this works, say you want to have six separate conditions in the range A1:A10 on a particular worksheet. Set up some data such as that shown in Figure 7-9.

	A
1	**Numbers**
2	3
3	
4	8
5	
6	13
7	
8	18
9	23
10	28
11	3
12	7
13	12
14	17
15	23
16	28

Figure 7-9. Data setup for conditional formatting experiment

Save your workbook, then activate the worksheet, right-click its Sheet Name tab, select View Code, and enter the following code:

```
Private Sub Worksheet_Change(ByVal Target As Range)

Dim icolor As Integer
If Not Intersect(Target, Range("A1:A10")) is Nothing Then
  Select Case Target
  Case 1 To 5
     icolor = 6
  Case 6 To 10
     icolor = 12
  Case 11 To 15
     icolor = 7
  Case 16 To 20
     icolor = 53
  Case 21 To 25
     icolor = 15
  Case 26 To 30
     icolor = 42
  Case Else
     'Whatever
```

```
    End Select
      Target.Interior.ColorIndex = icolor
    End If

    End Sub
```

Close the window to get back to your worksheet. Your results should look like Figure 7-10.

	A
1	**Numbers**
2	3
3	
4	8
5	
6	13
7	
8	18
9	23
10	28
11	3
12	7
13	12
14	17
15	23
16	28

Figure 7-10. What data should look like once the code is entered

The background color of each cell should have changed based on the number passed to the variable `icolor`, which in turn passes this number to `Target.Interior.ColorIndex`. The number that is passed is determined by the line `Case x To x`. For example, if you enter the number 22 in any cell within the range A1:A10, the number 15 is passed to `icolor`, and then `icolor` (now having a value of 15) is passed to `Target.Interior.ColorIndex`, making the cell gray. `Target` is always the cell that changed and, thus, fired the code.

HACK #93 Run Procedures on Protected Worksheets

Excel macros are a great way to save time and eliminate errors. However, sooner or later you might try to run your favorite Excel macro on a worksheet that has been protected, with or without a password, resulting in a runtime error. Avoid that problem with the following hack.

If you have ever tried to run an Excel macro on a worksheet that's been protected, you know that as soon as the worksheet is encountered, your macro probably won't work and instead will display a runtime error.

One way to get around this is to use some code such as the following to unprotect and then protect your worksheet:

```
Sub MyMacro( )

Sheet1.Unprotect Password:="Secret"

'YOUR CODE

Sheet1.Protect Password:="Secret"
End Sub
```

As you can see, the code unprotects Sheet1 with the password Secret, runs the code, and then password-protects it again. This will work, but it has a number of drawbacks. For one, the code could bug out and stop before it encounters the Sheet1.Protect Password:="Secret" line of code. This, of course, would leave your worksheet fully unprotected. Another drawback is that you will need similar code for all macros and all worksheets.

Another way to avoid this problem is to use UserInterFaceOnly, which is an optional argument of the Protect method that you can set to True. (The default is False.) By setting this argument to True, Excel will allow all Excel VBA macros to run on the worksheets that are protected with or without a password.

However, if you use the Protect method with the UserInterfaceOnly argument set to True on a worksheet and then save the workbook, the entire worksheet (not just the interface) will be fully protected when you reopen the workbook. To set the UserInterfaceOnly argument back to True after the workbook is opened, you must again apply the Protect method with UserInterfaceOnly set to True.

To avoid this hassle, you need to use the Workbook_Open event, which is fired as soon as the workbook is opened. Because this is an event of the Workbook object ThisWorkbook, you must place the following code in the private module of ThisWorkbook. To do this in Windows versions of Excel, right-click the Excel icon and select View Code. On Macs, open the Workbook object from the Projects window of the VBE. Then enter the following:

```
Private Sub Workbook_Open( )
'If you have different passwords
'for each worksheet.

Sheets(1).Protect Password:="Secret", UserInterFaceOnly:=True
Sheets(2).Protect Password:="Carrot", UserInterFaceOnly:=True

'Repeat as needed.
End Sub
```

The preceding code is good if each worksheet on which you want your macros to operate has a different password, or if you do not want to protect all worksheets. You can set the UserInterfaceOnly argument to True without having to unprotect first.

If you want to set the UserInterfaceOnly argument to True on all worksheets and they have the same password, you can use the following code, which must be placed in the same place as the preceding code:

```
Private Sub Workbook_Open( )
Dim wSheet As Worksheet

    For Each wSheet In Worksheets
        wSheet.Protect Password:="Secret", _
                    UserInterFaceOnly:=True
    Next wSheet
End Sub
```

Now, each time you open the workbook, the code will run and will set the UserInterfaceOnly property to True, allowing your macros to operate while still preventing any user changes.

H A C K Distribute Macros
#94

Although you can distribute a macro along with a workbook, if you want to distribute only the macro's functionality, an Excel add-in is the way to go.

An Excel add-in is nothing more than an Excel workbook that was saved as an add-in by selecting File → Save As... → Microsoft Excel Add-in (*.xla). Once it's saved and reopened, the workbook will be hidden and can be seen only in the Project Explorer via the VBE. It is not hidden in the same way as the *Personal.xls* file, as this can be seen (and made visible) via Windows → Unhide.

Once you have completed the workbook you want to use as an add-in, you need to save a copy of it. You can save it to any location you want, but make sure to note where you placed it.

Open any workbook, and on the Tools menu, select Add-Ins, then click Browse. Locate your add-in from where you saved it, select it, and then click OK.

Ensure that your add-in is in the Add-Ins Available: box and that the box is checked. Then click OK to install the add-in. You can save most code to an Excel add-in without too many changes. There are a few issues worth considering, however:

- The ThisWorkbook object will always refer to the add-in, not to the user's workbook. Use the ActiveWorkbook object instead.
- You cannot refer to sheets in the ActiveWorkbook with CodeNames.

- You should always put toolbars, etc., back to the way the user had them originally. There is nothing worse than an add-in that changes all your Excel settings without your knowledge.

- Always include some sort of error handling (yes, most add-ins will cause errors at some time).

- Be very aware that the user might have many sorts of protection applied. *Never* use code to unprotect any part of the user's workbook. Simply display a message asking the user to unprotect.

- Make full and good use of the worksheet you have in the add-in. We use the worksheet(s) to store user settings such as toolbars.

- Holding down the Shift key will *not* prevent add-in workbook events from running (holding down the Shift key will prevent a normal *.xls* file from running, however).

- If you need to see or work with the add-in workbook again to incorporate updates or modifications, go into the VBE while the add-in is installed and, from the Properties window, select the IsAddin property and set it to False. Saving the workbook as an add-in sets this property to True.

- Apply protection to the modules of your add-in by selecting Tools → VBAProject Properties → Protection.

Once you have created your add-in you will need to make the macros within it easy for the user to run. This is best achieved by using the Workbook_ AddinInstall and Workbook_AddinUnInstall events in the private module of the ThisWorkbook object. Simply double-click ThisWorkbook for the *.xla* file, and Excel will take you into the private module where the code is placed, as shown in Figure 7-11.

Here is a simple example of the code:

```
Option Explicit
Dim cControl As CommandBarButton
Private Sub Workbook_AddinInstall( )

On Error Resume Next 'Just in case
    'Delete any existing menu item that may have been left.
    Application.CommandBars("Worksheet Menu Bar").Controls("Super Code").
Delete
    'Add the new menu item and set a CommandBarButton variable to it
    Set cControl = Application.CommandBars("Worksheet Menu Bar").Controls.
Add
        'Work with the Variable
        With cControl
            .Caption = "Super Code"
            .Style = msoButtonCaption
            .OnAction = "MyGreatMacro" 'Macro stored in a Standard Module
        End With
```

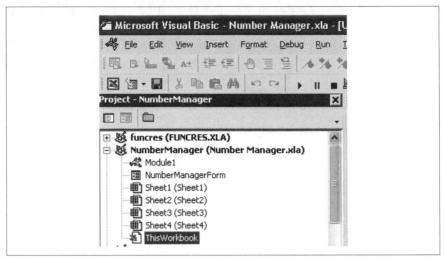

Figure 7-11. Project Explorer with ThisWorkbook selected for an add-in named Number Manager.xla

```
On Error GoTo 0

End Sub


Private Sub Workbook_AddinUninstall( )

    On Error Resume Next 'In case it has already gone.
    Application.CommandBars("Worksheet Menu Bar").Controls("Super Code).
Delete
    On Error GoTo 0

End Sub
```

This is all the code you'll need to add a single menu item (called Super Code) to the end of the existing worksheet menu bar as soon as the user installs the add-in via Tools → Add-ins. When the Super Code menu item is clicked, a macro (that is within a standard module of the add-in) is run. Remember that the preceding code *must* be placed in the private module of ThisWorkbook for the add-in.

If you want the Super Code menu item added, say, before the format menu item, you can use this code:

```
Option Explicit
Dim cControl As CommandBarButton

Private Sub Workbook_AddinInstall( )

Dim iContIndex As Integer
```

```
On Error Resume Next 'Just in case
    'Delete any existing menu item that may have been left.
    Application.CommandBars("Worksheet Menu Bar").Controls("Super
Code").Delete
    'Pass the index of the "Format" menu item number to a variable.
    'Use the FindControl method to find its Index number. ID number _
    is used in case of customization
    iContIndex = Application.CommandBars.FindControl(ID:=30006).Index
    'Add the new menu item and set a CommandBarButton variable to it.
    'Use the number passed to our Integer variable to position it.
    Set cControl = Application.CommandBars("Worksheet Menu Bar") _
                        .Controls.Add(Before:=iContIndex)
            'Work with the Variable
            With cControl
                .Caption = "Super Code"
                .Style = msoButtonCaption
                .OnAction = "MyGreatMacro" 'Macro stored in a standard
module
            End With
    On Error GoTo 0
End Sub
```

You would not have to change the Workbook_AddinUninstall( ) code in this
case.

In these examples, all the menu item code is in Workbook_AddinInstall and
Workbook_AddinUnInstall. This is not a problem when the code is adding
only one menu item. If, however, you will be adding more than one item
and, perhaps, even submenus, you should place the menu item code in a
procedure (or two) inside a standard module. Then use some code such as
this:

```
Private Sub Workbook_AddinInstall( )
    Run "AddMenus"
End Sub

Private Sub Workbook_AddinUninstall( )
    Run "DeleteMenu"
End Sub
```

In the standard module, put some code such as this:

```
Sub AddMenus( )
Dim cMenu1 As CommandBarControl
Dim cbMainMenuBar As CommandBar
Dim iHelpMenu As Integer
Dim cbcCutomMenu As CommandBarControl

    '(1)Delete any existing one. We must use On Error Resume next _
        in case it does not exist.
        On Error Resume Next
        Application.CommandBars("Worksheet Menu Bar").Controls("&New Menu").
Delete
```

```
            '(2)Set a CommandBar variable to the worksheet menu bar
                Set cbMainMenuBar = _
                    Application.CommandBars("Worksheet Menu Bar")

            '(3)Return the index number of the Help menu. We can then use _
                this to place a custom menu before it.
                iHelpMenu = _
                cbMainMenuBar.Controls("Help").Index

            '(4)Add a control to the "Worksheet Menu Bar" before Help.
            'Set a CommandBarControl variable to it
                Set cbcCutomMenu = _
                    cbMainMenuBar.Controls.Add(Type:=msoControlPopup, _
                                                Before:=iHelpMenu)

            '(5)Give the control a caption
              cbcCutomMenu.Caption = "&New Menu"

            '(6)Working with our new control, add a sub control and _
              give it a caption and tell it which macro to run (OnAction).
                With cbcCutomMenu.Controls.Add(Type:=msoControlButton)
                    .Caption = "Menu 1"
                    .OnAction = "MyMacro1"
                End With

            '(6a)Add another sub control and give it a caption _
              and tell it which macro to run (OnAction)
                With cbcCutomMenu.Controls.Add(Type:=msoControlButton)
                    .Caption = "Menu 2"
                    .OnAction = "MyMacro2"
                End With
            'Repeat step "6a" for each menu item you want to add.


            'Add another menu that will lead off to another menu
            'Set a CommandBarControl variable to it
             Set cbcCutomMenu = cbcCutomMenu.Controls.Add(Type:=msoControlPopup)
            ' Give the control a caption
             cbcCutomMenu.Caption = "Ne&xt Menu"

            'Add a control to the sub menu just created above
                With cbcCutomMenu.Controls.Add(Type:=msoControlButton)
                    .Caption = "&Charts"
                    .FaceId = 420
                    .OnAction = "MyMacro2"
                End With


        On Error GoTo 0
    End Sub

    Sub DeleteMenu()
        On Error Resume Next
```

```
        Application.CommandBars("Worksheet Menu Bar").Controls("&New Menu").
Delete
    On Error GoTo 0
End Sub
```

When using the OnAction property, it is possible that you may encounter
problems if there is a macro in the user's workbook that has the exact same
name as a macro that resides in your add-in. To play it safe, it is often a
good idea to use a method like this:

```
With cbcCutomMenu.Controls.Add(Type:=msoControlButton)
    .Caption = "&Charts"
    .FaceId = 420
    .OnAction = ThisWorkbook.Name & "!MyMacro2"
End With
```

By doing this, you ensure that Excel knows which macro you want run
when the user clicks the button. With these snippets of code, you'll find it
easy to distribute and use macros to their fullest potential.

CHAPTER EIGHT

Connecting Excel to the World
Hacks 95-100

Excel has long had connections to other members of the Microsoft Office family, as well as to databases. With the growth of the Web, Excel developed HTML export capabilities as well, making it easy to publish information created in Excel. Over the last few years, however, Microsoft has developed features that enable you to use Excel as an interface to information published anywhere, and to get your information out of Excel and into other forms—whatever forms you want, given whatever data you have. At the same time, a number of developers have created ways to get information into and out of Excel spreadsheets without using Excel, and these also have become important gateways.

HACK #95 Load an XML Document into Excel

If someone sends you an XML file containing data that fits into tables, you don't need to read the text and all its angle brackets. You can load the document into Excel directly, tell Excel how you want to present it, and work with the data through maps.

Extensible Markup Language (XML) has become a common interchange format over the past few years, and it's not unusual for people and organizations to send each other XML files. XML's simple core structures make it easy to exchange information with much less concern that all parties are using the same software. Until recently, however, although generic XML tools were widely available, bridging the gap between XML documents and the user interface was difficult. Excel 2003 makes it much easier, at least for data that fits on a grid.

This hack uses Excel features that are available only in Excel 2003 on Windows. Earlier versions of Excel do not support this, and neither do current or announced Macintosh versions of Excel.

We'll start with a sample XML document, shown in Example 8-1.

Example 8-1. A simple XML document for analysis in Excel

```
<?xml version="1.0" encoding="UTF-8"?>
<sales>

<sale>
<date>2003-10-05</date>
<ISBN>0596005385</ISBN>
<Title>Office 2003 XML Essentials</Title>
<PriceUS>34.95</PriceUS>
<quantity>200</quantity>
<customer ID="1025">Zork's Books</customer>
</sale>

<sale>
<date>2003-10-05</date>
<ISBN>0596002920</ISBN>
<Title>XML in a Nutshell, 2nd Edition</Title>
<PriceUS>39.95</PriceUS>
<quantity>90</quantity>
<customer ID="1025">Zork's Books</customer>
</sale>

<sale>
<date>2003-10-05</date>
<ISBN>0596002378</ISBN>
<Title>SAX2</Title>
<PriceUS>29.95</PriceUS>
<quantity>300</quantity>
<customer ID="1025">Zork's Books</customer>
</sale>

<sale>
<date>2003-10-05</date>
<ISBN>0596005385</ISBN>
<Title>Office 2003 XML Essentials</Title>
<PriceUS>34.95</PriceUS>
<quantity>10</quantity>
<customer ID="1029">Books of Glory</customer>
</sale>

<sale>
<date>2003-10-05</date>
<ISBN>0596002920</ISBN>
<Title>XML in a Nutshell, 2nd Edition</Title>
<PriceUS>39.95</PriceUS>
<quantity>25</quantity>
<customer ID="1029">Books of Glory</customer>
</sale>

<sale>
```

Example 8-1. A simple XML document for analysis in Excel (continued)

```
<date>2003-10-07</date>
<ISBN>0596002378</ISBN>
<Title>SAX2</Title>
<PriceUS>29.95</PriceUS>
<quantity>5</quantity>
<customer ID="1029">Books of Glory</customer>
</sale>

<sale>
<date>2003-10-18</date>
<ISBN>0596002378</ISBN>
<Title>SAX2</Title>
<PriceUS>29.95</PriceUS>
<quantity>15</quantity>
<customer ID="2561">Title Wave</customer>
</sale>

<sale>
<date>2003-10-21</date>
<ISBN>0596002920</ISBN>
<Title>XML in a Nutshell, 2nd Edition</Title>
<PriceUS>39.95</PriceUS>
<quantity>15</quantity>
<customer ID="9021">Books for You</customer>
</sale>

</sales>
```

You can open this directly from Excel 2003 by selecting File → Open.... The dialog box shown in Figure 8-1 will appear.

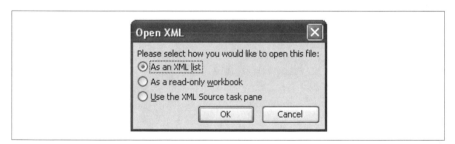

Figure 8-1. Opening an XML file in Excel 2003

If you select "As an XML list," you'll first be warned that Excel will be creating its own schema for this schema-free document, as shown in Figure 8-2. After clicking OK, you'll be rewarded with Excel's best guess as to how to present the information in the document as a spreadsheet, as shown in Figure 8-3.

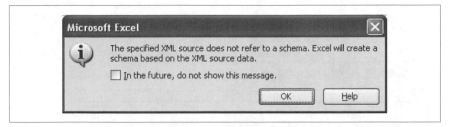

Figure 8-2. Excel 2003 warning about lack of schema references

Figure 8-3. XML data presented as an XML list in Excel 2003

Note that Excel expected the date format used by the date element, so it is now displaying dates imported as 2003-10-05 as 10/5/2003.

Once you have the document loaded into Excel, you can treat the data much like you would any other data in Excel—incorporating it into formulas, creating named ranges for it, making charts based on its contents, etc. To help you, Excel provides some built-in functionality for analyzing the data. The drop-down boxes in the column headers enable you to choose how to sort the data (the default is the order the document had originally). You also can turn on a total row, either from the List toolbar or by right-clicking anywhere on the list and selecting List → Total Row from the pop-up menu. Once the total row appears, you can choose what kind of total you prefer from the drop-down menu displayed in Figure 8-4.

You also can refresh the data, updating that area with information from an XML document with the same structure. If you had another document with the same structure, you could right-click the list, select XML → Import... from the pop-up menu, and choose a different document. With more data, it might look like Figure 8-5.

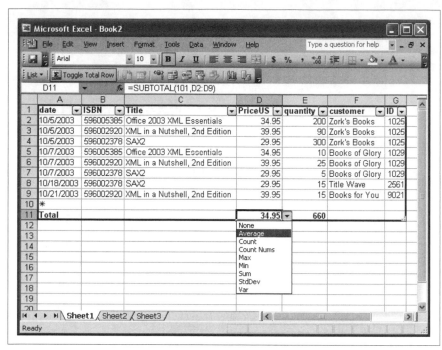

Figure 8-4. Choosing totals for an XML list in Excel 2003

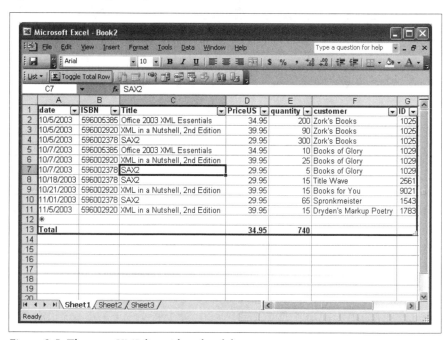

Figure 8-5. The same XML list with updated data

In addition, you can export the data back to an XML file after editing it by right-clicking the list and selecting XML → Export... from the pop-up menu. This makes Excel a very convenient editing tool for simple XML documents with tabular structures.

For simple data, you can usually trust Excel to guess what a file's contents are and use the default view it provides. As data gets more complicated, however, especially if it contains dates or text that looks like numbers (note the missing initial zeros on the ISBNs in the preceding figures!), you might want to use XML schemas to constrain how Excel reads your data and what kinds of data will fit in a given map. For this document, an XML schema might look like Example 8-2.

Example 8-2. A schema for the book sales data

```
<?xml version="1.0" encoding="UTF-8"?>
<xs:schema xmlns:xs="http://www.w3.org/2001/XMLSchema"
elementFormDefault="qualified">
  <xs:element name="sales">
    <xs:complexType>
      <xs:sequence>
        <xs:element maxOccurs="unbounded" ref="sale"/>
      </xs:sequence>
    </xs:complexType>
  </xs:element>
  <xs:element name="sale">
    <xs:complexType>
      <xs:sequence>
        <xs:element ref="date"/>
        <xs:element ref="ISBN"/>
        <xs:element ref="Title"/>
        <xs:element ref="PriceUS"/>
        <xs:element ref="quantity"/>
        <xs:element ref="customer"/>
      </xs:sequence>
    </xs:complexType>
  </xs:element>
  <xs:element name="date" type="xs:date"/>
  <xs:element name="ISBN" type="xs:string"/>
  <xs:element name="Title" type="xs:string"/>
  <xs:element name="PriceUS" type="xs:decimal"/>
  <xs:element name="quantity" type="xs:integer"/>
  <xs:element name="customer">
    <xs:complexType mixed="true">
      <xs:attribute name="ID" use="required" type="xs:integer"/>
    </xs:complexType>
  </xs:element>
</xs:schema>
```

Note that the date element is defined as a date, and the ISBN element is defined as a string here, not an integer. If you start by opening this schema rather than the document, you can have Excel load the document while preserving the initial zero on the ISBNs. This time, you'll create a list before loading the XML document, starting from a blank worksheet.

You'll need to open the XML Source task pane. If the task pane isn't open already, open it by selecting View → Task Pane or by pressing Control-F1. Then select XML Source from the drop-down box at the top of the task pane, and you'll see something such as that shown in Figure 8-6.

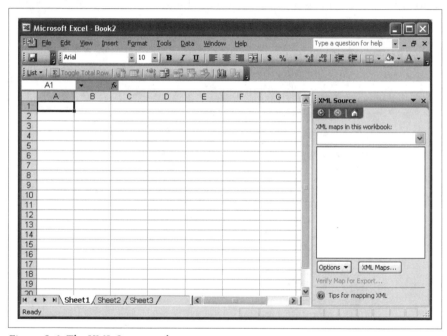

Figure 8-6. The XML Source task pane

To load the schema, click the XML Maps... button. This will bring up the XML Maps dialog box, shown in Figure 8-7.

Click the Add... button to open the schema, and select the schema as shown in Figure 8-8.

If your schema doesn't restrict documents to having only one possible starting element, Excel will ask you which element to use as the root element, as shown in Figure 8-9. Because the documents in this example start with the sales element, pick "sales."

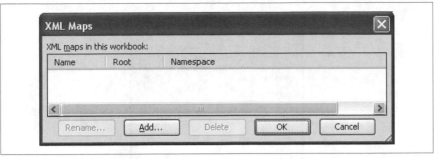

Figure 8-7. The XML Maps dialog box

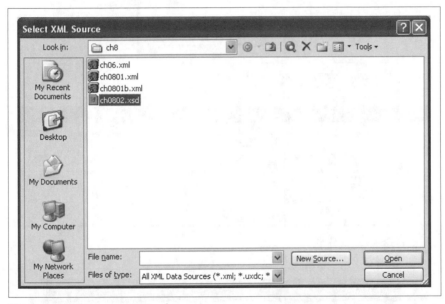

Figure 8-8. Selecting an XML schema

After you click OK, Excel warns about possible difficulties it might have in interpreting schemas in the dialog box shown in Figure 8-10. XML Schema is an enormous specification that supports a wide variety of structures that don't fit well with Excel's perspective on information, so Excel has some limitations.

Excel will show that your schema has been added to the spreadsheet in the XML Maps dialog, which should look like that shown in Figure 8-11.

If you click OK, you'll be returned to the main Excel interface, and the XML Source task pane will be populated with a diagram of the structure the schema described, such as that shown at the right of Figure 8-12. Now that you have the structure, you can lay out the list. The easiest way to do this—

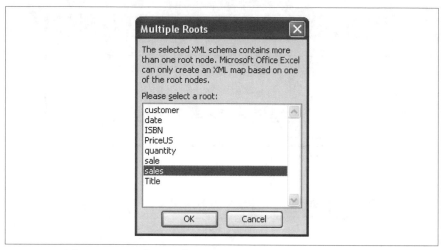

Figure 8-9. Selecting a root element for the schema

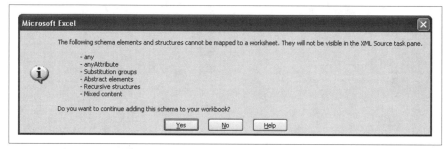

Figure 8-10. Warning label for schema processing

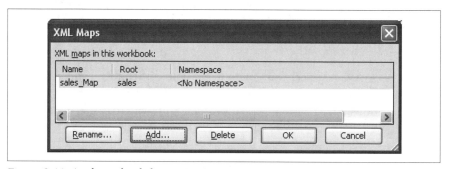

Figure 8-11. A schema loaded as an XML map

especially with a small document such as this one—is to drag the sales icon to cell A1, producing the result in Figure 8-12.

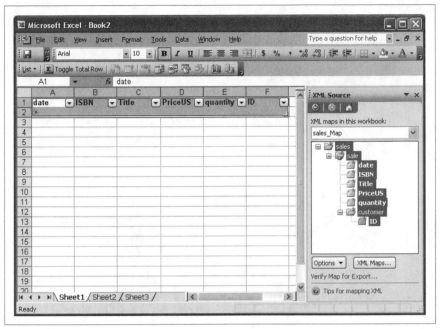

Figure 8-12. An XML list created from the schema information in the XML Source task pane

 You also can drag items over individually, if you want to change the order or want to put different pieces in different places on the spreadsheet.

Now that you have a home for the data, it's time to populate it. You can either click the Import XML Data button on the list toolbar, or right-click the list and select XML → Import. If you choose the file you used earlier (Example 8-1), you'll see a result such as that shown in Figure 8-13. Note the addition of the leading zeros to the ISBNs, which are now text, as they should be.

Excel's support for XML maps and lists means you can create spreadsheets that work on data arriving in separate files with more flexibility than prior formats such as CSV or tab-delimited formats provided. Instead of having to be connected to a database to edit data interactively, a user can edit XML files while on an airplane and feed that XML to an appropriate consumer when he lands. Perhaps the best aspect of Excel's new XML features is their flexibility; so long as the data is in a structure that fits on a grid, Excel has very few rules about what kinds of XML it will accept. With a few mouse clicks and no programming, you can integrate XML data with your spreadsheets.

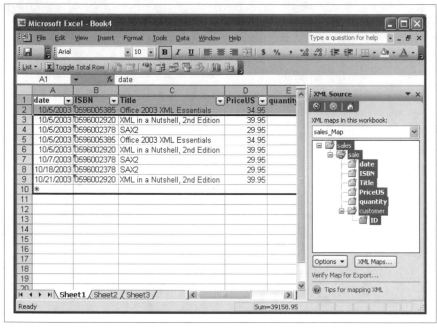

Figure 8-13. The XML list, populated with data

—*Simon St.Laurent*

HACK #96 Save to SpreadsheetML and Extracting Data

Since Excel XP, Excel has included an XML export option. SpreadsheetML provides an XML representation of your spreadsheets, complete with formatting and formula information.

Although there are several ways to read Excel spreadsheet files without using Excel (see "Create Excel Spreadsheets Using Other Environments" [Hack #100] for details), one of the easiest options is to export XML files that use Microsoft's SpreadsheetML vocabulary. SpreadsheetML isn't complete—most notably, charts and VBA code are omitted—but it does represent the core components of a spreadsheet, including formulas, named ranges, and formatting.

> This hack uses Excel features that are available only in Excel XP and Excel 2003 on Windows. Earlier versions of Excel do not support this, and neither do current or announced Macintosh versions of Excel.

The easiest way to get started with SpreadsheetML is to save a spreadsheet as XML. The spreadsheet shown in Figure 8-14 includes data, formulas, named ranges and cells, and some simple formatting.

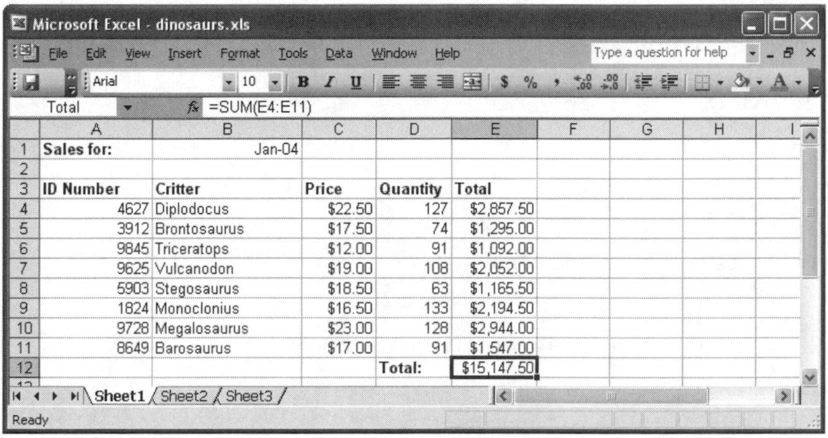

Figure 8-14. A test spreadsheet for SpreadsheetML

If you save the spreadsheet using the XML Spreadsheet (*.xml) format, which you can access by selecting File → Save As..., you'll get a long XML document containing the markup shown in Example 8-3. Key portions are highlighted in bold.

Example 8-3. A SpreadsheetML document

```
<?xml version="1.0"?>
<?mso-application progid="Excel.Sheet"?>
<Workbook xmlns="urn:schemas-microsoft-com:office:spreadsheet"
 xmlns:o="urn:schemas-microsoft-com:office:office"
 xmlns:x="urn:schemas-microsoft-com:office:excel"
 xmlns:ss="urn:schemas-microsoft-com:office:spreadsheet"
 xmlns:html="http://www.w3.org/TR/REC-html40">
 <DocumentProperties xmlns="urn:schemas-microsoft-com:office:office">
  <Author>Simon St.Laurent</Author>
  <LastAuthor>Simon St.Laurent</LastAuthor>
  <Created>2003-12-03T15:48:38Z</Created>
  <LastSaved>2004-01-26T21:04:14Z</LastSaved>
  <Company>O'Reilly &amp; Associates</Company>
  <Version>11.5703</Version>
 </DocumentProperties>
 <ExcelWorkbook xmlns="urn:schemas-microsoft-com:office:excel">
  <WindowHeight>6150</WindowHeight>
  <WindowWidth>8475</WindowWidth>
  <WindowTopX>120</WindowTopX>
  <WindowTopY>30</WindowTopY>
```

Example 8-3. A SpreadsheetML document (continued)

```
      <ProtectStructure>False</ProtectStructure>
      <ProtectWindows>False</ProtectWindows>
     </ExcelWorkbook>
     <Styles>
      <Style ss:ID="Default" ss:Name="Normal">
       <Alignment ss:Vertical="Bottom"/>
       <Borders/>
       <Font/>
       <Interior/>
       <NumberFormat/>
       <Protection/>
      </Style>
      <Style ss:ID="s21">
       <NumberFormat ss:Format="mmm\-yy"/>
      </Style>
      <Style ss:ID="s22">
       <NumberFormat ss:Format="&quot;$&quot;#,##0.00"/>
      </Style>
      <Style ss:ID="s23">
       <Font x:Family="Swiss" ss:Bold="1"/>
      </Style>
     </Styles>
     <Names>
      <NamedRange ss:Name="Critters" ss:RefersTo="=Sheet1!R4C2:R11C2"/>
      <NamedRange ss:Name="Date" ss:RefersTo="=Sheet1!R1C2"/>
      <NamedRange ss:Name="ID" ss:RefersTo="=Sheet1!R4C1:R11C1"/>
      <NamedRange ss:Name="Price" ss:RefersTo="=Sheet1!R4C3:R11C3"/>
      <NamedRange ss:Name="Quantity" ss:RefersTo="=Sheet1!R4C4:R11C4"/>
      <NamedRange ss:Name="Total" ss:RefersTo="=Sheet1!R12C5"/>
     </Names>
     <Worksheet ss:Name="Sheet1">
      <Table ss:ExpandedColumnCount="5" ss:ExpandedRowCount="12" x:FullColumns="1"
       x:FullRows="1">
       <Column ss:AutoFitWidth="0" ss:Width="73.5"/>
       <Column ss:AutoFitWidth="0" ss:Width="96.75"/>
       <Column ss:Index="5" ss:AutoFitWidth="0" ss:Width="56.25"/>
       <Row>
        <Cell ss:StyleID="s23"><Data ss:Type="String">Sales for:</Data></Cell>
        <Cell ss:StyleID="s21"><Data ss:Type="DateTime">2004-01-01T00:00:00.000</
     Data><NamedCell
         ss:Name="Date"/></Cell>
       </Row>
       <Row ss:Index="3" ss:StyleID="s23">
        <Cell><Data ss:Type="String">ID Number</Data></Cell>
        <Cell><Data ss:Type="String">Critter</Data></Cell>
        <Cell><Data ss:Type="String">Price</Data></Cell>
        <Cell><Data ss:Type="String">Quantity</Data></Cell>
        <Cell><Data ss:Type="String">Total</Data></Cell>
       </Row>
       <Row>
        <Cell><Data ss:Type="Number">4627</Data><NamedCell ss:Name="ID"/></Cell>
```

Example 8-3. A SpreadsheetML document (continued)

```
    <Cell><Data ss:Type="String">Diplodocus</Data><NamedCell ss:
Name="Critters"/></Cell>
    <Cell ss:StyleID="s22"><Data ss:Type="Number">22.5</Data><NamedCell
      ss:Name="Price"/></Cell>
    <Cell><Data ss:Type="Number">127</Data><NamedCell ss:Name="Quantity"/></
Cell>
    <Cell ss:StyleID="s22" ss:Formula="=RC[-2]*RC[-1]"><Data ss:Type="Number">
2857.5</Data></Cell>
    </Row>
    <Row>
    <Cell><Data ss:Type="Number">3912</Data><NamedCell ss:Name="ID"/></Cell>
    <Cell><Data ss:Type="String">Brontosaurus</Data><NamedCell ss:
Name="Critters"/></Cell>
    <Cell ss:StyleID="s22"><Data ss:Type="Number">17.5</Data><NamedCell
      ss:Name="Price"/></Cell>
    <Cell><Data ss:Type="Number">74</Data><NamedCell ss:Name="Quantity"/></
Cell>
    <Cell ss:StyleID="s22" ss:Formula="=RC[-2]*RC[-1]"><Data ss:Type="Number">
1295</Data></Cell>
    </Row>
    <Row>
    <Cell><Data ss:Type="Number">9845</Data><NamedCell ss:Name="ID"/></Cell>
    <Cell><Data ss:Type="String">Triceratops</Data><NamedCell ss:
Name="Critters"/></Cell>
    <Cell ss:StyleID="s22"><Data ss:Type="Number">12</Data><NamedCell
      ss:Name="Price"/></Cell>
    <Cell><Data ss:Type="Number">91</Data><NamedCell ss:Name="Quantity"/></
Cell>
    <Cell ss:StyleID="s22" ss:Formula="=RC[-2]*RC[-1]"><Data ss:Type="Number">
1092</Data></Cell>
    </Row>
    <Row>
    <Cell><Data ss:Type="Number">9625</Data><NamedCell ss:Name="ID"/></Cell>
    <Cell><Data ss:Type="String">Vulcanodon</Data><NamedCell ss:
Name="Critters"/></Cell>
    <Cell ss:StyleID="s22"><Data ss:Type="Number">19</Data><NamedCell
      ss:Name="Price"/></Cell>
    <Cell><Data ss:Type="Number">108</Data><NamedCell ss:Name="Quantity"/></
Cell>
    <Cell ss:StyleID="s22" ss:Formula="=RC[-2]*RC[-1]"><Data ss:Type="Number">
2052</Data></Cell>
    </Row>
    <Row>
    <Cell><Data ss:Type="Number">5903</Data><NamedCell ss:Name="ID"/></Cell>
    <Cell><Data ss:Type="String">Stegosaurus</Data><NamedCell ss:
Name="Critters"/></Cell>
    <Cell ss:StyleID="s22"><Data ss:Type="Number">18.5</Data><NamedCell
      ss:Name="Price"/></Cell>
    <Cell><Data ss:Type="Number">63</Data><NamedCell ss:Name="Quantity"/></
Cell>
```

Example 8-3. A SpreadsheetML document (continued)

```
     <Cell ss:StyleID="s22" ss:Formula="=RC[-2]*RC[-1]"><Data ss:Type="Number">
1165.5</Data></Cell>
    </Row>
    <Row>
    <Cell><Data ss:Type="Number">1824</Data><NamedCell ss:Name="ID"/></Cell>
    <Cell><Data ss:Type="String">Monoclonius</Data><NamedCell ss:
Name="Critters"/></Cell>
     <Cell ss:StyleID="s22"><Data ss:Type="Number">16.5</Data><NamedCell
       ss:Name="Price"/></Cell>
     <Cell><Data ss:Type="Number">133</Data><NamedCell ss:Name="Quantity"/></
Cell>
     <Cell ss:StyleID="s22" ss:Formula="=RC[-2]*RC[-1]"><Data ss:Type="Number">
2194.5</Data></Cell>
    </Row>
    <Row>
    <Cell><Data ss:Type="Number">9728</Data><NamedCell ss:Name="ID"/></Cell>
    <Cell><Data ss:Type="String">Megalosaurus</Data><NamedCell ss:
Name="Critters"/></Cell>
     <Cell ss:StyleID="s22"><Data ss:Type="Number">23</Data><NamedCell
       ss:Name="Price"/></Cell>
     <Cell><Data ss:Type="Number">128</Data><NamedCell ss:Name="Quantity"/></
Cell>
     <Cell ss:StyleID="s22" ss:Formula="=RC[-2]*RC[-1]"><Data ss:Type="Number">
2944</Data></Cell>
    </Row>
    <Row>
    <Cell><Data ss:Type="Number">8649</Data><NamedCell ss:Name="ID"/></Cell>
    <Cell><Data ss:Type="String">Barosaurus</Data><NamedCell ss:
Name="Critters"/></Cell>
     <Cell ss:StyleID="s22"><Data ss:Type="Number">17</Data><NamedCell
       ss:Name="Price"/></Cell>
     <Cell><Data ss:Type="Number">91</Data><NamedCell ss:Name="Quantity"/></
Cell>
     <Cell ss:StyleID="s22" ss:Formula="=RC[-2]*RC[-1]"><Data ss:Type="Number">
1547</Data></Cell>
    </Row>
    <Row>
    <Cell ss:Index="4" ss:StyleID="s23"><Data ss:Type="String">Total:</Data></
Cell>
    <Cell ss:StyleID="s22" ss:Formula="=SUM(R[-8]C:R[-1]C)"><Data ss:
Type="Number">15147.5</Data><NamedCell
       ss:Name="Total"/></Cell>
    </Row>
   </Table>
   <WorksheetOptions xmlns="urn:schemas-microsoft-com:office:excel">
    <Print>
    <ValidPrinterInfo/>
    <HorizontalResolution>600</HorizontalResolution>
    <VerticalResolution>600</VerticalResolution>
    </Print>
    <Selected/>
    <Panes>
```

Example 8-3. A SpreadsheetML document (continued)

```
        <Pane>
         <Number>3</Number>
         <ActiveRow>11</ActiveRow>
         <ActiveCol>4</ActiveCol>
        </Pane>
       </Panes>
       <ProtectObjects>False</ProtectObjects>
       <ProtectScenarios>False</ProtectScenarios>
      </WorksheetOptions>
     </Worksheet>
     <Worksheet ss:Name="Sheet2">
      <WorksheetOptions xmlns="urn:schemas-microsoft-com:office:excel">
       <ProtectObjects>False</ProtectObjects>
       <ProtectScenarios>False</ProtectScenarios>
      </WorksheetOptions>
     </Worksheet>
     <Worksheet ss:Name="Sheet3">
      <WorksheetOptions xmlns="urn:schemas-microsoft-com:office:excel">
       <ProtectObjects>False</ProtectObjects>
       <ProtectScenarios>False</ProtectScenarios>
      </WorksheetOptions>
     </Worksheet>
    </Workbook>
```

The first highlighted line, `<?mso-application progid="Excel.Sheet"?>`, is an XML processing instruction that tells Windows (actually a component Office 2003 adds to Windows) that this XML document is, in fact, an Excel spreadsheet. When Windows displays the file, it will have an Excel logo on it, and double-clicking it will open it in Excel.

The root element of the document, `Worksheet`, appears immediately after the processing instruction. Its attributes define namespaces used for various pieces of SpreadsheetML. The next few lines comprise mostly metadata, window presentation, and formatting information, and it isn't until you get to the `Names` and `Worksheet` elements that there's much worth examining closely.

The `Names` element identifies the named ranges and cells in the document. These two `NamedRange` elements define the `Quantity` named range—which extends from row 4, column 4, to row 11, column 4—and the Total named range, which is just the cell in row 12 of column 5:

```
<NamedRange ss:Name="Quantity" ss:RefersTo="=Sheet1!R4C4:R11C4"/>
<NamedRange ss:Name="Total" ss:RefersTo="=Sheet1!R12C5"/>
```

The meat of the spreadsheet is in the `Worksheet` element. It starts out by defining how large the actual table of data is:

```
<Worksheet ss:Name="Sheet1">
 <Table ss:ExpandedColumnCount="5" ss:ExpandedRowCount="12" x:
FullColumns="1"
  x:FullRows="1">
```

This sheet, named Sheet1, used 5 columns and 12 rows. (The x:FullColumns and x:FullRows attributes are in another namespace that Excel won't use for layout.) The actual information in the table is stored in Row and Cell elements:

```
<Row>
  <Cell ss:StyleID="s23"><Data ss:Type="String">Sales for:</Data></Cell>
  <Cell ss:StyleID="s21"><Data ss:Type="DateTime">2004-01-01T00:00:00.
000</Data><NamedCell
     ss:Name="Date"/></Cell>
</Row>
<Row ss:Index="3" ss:StyleID="s23">
  <Cell><Data ss:Type="String">ID Number</Data></Cell>
```

This Row, the first in the spreadsheet, contains two Cell elements. The first, formatted as s23 (bold, in this spreadsheet) and using the datatype String, contains the text "Sales for:". The second cell is formatted as s21 (plain) and uses the datatype DateTime. Its contents are given in a verbose ISO 8601 format. This cell also is part of a named range, in this case, "Date".

Most of the other Row elements follow similar patterns, but there are a few items worth extra attention. The second Row element has an extra attribute on it, ss:Index:

```
<Row ss:Index="3" ss:StyleID="s23">
```

Excel doesn't represent empty rows or empty columns with empty Row or Cell elements. It just adds an ss:Index attribute to the next Row or Cell with content to tell you where you are. This requires programs that process this XML to pay a little more attention when assembling their tables. The other thing to watch is formulas:

```
<Cell ss:StyleID="s22" ss:Formula="=SUM(R[-8]C:R[-1]C)"><Data ss:
Type="Number">15147.5</Data><NamedCell
     ss:Name="Total"/></Cell>
```

In Figure 8-15, this cell had a name of Total, a value of $15,147.50, and a formula of =SUM(E4:E11). All of those parts are here. But you must assemble them from the style of s22 (defined earlier in the document as a monetary number format), the value 15147.5, and a formula that uses relative references to say "the sum of the values in the same column as this one from 8 rows up to 1 row up."

This might not seem like much fun to process, but it's actually not that hard to do once you have an XML toolkit. You can use C#, Java, Perl, Python, VB, or your favorite XML-enabled programming language to extract the information, but we'll use XSLT to demonstrate.

There are many choices of XSLT processors out there, from command-line tools to Windows applications. You might want to try Architags XRay, available from *http://architag.com/xray/*, or Michael Kay's SAXON, at *http://saxon.sourceforge.net/*. Microsoft offers various XSLT tools, including a command-line tool, at *http://msdn.microsoft.com/library/default.asp?url=/downloads/list/xmlgeneral.asp*. If this is intriguing enough that you want to learn XSLT, you might try Mike Fitzgerald's *Learning XSLT* (O'Reilly).

The stylesheet in Example 8-4, run against the XML in Example 8-3, will produce the much simpler XML in Example 8-5.

Example 8-4. An XSLT stylesheet for extracting content from the SpreadsheetML in Example 8-3

```
<xsl:stylesheet version="1.0"
  xmlns:xsl="http://www.w3.org/1999/XSL/Transform"
  xmlns="http://simonstl.com/ns/dinosaurs/"
  xmlns:ss="urn:schemas-microsoft-com:office:spreadsheet"
 >

<xsl:output method="xml" omit-xml-declaration="yes" indent="yes" encoding="US-
ASCII"/>

<xsl:template match="/">
  <xsl:apply-templates select="ss:Workbook"/>
</xsl:template>

<xsl:template match="ss:Workbook">
  <dinosaurs>
      <xsl:apply-templates select="ss:Worksheet[@ss:Name = 'Sheet1']"/>
  </dinosaurs>
</xsl:template>

<xsl:template match="ss:Worksheet">
  <date><xsl:value-of select="ss:Table/ss:Row/ss:Cell[@ss:StyleID = 's21']" /
></date>
  <xsl:apply-templates select="ss:Table" />
</xsl:template>

<xsl:template match="ss:Table">
  <xsl:apply-templates select="ss:Row[position() &gt; 2]" />
<!--Note that because Excel skips the blank row, the third row is in position
2-->
</xsl:template>

<xsl:template match="ss:Row[ss:Cell[4]]">
<sale>
  <IDnum><xsl:apply-templates select="ss:Cell[1]" /></IDnum>
```

Example 8-4. An XSLT stylesheet for extracting content from the SpreadsheetML in Example 8-3 (continued)

```
        <critter><xsl:apply-templates select="ss:Cell[2]" /></critter>
        <price><xsl:apply-templates select="ss:Cell[3]" /></price>
        <quantity><xsl:apply-templates select="ss:Cell[4]" /></quantity>
        <total><xsl:apply-templates select="ss:Cell[5]" /></total>
    </sale>
    </xsl:template>

    <xsl:template match="ss:Row">
    <total><xsl:apply-templates select="ss:Cell[2]" /></total>
    </xsl:template>

    </xsl:stylesheet>
```

The heart of the stylesheet is the template that matches all rows with four or more child cell elements. It extracts the information from the cells and puts it into XML elements that reflect the data, producing the result shown in Example 8-5.

Example 8-5. Information extracted from SpreadsheetML to a custom XML vocabulary

```
<dinosaurs xmlns="http://simonstl.com/ns/dinosaurs/" xmlns:ss="urn:schemas-
microsoft-com:office:spreadsheet">
<date>2004-01-01T00:00:00.000</date>
<sale>
<IDnum>4627</IDnum>
<critter>Diplodocus</critter>
<price>22.5</price>
<quantity>127</quantity>
<total>2857.5</total>
</sale>
<sale>
<IDnum>3912</IDnum>
<critter>Brontosaurus</critter>
<price>17.5</price>
<quantity>74</quantity>
<total>1295</total>
</sale>
<sale>
<IDnum>9845</IDnum>
<critter>Triceratops</critter>
<price>12</price>
<quantity>91</quantity>
<total>1092</total>
</sale>
<sale>
<IDnum>9625</IDnum>
<critter>Vulcanodon</critter>
<price>19</price>
```

Example 8-5. Information extracted from SpreadsheetML to a custom XML vocabulary (continued)

```
<quantity>108</quantity>
<total>2052</total>
</sale>
<sale>
<IDnum>5903</IDnum>
<critter>Stegosaurus</critter>
<price>18.5</price>
<quantity>63</quantity>
<total>1165.5</total>
</sale>
<sale>
<IDnum>1824</IDnum>
<critter>Monoclonius</critter>
<price>16.5</price>
<quantity>133</quantity>
<total>2194.5</total>
</sale>
<sale>
<IDnum>9728</IDnum>
<critter>Megalosaurus</critter>
<price>23</price>
<quantity>128</quantity>
<total>2944</total>
</sale>
<sale>
<IDnum>8649</IDnum>
<critter>Barosaurus</critter>
<price>17</price>
<quantity>91</quantity>
<total>1547</total>
</sale>
<total>15147.5</total>
</dinosaurs>
```

It's the same data, but in a very different form. The formula information has been discarded in this case, but because Excel provides the values as well as the formulas, this particular application didn't need to understand the formulas.

HACK #97 Create Spreadsheets using SpreadsheetML

While exporting spreadsheets as XML is useful, Excel also lets you import information this way, letting you create spreadsheets using SpreadsheetML.

Excel supports SpreadsheetML for both import and export, providing a complete pathway for information. You can open a SpreadsheetML document, make a few changes, and re-open it in Excel if you want. (This is the only way to edit the schemas for XML Maps, for instance.) Perhaps more importantly, though, you can generate SpreadsheetML documents from whatever data you happen to have, providing a relatively easy and automatable path for transforming raw information into Excel spreadsheets.

To demonstrate, the code in Example 8-6 will transform the XML shown in Example 8-5 of the previous hack back into Excel again using XSLT. The stylesheet in Example 8-6 uses the original spreadsheet as a template, and will produce XML very much like the SpreadsheetML you saved from Excel originally. The example leaves out some formatting so that there's a visible difference.

> This hack uses Excel features that are available only in Excel XP and Excel 2003 on Windows. Earlier versions of Excel do not support this, and neither do current or announced Macintosh versions of Excel.

Example 8-6. XSLT for converting the custom XML vocabulary back to SpreadsheetML

```
<xsl:stylesheet version="1.0"
  xmlns:xsl="http://www.w3.org/1999/XSL/Transform"
  xmlns:d="http://simonstl.com/ns/dinosaurs/"
  xmlns:ss="urn:schemas-microsoft-com:office:spreadsheet"
  xmlns="urn:schemas-microsoft-com:office:spreadsheet"
 >

<xsl:output method="xml" omit-xml-declaration="no" indent="yes" encoding="US-ASCII"/>

<xsl:template match="/">
  <xsl:apply-templates select="d:dinosaurs" />
</xsl:template>

<xsl:template match="d:dinosaurs">

<xsl:processing-instruction name="mso-application">progid="Excel.Sheet"</xsl:processing-instruction>
<Workbook xmlns="urn:schemas-microsoft-com:office:spreadsheet"
  xmlns:o="urn:schemas-microsoft-com:office:office"
  xmlns:x="urn:schemas-microsoft-com:office:excel"
  xmlns:ss="urn:schemas-microsoft-com:office:spreadsheet"
  xmlns:html="http://www.w3.org/TR/REC-html40">
  <DocumentProperties xmlns="urn:schemas-microsoft-com:office:office">
   <Author>Simon St.Laurent</Author>
   <LastAuthor>Simon St.Laurent</LastAuthor>
   <Created>2003-12-03T15:48:38Z</Created>
   <LastSaved>2003-12-03T15:57:46Z</LastSaved>
   <Company>O'Reilly &amp; Associates</Company>
   <Version>11.5606</Version>
  </DocumentProperties>
```

Example 8-6. XSLT for converting the custom XML vocabulary back to SpreadsheetML (continued)

```
<ExcelWorkbook xmlns="urn:schemas-microsoft-com:office:excel">
 <WindowHeight>6150</WindowHeight>
 <WindowWidth>8475</WindowWidth>
 <WindowTopX>120</WindowTopX>
 <WindowTopY>30</WindowTopY>
 <ProtectStructure>False</ProtectStructure>
 <ProtectWindows>False</ProtectWindows>
</ExcelWorkbook>
<Styles>
 <Style ss:ID="Default" ss:Name="Normal">
  <Alignment ss:Vertical="Bottom"/>
  <Borders/>
  <Font/>
  <Interior/>
  <NumberFormat/>
  <Protection/>
 </Style>
 <Style ss:ID="s21">
  <NumberFormat ss:Format="mmm\-yy"/>
 </Style>
 <Style ss:ID="s22">
  <NumberFormat ss:Format="&quot;$&quot;#,##0.00"/>
 </Style>
</Styles>
<Worksheet ss:Name="Sheet1">
 <Table ss:ExpandedColumnCount="5" ss:ExpandedRowCount="{count(d:sale)+4}" x:
FullColumns="1"
  x:FullRows="1">
  <Column ss:AutoFitWidth="0" ss:Width="73.5"/>
  <Column ss:AutoFitWidth="0" ss:Width="96.75"/>
  <Column ss:Index="5" ss:AutoFitWidth="0" ss:Width="56.25"/>
  <Row>
   <Cell><Data ss:Type="String">Sales for:</Data></Cell>
   <Cell ss:StyleID="s21"><Data ss:Type="DateTime"><xsl:value-of select="d:
date"/></Data></Cell>
  </Row>
  <Row ss:Index="3">
   <Cell><Data ss:Type="String">ID Number</Data></Cell>
   <Cell><Data ss:Type="String">Critter</Data></Cell>
   <Cell><Data ss:Type="String">Price</Data></Cell>
   <Cell><Data ss:Type="String">Quantity</Data></Cell>
   <Cell><Data ss:Type="String">Total</Data></Cell>
  </Row>

<xsl:apply-templates select="d:sale" />

  <Row>
   <Cell ss:Index="4"><Data ss:Type="String">Total:</Data></Cell>
   <Cell ss:StyleID="s22" ss:Formula="=SUM(R[-{count(d:sale)}]C:R[-1]C)">
<Data ss:Type="Number"></Data></Cell>
```

Example 8-6. XSLT for converting the custom XML vocabulary back to SpreadsheetML (continued)

```
      </Row>
     </Table>
     <WorksheetOptions xmlns="urn:schemas-microsoft-com:office:excel">
      <Print>
       <ValidPrinterInfo/>
       <HorizontalResolution>600</HorizontalResolution>
       <VerticalResolution>600</VerticalResolution>
      </Print>
      <Selected/>
      <Panes>
       <Pane>
        <Number>3</Number>
        <ActiveRow>12</ActiveRow>
        <ActiveCol>1</ActiveCol>
       </Pane>
      </Panes>
      <ProtectObjects>False</ProtectObjects>
      <ProtectScenarios>False</ProtectScenarios>
     </WorksheetOptions>
    </Worksheet>
    <Worksheet ss:Name="Sheet2">
     <WorksheetOptions xmlns="urn:schemas-microsoft-com:office:excel">
      <ProtectObjects>False</ProtectObjects>
      <ProtectScenarios>False</ProtectScenarios>
     </WorksheetOptions>
    </Worksheet>
    <Worksheet ss:Name="Sheet3">
     <WorksheetOptions xmlns="urn:schemas-microsoft-com:office:excel">
      <ProtectObjects>False</ProtectObjects>
      <ProtectScenarios>False</ProtectScenarios>
     </WorksheetOptions>
    </Worksheet>
   </Workbook>
  </xsl:template>

  <xsl:template match="d:sale">
    <Row>
     <Cell><Data ss:Type="Number"><xsl:value-of select="d:IDnum" /></Data>
<NamedCell ss:Name="ID"/></Cell>
     <Cell><Data ss:Type="String"><xsl:value-of select="d:critter" /></Data>
<NamedCell ss:Name="Critters"/></Cell>
     <Cell ss:StyleID="s22"><Data ss:Type="Number"><xsl:value-of select="d:
price" /></Data><NamedCell
        ss:Name="Price"/></Cell>
     <Cell><Data ss:Type="Number"><xsl:value-of select="d:quantity" /></Data>
<NamedCell ss:Name="Quantity"/></Cell>
     <Cell ss:StyleID="s22" ss:Formula="=RC[-2]*RC[-1]"><Data ss:Type="Number">
<xsl:value-of select="d:total" /></Data></Cell>
    </Row>
  </xsl:template>
```

*Example 8-6. XSLT for converting the custom XML vocabulary back
to SpreadsheetML (continued)*

```
<xsl:template match="d:date" />
<xsl:template match="d:total" />

</xsl:stylesheet>
```

A few pieces of this example are worth special attention. First, note that the SpreadsheetML is wrapped in XSLT; the SpreadsheetML becomes part of the stylesheet. There's one piece of the SpreadsheetML you can't re-create with this method: the processing instruction noted earlier that tells Windows this is an Excel spreadsheet. For that, you have to use the following:

```
<xsl:processing-instruction name="mso-application">progid=⌐
    "Excel.Sheet"</xsl:processing-instruction>
```

Because XSLT won't allow you to use the default namespace (no prefix) to refer to content that has a namespace, all the references to content in the source document now have the prefix `d:`, such as `d:sale`, `d:date`, etc.

Also, because the named ranges will vary depending on the number of `sale` elements in the original, this stylesheet won't generate the `Names` element and its contents. Excel will re-create the named ranges from the `NamedCell` elements in any case. The heart of this stylesheet is again the part that generates the `Row` and `Cell` elements, as shown in the following:

```
<xsl:template match="d:sale">
  <Row>
    <Cell><Data ss:Type="Number"><xsl:value-of select="d:IDnum" /></Data>
<NamedCell ss:Name="ID"/></Cell>
```

The `xsl:template` element will collect every `sale` element in the original and produce a `Row` element that contains `Cell` elements matching its contents. If you open in Excel the SpreadsheetML that this stylesheet produces (which looks much like that in Example 8-3, minus named ranges and some formatting), you get the result shown in Figure 8-15.

SpreadsheetML might not look very beautiful, but there are lots of reasons you might want to use it. For one, saving as SpreadsheetML gives you better access to the XML map information described in the previous hack than Excel's GUI offers at present. More importantly in the long run, SpreadsheetML is portable, and you can process it and generate it on virtually any computer that has basic XML facilities.

—*Simon St.Laurent*

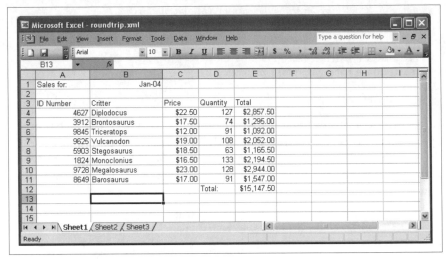

Figure 8-15. The test spreadsheet after its data has gone from SpreadsheetML to another vocabulary and back again

Import Data Directly into Excel

#98 Using Amazon's Web Services as a source of data, you can easily integrate live information about books into Excel spreadsheets. This example imports sales rank data for particular books and calculates the average rank.

This hack relies on Excel's ability to perform *web queries*, so you'll need Excel 97 or higher. Excel's Web Queries tool transforms simple HTML tables into Excel spreadsheets.

> To make this work, you'll need to sign up with Amazon and get an associate tag. To do this, visit *http://www.amazon. com/associates/*. Then you'll need to go to *http://amazon.com/ webservices/* and click on "Apply for a free developer's token". Both of these pieces are required to use Amazon's web services.

This code uses several features of both Amazon Web Services and Excel. Once you see how it's put together, building your own queries is a snap.

This hack starts with a standard XML/HTTP query. We want to analyze sales ranks of O'Reilly's Hacks series, so we build a standard query to retrieve those results.

```
http://xml.amazon.com/onca/xml3?t=insert associate tag ↵
&dev-t=insert developer token&PowerSearch=publisher:O'Reilly ↵
%20and%20keywords:Hack&type=heavy&mode=books&f=xml
```

This request uses an Amazon Power Search to specify a publisher (O'Reilly) and a keyword (Hack).

The next task is to get the Amazon response data into a form that Excel can work with. Because Excel Web Queries rely on simple HTML, Amazon's response must be transformed. As was done in the last two Hacks, XSL stylesheets are a quick way to make that happen.

Put the following code into a file called *excel_SalesRank.xsl*. This file will narrow the Amazon response to the fields needed and turn it into HTML.

```
<?xml version="1.0" ?>
<xsl:stylesheet version="1.0" xmlns:xsl="http://www.w3.org/1999/XSL/
Transform">
<xsl:output method="html"/>
<xsl:template match="/">
<html xmlns:o="urn:schemas-microsoft-com:office:office"
xmlns:x="urn:schemas-microsoft-com:office:excel"
xmlns="http://www.w3.org/TR/REC-html40">
<body>
<table id="basic">
<tr>
    <th bgcolor="#cccccc" colspan="3">Sales Data</th>
</tr>
<tr>
    <th bgcolor="#999999">ASIN</th>
    <th bgcolor="#999999">Title</th>
    <th bgcolor="#999999">Sales Rank</th>
</tr>
<xsl:for-each select="ProductInfo/Details">
<tr>
    <td><xsl:value-of select="Asin" /></td>
    <td><xsl:value-of select="ProductName" /></td>
    <td><xsl:value-of select="SalesRank" /></td>
</tr>
</xsl:for-each>
<tr><td colspan="3"></td></tr>
<tr>
    <td bgcolor="#ffcc00" colspan="2" align="right">
        <b>Average Sales Rank</b>
    </td>
    <td bgcolor="#ffcc00">=ROUND(AVERAGE(C3:C<xsl:value-of
select="count(ProductInfo/Details) + 2" />),0)</td>
    </tr>
</table>
</body>
</html>
</xsl:template>
</xsl:stylesheet>
```

This file takes an AWS response and turns it into a simple HTML table. The xsl:for-each section loops through the Details node and adds a table row for each result. Once you upload this file to a publicly accessible server, you should be able to view the results of the transformation in a web browser by specifying the XSL file's URL in the request. Just modify the URL from the last step by replacing f=xml with f=http://example.com/excel_SalesRank.xsl.

```
http://xml.amazon.com/onca/xml3?t=insert associate tag↵
&dev-t=insert developer token&PowerSearch=publisher:O'Reilly↵
%20and%20keywords:Hack&type=heavy&mode=books↵
&f=http://example.com/excel_SalesRank.xsl
```

You should see a table like the one in Figure 8-16 with the data from the previous request. Note that the last cell of the table contains an Excel function. It looks like gibberish at this point, but serves an important purpose once it's inside Excel.

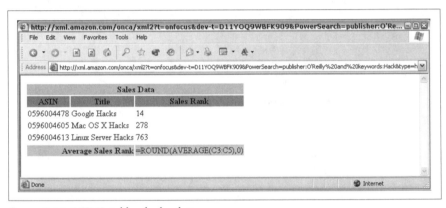

Figure 8-16. HTML table of sales data

To glue the two applications together, use an Excel Query (IQY) file. The file will hold all of the information about the query, including the URL that points to the data. Create a new file called *amzn_avg_sales.iqy* and add this code:

```
WEB
1
http://xml.amazon.com/onca/xml3?t=insert associate tag↵
&dev-t=insert developer token&PowerSearch=publisher:O'Reilly↵
%20and%20keywords:Hack&type=heavy&mode=books&f=http://example.com↵
/excel_SalesRank.xsl
```

The top line lets Excel know that this is a Web Query. The 1 is a Web Query version number (this will always be set to 1) followed by the URL of the AWS query that includes the XSL file. Save the file and note its location.

Running the Hack

To run the hack, double-click the *amzn_avg_sales.iqy* file. Excel should open, contact the URL, and populate a spreadsheet resembling Figure 8-17.

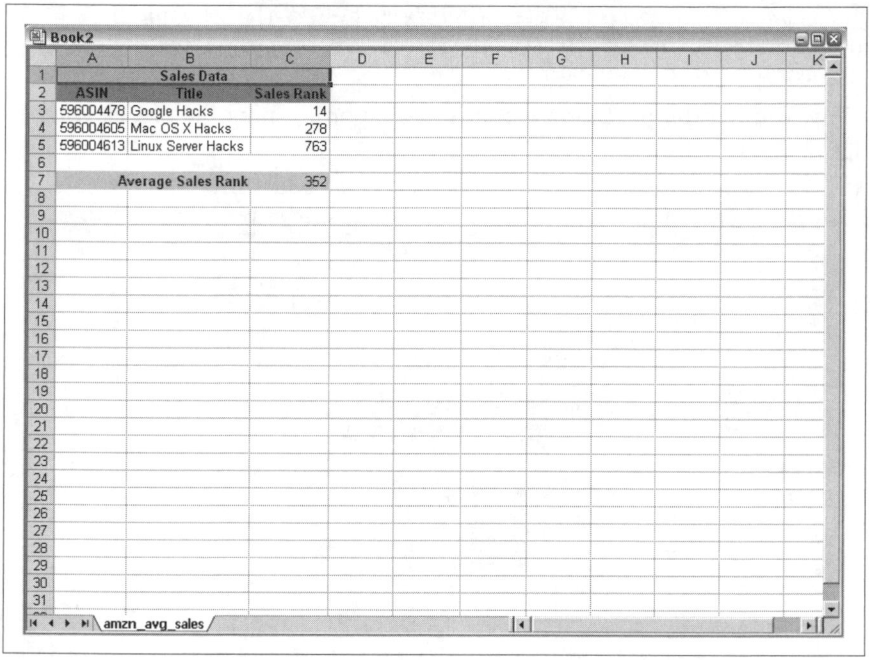

Figure 8-17. Excel spreadsheet with Amazon sales rank data

You now have some useful data—the average sales rank of the books in an application well-suited to manipulation and data analysis. You can update the data at any time by right-clicking any of the data cells in the spreadsheet and choosing Refresh Data.

Hacking the Hack

The tough part of this hack is knowing how to get data directly from AWS into Excel. Once inside Excel the data is available to all of the features Excel offers: calculations, graphing, user input, etc. Here are a few quick ways to extend this example further.

Making the Query Dynamic. Instead of limiting the data to static information built into the query inside the IQY file, you can add a bit of interactivity. Suppose we have a list of ASINs and want to know the average sales rank, but we don't have the list when we're building the IQY file. Excel offers the ability to prompt the user for information before making the Web Query.

Import Data Directly into Excel

The only change you need to make is to place the prompt information inside the Web Query URL where you'd like the user input to go. Change the URL inside *amzn_avg_sales.iqy* to:

```
http://xml.amazon.com/onca/xml3?t=insert associate tag&dev-t=insert ↲
developer token&PowerSearch=isbn:["ASINs","Enter a list of ASINs ↲
separated by pipe symbols (|)."]&type=heavy&mode=books&f=http://↲
example.com/excel_SalesRank.xsl
```

Now, you're prompted for a list of ASINs upon opening the file, as you can see in Figure 8-18.

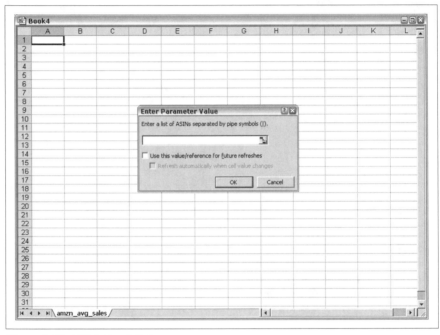

Figure 8-18. ASINs Excel dialogue

Try these if you don't have a list in mind:

```
1565927141|0596003595|0596002246|0596002505
```

This should give you the average sales rank for the ASINs you enter. It could be different every time!

Using Different Data. As in the previous example, changing the data you're working with is just a matter of changing the URL of the AWS query. But if you want to work with a different set of data (like the cost of each item rather than sales rank), you need to tweak the XSL stylesheet a bit.

To see how the stylesheet makes all the difference, create a new file called *excel_PriceDiff.xsl* and add the following code:

```
<?xml version="1.0" ?>
<xsl:stylesheet version="1.0" xmlns:xsl="http://www.w3.org/1999/XSL/
Transform">
<xsl:output method="html"/>
<xsl:template match="/">
<html xmlns:o="urn:schemas-microsoft-com:office:office"
xmlns:x="urn:schemas-microsoft-com:office:excel"
xmlns="http://www.w3.org/TR/REC-html40">
<body>
<table id="basic">
<tr>
    <th bgcolor="#cccccc" colspan="4">Sales Data</th>
</tr>
<tr>
    <th bgcolor="#999999">ASIN</th>
    <th bgcolor="#999999">Title</th>
    <th bgcolor="#999999">List Price</th>
    <th bgcolor="#999999">Amazon Price</th>
</tr>
<xsl:for-each select="ProductInfo/Details">
<tr>
<td>
  <xsl:value-of select="Asin" />
</td>
<td>
  <xsl:value-of select="ProductName" />
</td>
<td>
  <xsl:value-of select="ListPrice" />
</td>
<td>
  <xsl:value-of select="OurPrice" />
</td>
</tr>
</xsl:for-each>
<tr><td colspan="3"></td></tr>
<tr>
    <td bgcolor="#ffcc00" colspan="3" align="right">
        <b>Average List Price</b>
    </td>
    <td bgcolor="#ffcc00">=ROUND(AVERAGE(C3:C<xsl:value-of
select="count(ProductInfo/Details) + 2" />),2)
    </td>
</tr>
<tr>
    <td bgcolor="#ffcc00" colspan="3" align="right">
        <b>Average Amazon Price</b>
    </td>
    <td bgcolor="#ffcc00">=ROUND(AVERAGE(D3:D<xsl:value-of
select="count(ProductInfo/Details) + 2" />),2)
    </td>
</tr>
</table>
```

```
</body>
</html>
</xsl:template>
</xsl:stylesheet>
```

Upload this XSL file to a public server and note the URL. Create a new query file called *amzn_price_diff.iqy* and use the same code as in previous examples, but change the f= variable to the URL of the new stylesheet. Open the file and you should see a new spreadsheet with the list price and the Amazon price, as shown in Figure 8-19.

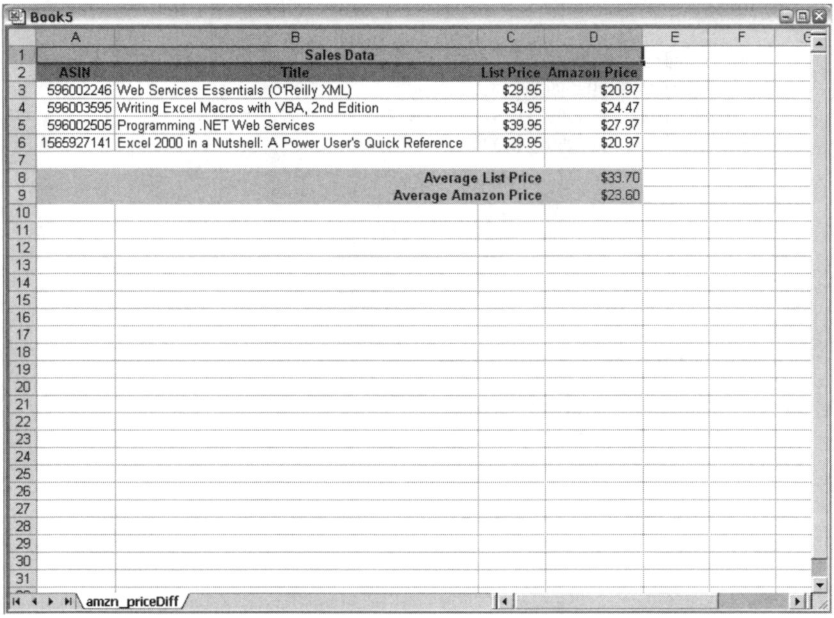

Figure 8-19. Excel spreadsheet with price data

Graphing Results. Once the data is in Excel, it's easy to create graphs to get a sense of what the data means at a glance. Here's how to add a graph to the spreadsheet:

1. Building on the last example, run the *amzn_price_diff.iqy* file. You should see data that includes a list of books along with the list price and Amazon price.

2. Highlight all of the Title, List Price, and Amazon Price cells.

3. Choose Insert → Chart from the menu. This will start the chart wizard.

4. Click "Finish."

You should now have a nice graphic representation of the data (Figure 8-20).

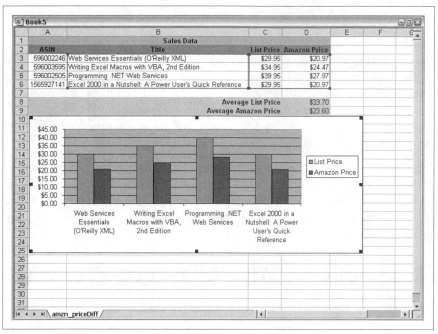

Figure 8-20. Graph of price data

—Paul Bausch (Amazon Hacks)

Access SOAP Web Services from Excel

HACK #99

> If your spreadsheet needs to access constantly updated data, or if you need to access services hosted on another computer, Excel's Web Services support will enable you to get connected.

SOAP-based Web Services have been a key part of Microsoft's plans for .NET, as well as a common feature of toolkits from other vendors. SOAP (the acronym doesn't mean anything) is a protocol that uses XML to transmit information between systems. In the case you'll explore here, it's used to call procedures and return values. A companion specification, Web Service Definition Language (WSDL), describes Web Services so that applications can connect to them easily. Microsoft's Web Services Reference Tool can take a WSDL file and generate VBA code your application can use to access SOAP-based web services.

This hack uses Excel features that are available only in Excel XP and Excel 2003 on Windows. Earlier versions of Excel do not support this, and neither do current or announced Macintosh versions of Excel.

Making this work requires downloading the Office Web Services Toolkit. As its location has changed a few times, it's easiest to go to *http://www. microsoft.com/downloads/search.aspx* and search for "Office Web Services Toolkit". Separate versions are available for Office XP and Office 2003. You'll need to install this toolkit, using the directions that come with it, before proceeding with this hack.

Once you've installed the toolkit, you can start connecting your spreadsheet to web services. To get to the Web Service References Tool (its name inside of Excel), you'll need to select Tools → Macro → Visual Basic Editor. On the Tools menu of the VBE, you'll find Web Services References.... Selecting this brings up the dialog box shown in Figure 8-21.

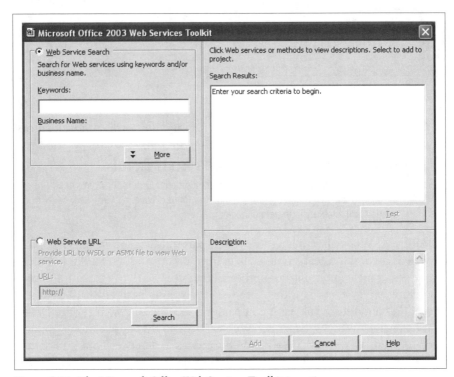

Figure 8-21. The Microsoft Office Web Services Toolkit in action

You can use the search features in the top left of this dialog to find services through Microsoft's Universal Discovery, Description and Integration (UDDI) service, or you can enter a URL for the WSDL file at the lower left. You can find a listing of public services at *http://xmethods.net/*, though you should definitely test to make sure the services still work before you integrate them with your spreadsheets. Many services also require license keys and sometimes license payments, but for this example you'll use one that is available for free. It returns the IP address for a given domain name.

Start by telling Excel which service you want to use—in this case, *http://www.cosme.nu/services/dns.php?wsdl*. Enter that value in the URL: box at the bottom left and click Search. A search result of dns will appear in the top right, as shown in Figure 8-22. Check the box to its left.

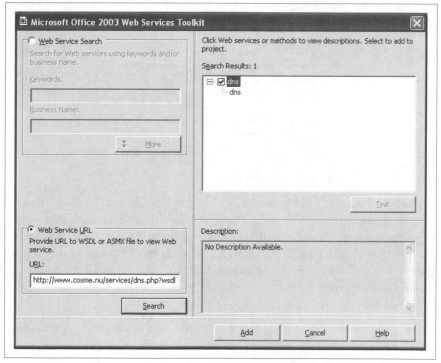

Figure 8-22. Telling the Web Services Toolkit to generate code for a web service

Clicking the Add button will make Excel generate VBA code for the service, as shown in Figure 8-23.

Next, close the VBE and set up a very simple spreadsheet such as the one shown in Figure 8-24.

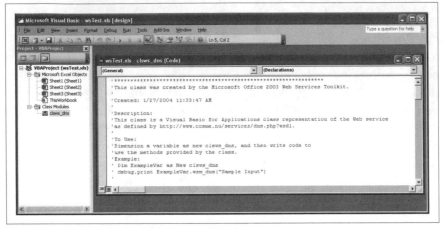

Figure 8-23. VBA code generated by the Web Services Toolkit for accessing the dns service

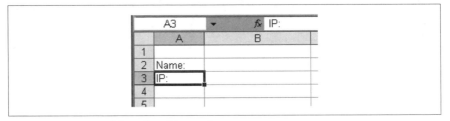

Figure 8-24. A spreadsheet for adding web services

To add a button for calling the service, display the Control toolbar by right-clicking a toolbar and choosing Control Toolbox from the pop-up menu. Click the button icon, and then click the spreadsheet wherever you want the button to go. Right-click the button, and choose Properties from the pop-up menu. Under Name, enter **GetData**; under Caption, enter **Get IP Address**. Close the Properties dialog box, and your spreadsheet should look something like that shown in Figure 8-25.

To add the final piece, right-click the button you added and choose View Code. In the window that appears, enter this subroutine:

```
Private Sub GetData_Click( )
    Dim info As New clsws_dns
    Dim name As String
    Dim IP As String

    name = Range("B2").Text

    IP = info.wsm_dns(name)
```

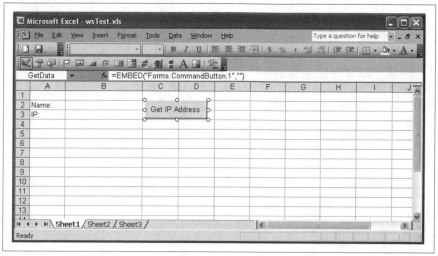

Figure 8-25. Spreadsheet with button for calling web services

```
Set IPRange = Range("B3")

IPRange.Value = IP

End Sub
```

This code is pretty simple. It references the object the toolkit created for the web service, and creates variables for the name and IP address. It collects the name from cell B2, calls the web service with the name as an argument, and then puts the value returned into cell B3. Once you've entered this code and closed the VBE, you can leave design mode by making sure the triangle and ruler icon at the left of the Control toolbar isn't highlighted. The spreadsheet will now enable you to enter a domain name in cell B2. Clicking the Get IP Address button will put the IP address corresponding to that domain name in cell B3. Figures 8-26 and 8-27 show this spreadsheet in action with different domain names.

IP address resolution is one of the simpler services out there, but many times services this simple can be very useful in a spreadsheet—for instance, for currency converters, price retrieval, postal code processing, and much more. You don't even need to learn about SOAP or WSDL to use these services, as the Web Services Toolkit takes care of all of that for you.

A few caveats are worth mentioning, however. First, the computer has to be connected to a network for a web service to work. You probably don't want to create spreadsheets that depend heavily on web services if their users will be working on them at 30,000 feet and will be thoroughly disconnected. (Spreadsheets such as this one, which uses a web service to populate fields but doesn't need to be connected constantly, are probably OK.)

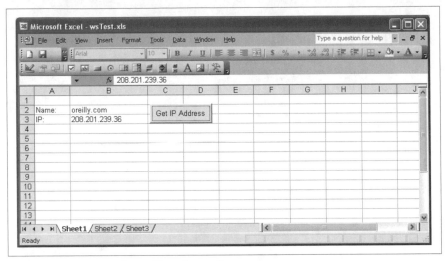

Figure 8-26. A retrieved IP address for oreilly.com

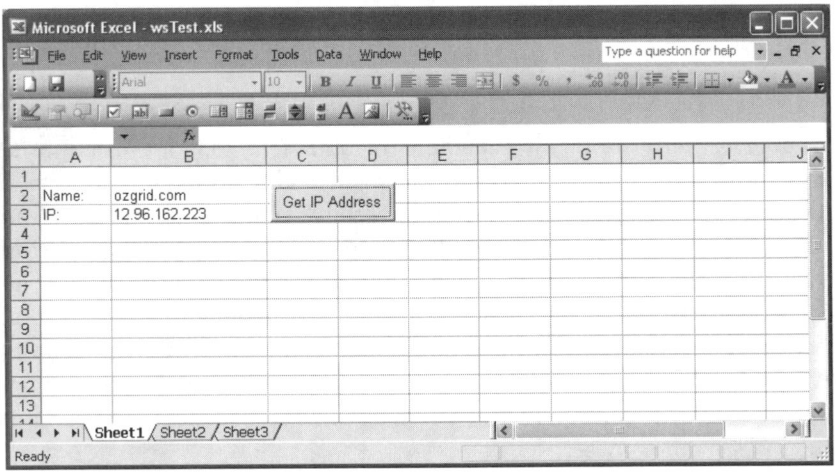

Figure 8-27. A retrieved IP address for ozgrid.com

The other major issue with web services generally is that the field is in significant flux. At the time of this writing, SOAP had moved from Version 1.1 to 1.2, and a new version of WSDL was under development; what's more, many people feel UDDI might eventually be replaced with other technologies. For now, be certain to test the services you use, and keep an eye out for new versions of the Office Web Services Toolkit.

—Simon St.Laurent

Create Excel Spreadsheets Using Other Environments

HACK #100

Although Excel and other spreadsheet programs are the traditional interfaces for creating and reading spreadsheets, sometimes you might need to create .xls files directly from other programs.

Whether you're creating Excel files from databases on an Apache server or you just want to present the information stored in a Java program to Excel users, there are a variety of packages out there that will enable you to create and access *.xls* files without actually using Excel. Although these packages are frequently more difficult to use than the SpreadsheetML described in "Save to SpreadsheetML and Extracting Data" **[Hack #96]** and "Create Spreadsheets using SpreadsheetML" **[Hack #97]**, they generally produce files readable by any version of Excel since Excel 97 (including Macintosh versions of Excel), and often support more Excel features as well.

Some of the more popular (free) packages for working with Excel data include the following:

Spreadsheet::WriteExcel
A Perl package for creating Excel documents, available at *http://search.cpan.org/dist/Spreadsheet-WriteExcel/*

Spreadsheet::ParseExcel
A toolkit that enables Perl programs to read Excel files, available at *http://search.cpan.org/~kwitknr/Spreadsheet-ParseExcel-0.2602/*

Jakarta POI
A product of the Apache Project that provides both read and write access to Excel spreadsheets through a Java API, available at *http://jakarta.apache.org/poi/index.html*

JExcelApi
A Java API for reading and writing Excel spreadsheets that includes Excel-to-CSV and Excel-to-XML converters, available at *http://www.andykhan.com/jexcelapi/*

You also can automate Excel in various ways, often through the use of Microsoft's .NET Framework. To see an example of how to do this in the C# language, visit *http://www.eggheadcafe.com/articles/20021012.asp*.

As an example of how this process works, the Java code in Example 8-7 will generate an Excel spreadsheet using the POI API. (Even if you aren't a Java programmer, you'll probably get the idea.) You can skip reading the license, though it's required to be included in the code.

Example 8-7. Java code for generating an Excel spreadsheet with POI

```
// This code is derived from the org.apache.poi.hssf.dev.HSSF class,
// hence the long license.
/* =====================================================================
 * The Apache Software License, Version 1.1
 *
 * Copyright (c) 2003 The Apache Software Foundation.  All rights
 * reserved.
 *
 * Redistribution and use in source and binary forms, with or without
 * modification, are permitted provided that the following conditions
 * are met:
 *
 * 1. Redistributions of source code must retain the above copyright
 *    notice, this list of conditions and the following disclaimer.
 *
 * 2. Redistributions in binary form must reproduce the above copyright
 *    notice, this list of conditions and the following disclaimer in
 *    the documentation and/or other materials provided with the
 *    distribution.
 *
 * 3. The end-user documentation included with the redistribution,
 *    if any, must include the following acknowledgment:
 *       "This product includes software developed by the
 *        Apache Software Foundation (http://www.apache.org/)."
 *    Alternately, this acknowledgment may appear in the software itself,
 *    if and wherever such third-party acknowledgments normally appear.
 *
 * 4. The names "Apache" and "Apache Software Foundation" and
 *    "Apache POI" must not be used to endorse or promote products
 *    derived from this software without prior written permission. For
 *    written permission, please contact apache@apache.org.
 *
 * 5. Products derived from this software may not be called "Apache",
 *    "Apache POI", nor may "Apache" appear in their name, without
 *    prior written permission of the Apache Software Foundation.
 *
 * THIS SOFTWARE IS PROVIDED ``AS IS'' AND ANY EXPRESSED OR IMPLIED
 * WARRANTIES, INCLUDING, BUT NOT LIMITED TO, THE IMPLIED WARRANTIES
 * OF MERCHANTABILITY AND FITNESS FOR A PARTICULAR PURPOSE ARE
 * DISCLAIMED.  IN NO EVENT SHALL THE APACHE SOFTWARE FOUNDATION OR
 * ITS CONTRIBUTORS BE LIABLE FOR ANY DIRECT, INDIRECT, INCIDENTAL,
 * SPECIAL, EXEMPLARY, OR CONSEQUENTIAL DAMAGES (INCLUDING, BUT NOT
 * LIMITED TO, PROCUREMENT OF SUBSTITUTE GOODS OR SERVICES; LOSS OF
 * USE, DATA, OR PROFITS; OR BUSINESS INTERRUPTION) HOWEVER CAUSED AND
 * ON ANY THEORY OF LIABILITY, WHETHER IN CONTRACT, STRICT LIABILITY,
 * OR TORT (INCLUDING NEGLIGENCE OR OTHERWISE) ARISING IN ANY WAY OUT
 * OF THE USE OF THIS SOFTWARE, EVEN IF ADVISED OF THE POSSIBILITY OF
 * SUCH DAMAGE.
 * =====================================================================
 *
 * This software consists of voluntary contributions made by many
```

Example 8-7. Java code for generating an Excel spreadsheet with POI (continued)

```
 * individuals on behalf of the Apache Software Foundation.  For more
 * information on the Apache Software Foundation, please see
 * <http://www.apache.org/>.
 */

import java.io.*;

import java.util.Random;

import org.apache.poi.poifs.filesystem.POIFSFileSystem;
import org.apache.poi.hssf.record.*;
import org.apache.poi.hssf.model.*;
import org.apache.poi.hssf.usermodel.*;
import org.apache.poi.hssf.util.*;

public class PoiDemo {

    public static void main (String[] args) throws Exception {
        short rownum;

// create a destination file
        FileOutputStream out = new FileOutputStream("zingot.xls");

// create a new workbook object; note that the workbook
// and the file are two separate things until the very
// end, when the workbook is written to the file.
        HSSFWorkbook wb = new HSSFWorkbook();

// create a new worksheet
        HSSFSheet ws = wb.createSheet();

// create a row object reference for later use
        HSSFRow r = null;

// create a cell object reference
        HSSFCell c = null;
// create two cell styles - formats
//need to be defined before they are used
        HSSFCellStyle cs1 = wb.createCellStyle();
        HSSFCellStyle cs2 = wb.createCellStyle();
        HSSFDataFormat df = wb.createDataFormat();
// create two font objects for formatting
        HSSFFont f1 = wb.createFont();
        HSSFFont f2 = wb.createFont();

//set font 1 to 10 point bold type
        f1.setFontHeightInPoints((short) 10);
        f1.setBoldweight(HSSFFont.BOLDWEIGHT_BOLD);
```

Example 8-7. Java code for generating an Excel spreadsheet with POI (continued)

```
//set font 2 to 10 point red type
        f2.setFontHeightInPoints((short) 10);
        f2.setColor( (short)HSSFFont.COLOR_RED );

//for cell style 1, use font 1 and set data format
        cs1.setFont(f1);
        cs1.setDataFormat(df.getFormat("#,##0.0"));

//for cell style 2, use font 2, set a thin border, text format
        cs2.setBorderBottom(cs2.BORDER_THIN);
        cs2.setDataFormat(HSSFDataFormat.getBuiltinFormat("text"));
        cs2.setFont(f2);

// set the sheet name in Unicode
        wb.setSheetName(0, "Test sheet",
                HSSFWorkbook.ENCODING_UTF_16 );

// create a sheet with 10 rows (0-9)
        for (rownum = (short) 0; rownum < 10; rownum++)
        {
            // create a row
            r = ws.createRow(rownum);

            //r.setRowNum(( short ) rownum);
            // create six cells (0-5) (the += 2 becomes apparent later
            for (short cellnum = (short) 0; cellnum < 6; cellnum += 2)
            {
                // create a numeric cell
                c = r.createCell(cellnum);
                // fill with numbers based on position
                c.setCellValue(rownum * 10 + cellnum
                        + (((double) rownum / 10)
                        + ((double) cellnum / 100)));

                // create a string cell
                c = r.createCell((short) (cellnum + 1));

                // on every other row (this is why +=2)
                if ((rownum % 2) == 0)
                {
                    // set this cell to the first cell style we defined
                    c.setCellStyle(cs1);
                    // set the cell's string value to "Test"
                    c.setEncoding( HSSFCell.ENCODING_UTF_16 );
                    c.setCellValue( "Test" );
                }
                else
                {
                    c.setCellStyle(cs2);
                    // set the cell's string value to "1... 2... 3..."
```

Example 8-7. Java code for generating an Excel spreadsheet with POI (continued)

```
                        c.setEncoding( HSSFCell.ENCODING_UTF_16 );
                        c.setCellValue( "1... 2... 3..." );
                }
            }
        }

// use some formulas
// advance a row
        rownum++;
        r = ws.createRow(rownum);

//create formulas.
        for (short cellnum = (short) 0; cellnum < 6; cellnum += 2)
        {
            //produce SUMs for appropriate columns
            int column= 65+cellnum;
            char columnLabel=(char)column;
            String formula="SUM("+columnLabel+"1:"+columnLabel+"10)";
            c = r.createCell(cellnum);
            c.setCellStyle(cs1);
            c.setCellFormula(formula);
        }

// write the workbook to the output stream,
// remembering to close our file
        wb.write(out);
        out.close( );
    }
}
```

To run this code, you must first download the latest POI binary file and put the main POI jar file (*poi-2.0-final-20040126.jar* in this case) on your classpath, as appropriate to the platform on which you run it. When run, it takes no arguments and creates a single file, called *zingot.xls*. If you open that file, you'll see a spreadsheet such as the one in Figure 8-28 (or Figure 8-29, if you're using a Macintosh).

The logic in Example 8-7 is hardly an exemplary model of how to create a spreadsheet, but it shows off the basic functionality needed to create new sheets, cells, and formulas. If you use this to build spreadsheets for your own applications, you'll undoubtedly replace the loops with references to the data structures you're presenting, the destination files will be more logical and probably will vary depending on the data, and you might take advantage of more features than the basics shown here.

One other feature of POI is particularly worth noting if you're generating spreadsheets that are going to be part of a dynamically generated web site.

Create Excel Spreadsheets Using Other Environments

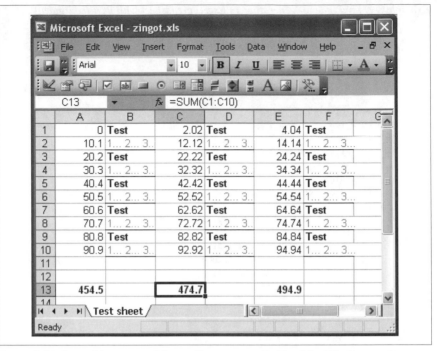

Figure 8-28. Spreadsheet created from a Java program in Excel for Windows

Figure 8-29. Spreadsheet created from a Java program in Excel for Macintosh

You can combine POI with Cocoon, a Java framework also from Apache, that uses XML documents and other sources to generate content accessible to web browsers. An XML.com article at *http://www.xml.com/pub/a/2003/01/22/cocoon-excel.html* provides details and a demonstration of how to do this.

—Simon St.Laurent

Glossary

ActiveX Controls
Fully programmable objects that can be used to help customize applications. In Excel use, these commonly include the Command button, the Option button, etc.

Add-In
A workbook saved with the extension *XLA*. It opens as a hidden workbook when installed via Tools → Add-Ins. An Add-In provides extra functionality to Excel.

Application
Another term for a program. Excel is an application; some people call their spreadsheets applications.

Arguments
The information a formula or function might require to return a value. Most functions within Excel require arguments for their execution. The arguments are enclosed within parentheses and are separated by commas.

Boolean
A mathematical means of expressing statements in logic. A Boolean value will be either True or False.

Brackets
See Parentheses.

Bug
An error in code. Unfortunately, some bugs can go undetected by the most stringent tests, and therefore they are hard to get rid of.

Command Bar
One of Excel's many objects, used to house menu items. The Worksheet menu bar is a Command bar that houses the menu items File, Edit, View, Insert, etc.

Constant
A named item that represents an unchanging value.

Contiguous
> A range of cells in which all boundaries of all cells are connected, with no gaps. For instance, A1:C20 is a contiguous range.

Control Toolbox Toolbar
> A toolbar that contains ActiveX controls (see ActiveX Controls).

Debugging
> The process of eliminating all possible errors from code.

Dialog
> A pop-up window, also referred to as a dialog box, that requests information from a user—for example, the File Open dialog box.

Event
> A call from Excel to your code that something has happened. For example, a mouse click, or the closing/ opening of a workbook, is reported as an event.

Forms Toolbar
> Toolbar used to store controls that are built into Excel (i.e., not ActiveX controls).

Formula
> A sequence of values, cell references, names, functions, or operator(s) in a cell that together produce a new value. All Excel formulas begin with = (an equals sign).

Function
> A type of procedure (see Procedure) that returns a value. Excel has built-in functions, such as the SUM function, but you also can create your own user-defined functions (see User-Defined Function).

Loop
> The continuous running of one or more lines of Visual Basic for Applications (VBA) code until a condition is met and the loop ends.

Macro
> An action or set of actions used to automate tasks. Excel enables you to record actions and use them later as macros.

Method
> A procedure (see Procedure) that acts on an object (see Object).

Module
> A self-contained unit in which VBA code is written and stored.

Name
> A human-readable term that can be applied to a constant, a range of cells, or a variable.

Non-Contiguous
> A range of cells in which all boundaries of some or all cells are not connected. For example, the range A1:C20, E10:F100 represents a non-contiguous range.

Object

A component of an application (see Application), such as a worksheet, a cell, or a chart. More than 100 objects are available within Excel, and they are fundamental to the usefulness of VBA code.

Operators

A mathematical symbol that instructs a formula or function to perform a specific task—for instance, the + operator instructs a formula or function to add.

Parentheses

The brackets ( ) used to indicate groupings in mathematics. In Excel, there must always be a matching set of closing parentheses for each opening set.

Parse

To divide a command or string of characters into its component parts.

Private Module

A module whose use is specific to a particular object, such as a workbook, sheet, or UserForm.

Procedure

A named sequence of statements executed as a whole. For example, function and sub are types of procedures (see the entries for Function and Sub, respectively).

Project Explorer

A window within the Visual Basic Editor (VBE) in which all objects can be viewed pertaining to a specific open workbook.

Property

A named attribute of an object (see Object). For example, the address of a specific cell is a property of a cell or range object.

Range

An area of one or many cells, contiguous or non-contiguous.

Runtime Error

An error within VBA code that occurs while the code is executing. Most runtime errors are followed by a numeric value to assist in their debugging.

Sheet

A generic term used to represent a worksheet, chart sheet, or macro sheet.

Spreadsheet

A software application or program that allows text, numbers, and functions to be entered into a matrix of individual cells.

String

A linear sequence of characters—e.g., the word carrot is a string of alpha characters.

Sub

A type of procedure that returns no value (see Procedure). Subs often are used to handle events.

Template

A predefined skeleton used as a standard base for use or modification.

User-Defined Function

A function (see Function) that is written in VBA specifically to return a value based on a distinct method of calculation.

UserForm

An object of Excel that can be used to house ActiveX controls. UserForms can be inserted and modified only from within the VBE.

Variable

A named item that houses a value that can be changed during its use.

Visual Basic Editor (VBE)

Also known as Visual Basic Environment. The VBE is an interface within Excel that enables users to access all elements pertaining to VBA.

Visual Basic for Applications (VBA)

The standard macro language used in most Microsoft Office Suite products. The word Applications can represent any one of the office suite programs it is used within—e.g., Excel. The VBA language is a derivative of Visual Basic (VB), which in turn is a derivative of the language Basic. The fundamental difference between VBA and VB is that VBA (as the name implies) can be used only within an applicable application, generally one of the Microsoft Office Suite products.

Wizard

A series of interfaces used to assist a user through a series of steps.

Workbook

A container for one or more sheets or worksheets. Each *.xls* file represents a workbook.

Worksheet

One of Excel's fundamental objects in which cells are housed. All workbooks must contain at least one worksheet, and at least one worksheet must be visible. The only limitation to the number of worksheets you can have open is your available PC memory.

Index

Symbols

{ } (curly brackets), 50, 134, 165
( ) (parentheses), 193
' (apostrophe)
    editing macros, 16
    INDIRECT function, 44, 61
    worksheets and spaces, 93
* (asterisk), 34, 77, 203
@ (at sign), 34, 153
, (comma), 13
< comparison operator, 187
<= comparison operator, 187
= comparison operator, 187
> comparison operator, 187
>= comparison operator, 187
$ (dollar sign), 33, 93, 153
= (equals sign)
    chart text elements and, 149
    Formula bar and, 178
    PivotTables and, 117
    replacing with @, 34, 153
! (exclamation mark), 93
+ (plus sign), 14
" (quotation marks)
    formulas and, 49
    INDIRECT function, 44, 61
    VBE and, 13
; (semicolon), 73
_ (underscore), 96
value, 174

Numbers

1904 date system, 174, 175
80/20 rule, 1

A

A1 cell (Start name), 22
absolute references
    anchoring cells as, 95
    boldfacing subtotals and, 80
    columns and, 53
    dollar sign and, 93, 153
    formulas and, 153
    moving cells and, 33–34
    named ranges and, 93
Activate command, 190
ActiveSheet, 194
ActiveSheet.ScrollArea, 26
ActiveWorkbook, 210
ActiveX controls, 194
Add button
    Source Data dialog box, 123
    XML Maps dialog box, 222
adding
    Calendar Control, 201–203
    CommandButton, 203
    data labels, 146
    data to validation lists, 83–86
    date extensions, 171–172
    documentation to
        formulas, 152–153
    graphs to spreadsheets, 246

We'd like to hear your suggestions for improving our indexes. Send email to *index@oreilly.com*.

C

MAX function
    date/time features, 88
    displaying negative times, 175
    extracting Grand Total, 118
    purpose, 98
    SUBTOTAL function and, 170
mega-formulas, 180–184
merged cells, 3
messages, displaying, 197–198
metadata (XML), 231
Microsoft
    .NET Framework, 253
    UDDI, 249
    XSLT tools, 233
Microsoft Office Download Center, 35
Microsoft Word, 41
MID function, 181, 182, 205
MIN function, 88, 170, 175
MINUTE function, 179
MOD function, 52–53, 165–166
modules
    accessing, 192
    empty, 14
    inserting, 23
    macros and, 38
    Project Explorer and, 14
    protecting add-ins, 211
    removing, 14
    (see also private modules)
months, days in, 179–180
mouse
    fill handle, 47
    Macintosh users, xviii
    referencing and, 183
MsgBox (VBE), 12
My Templates folder, 20

N

N function, 153
#N/A value
    avoiding, 161
    blank cells and, 150
    SUM function and, 161
Name box (Formula bar)
    assigning buttons to macros, 195
    checkboxes, 46
    drop-down lists, 91
    dynamic named ranges and, 97
    SUBTOTAL function, 170

Name in Workbook: box (Define Name)
    adding date extensions, 171
Name tab (see Sheet Name tab)
named ranges
    absolute references and, 93
    advantages of, 91
    data validation and, 43, 44, 60, 61
    help resources, 9
    PivotTables and, 117
    #REF! error, 61, 44
    SpreadsheetML and, 226
    stylesheets and, 239
    worksheets and, 92–94, 105–107
    XML document, 232
    (see also dynamic named ranges)
NamedCell element (XML), 239
NamedRange element (XML), 231
names
    cells and, 91, 92
    custom functions and, 94–96
    extracting last names, 181
    macro recorders and, 192
    retrieving for workbooks, 205
    workbooks and, 183, 205
Names element (XML), 231, 239
Names in Workbook: box (Define
        Name)
    adding date extensions, 171
    ComboBox, 58
    custom functions, 94
    dynamic ranges, 97, 101, 103–105
    hacking database functions, 186, 188
    named ranges, 93
    pivoting data in other
        workbooks, 119
    validation lists, 59, 84
namespaces
    XML documents, 231, 232
    XSLT and, 239
negative numbers/values
    custom formats and, 73, 76
    for time, 174–176
    relocating sign for, 172–174
    for time, 88
nesting
    ADDRESS function, 158
    COUNTA function, 97
    dynamic named ranges, 103–105
    extracting last name from
        strings, 182

nesting (*continued*)
  functions, 53, 94, 158, 183
  IF function, 176
  INDIRECT function and, 178, 182
  INT function and, 178
  ROW function, 165
  SUM function, 183
  TEXT function and, 175
  TODAY function, 163
  VLOOKUP function, 176
.NET Framework, 253
NETWORKDAYS function, 89
New Folder button, 20
New Workbook dialog box, 20
1904 date system, 174, 175
NOW function, 15, 163
#NUM! error, 185
numbers
  alignment of, 3, 62
  converting from text
      numbers, 62–64
  COUNT function and, 98
  custom formats, 73–77
  date and time as, 86, 174
  date extensions and, 172
  entering quickly, 47
  SUM function, 115
  (see also negative numbers/values)

O

Objects folder (Excel), 17
Objects option (Go To Special), 35
Office Web Services Toolkit, 248
OFFSET function
  charts and custom controls, 128, 131
  purpose, 97–102
OnAction property, 215
OnTime method (Application), 191,
      192
Open command (File menu), 5
Open dialog box, 218
opening
  files, 218
  VBE, 11, 14, 17
  VBE for Macintosh, 11
  workbooks, 40
OpenOffice.org web site, 41
operators, comparison, 76, 187
option buttons, 57

Option-F11 (opening VBE), 14, 17
Option-F8 (Macro dialog box), 14, 82
OR statement, 69
OzGrid Excel Forum, 106, 108

P

parentheses (), 193
password protection, 28, 203–205, 209
PasswordChar property, 203
Paste Function dialog box
      (Shift-F3), 64, 89, 206
Paste Name dialog box (F3), 35, 105
Paste Special → Formats, 163
pasting (Ctrl-V), 182
pathnames, retrieving, 205
Patterns tab
  checkboxes, 56
  Format Axis dialog box, 139
  Format Cells dialog box, 30, 31
  Format Data Series dialog box, 140
  speedometer charts, 143, 145, 146
performance considerations, 21, 51
Perl programming language, 232, 253
personal macro workbook
  creating Personal.xls file, 201, 203
  PivotTables and, 115
  private modules in, 16
  volatile functions and, 15
  XLSTART folder and, 20
Personal.xls file, 201, 203, 210
pick list (see validation lists)
pictures, inserting, 65
pie charts
  exploding single slices
      from, 121–123
  multiple sets of slices, 123–124
  reducing size of, 145
PivotChart Wizard, 112
PivotCharts, 39, 110
PivotTable → Select → Entire Table, 113
PivotTable Report, 115
PivotTable Wizard, 110–112, 115, 120
PivotTables
  alternatives to array formulas, 4
  blank cell problems and, 156
  creating quickly, 114–117
  databases and, 108, 115
  dynamic named ranges and, 97
  GETPIVOTDATA function, 117

V

validation lists
  adding data, 83–86
  based on selections, 58–60
  INDIRECT function, 61
  named ranges, 61
  (see also data validation)
#VALUE! error, 166
values
  for date/time, 86
  dollar values as words, 77
  finding nth occurrence of, 167–168
  formulas/functions, 81–83
  negative time values, 174–176
  serial values, 86
Values option (Paste Special), 157
VAR function, 170
VARP function, 170
VBA (Visual Basic for Applications)
  code performance, 197
  corrupted workbooks and, 41
  determining days in months, 179
  empty modules, 14
  grouping worksheets, 8–10
  hacks and, xvi
  multiple worksheets, 8
  PivotTables and, 115
  splash screens and, 195
  SpreadsheetML and, 226
  ticking cells upon selection, 198
  worksheet index numbers and, 193
VBE (Visual Basic Editor)
  Application.DisplayAlerts = False, 13
  CodeNames and, 193
  hidden workbooks, 210
  interface differences, xviii
  MsgBox recommendations, 12
  opening, 11, 14, 17, 120
  preventing printing, 12–13
  punctuation and, 13
  saving nonexistent changes, 16
  shortcut, 32
  splash screens, 195
  Web Services References, 248
  worksheet properties, 17
  (see also Project Explorer)
Vertical option (Window → Arrange), 5
View → Code (F7), 202, 204

View → Project Explorer (Ctrl-R)
  accessing sheet CodeNames, 193
  limiting scrolling, 24
  preventing prompts, 14
  Templates dialog, 17
View → Properties (F4)
  adding Calendar Control, 202
  password protecting worksheets, 203
  splash screens, 196
  viewing worksheet properties, 17
View → Task Pane (Ctrl-F1), 222
View → Toolbars → Customize, 114
View → Toolbars → Drawing, 65
View → Toolbars → Forms
  accessing buttons, 194
  checkboxes, 46
  ComboBox, 57, 170
  random sorting, 68
View → Toolbox, 195, 201, 203
View Code
  conditional formatting, 207
  creating indexes, 21
  custom toolbars, 32
  establishing boundaries, 24
  importing data, 250
  multiple worksheets, 8
  preventing actions, 11
  protected worksheets, 209
  running macros, 191
  ticking cells upon selection, 199
  validation lists, 85
Visible property (worksheets), 17–18
Visual Basic Editor (see VBE)
Visual Basic for Applications (see VBA)
VLOOKUP function, 167, 168, 176–178
volatile functions
  array formulas and, 165
  personal macro workbooks, 15
  recalculation and, 163–164

W

Walkenbach, John, 140, 143, 145
Web Query, 240, 242, 243
Web Service Definition Language (WSDL), 247
Web Services, 247–252
WEEKNUM function, 89
width for column charts, 138–141

Colophon

Our look is the result of reader comments, our own experimentation, and feedback from distribution channels. Distinctive covers complement our distinctive approach to technical topics, breathing personality and life into potentially dry subjects.

The tool on the cover of *Excel Hacks* is a trowel. The trowel shown is the type that is generally used in gardening tasks such as removing stones from dirt meant for planting, removing weeds, and digging up and/or planting the plants themselves.

Mary Brady was the production editor and proofreader for *Excel Hacks*. Audrey Doyle was the copyeditor. Philip Dangler and Claire Cloutier provided quality control. Lucie Haskins wrote the index.

Hanna Dyer designed the cover of this book, based on a series design by Edie Freedman. The cover image is from the Stockbyte Work Tools CD. Emma Colby produced the cover layout with QuarkXPress 4.1 using Adobe's Helvetica Neue and ITC Garamond fonts.

David Futato designed the interior layout. This book was converted by Julie Hawks to FrameMaker 5.5.6 with a format conversion tool created by Erik Ray, Jason McIntosh, Neil Walls, and Mike Sierra that uses Perl and XML technologies. The text font is Linotype Birka; the heading font is Adobe Helvetica Neue Condensed; and the code font is LucasFont's TheSans Mono Condensed. The illustrations that appear in the book were produced by Robert Romano and Jessamyn Read using Macromedia FreeHand 9 and Adobe Photoshop 6. This colophon was written by Mary Brady.